£5

MW00333247

Bill Maynard

Stand Up ... And Be Counted

The Other Side of Greengrass

Bill Maynard

Stand Up ... And Be Counted

WITH JOHN SHEARD

The Breedon Books
Publishing Company
Derby

First published in Great Britain by
The Breedon Books Publishing Company Limited
Breedon House, 44 Friar Gate, Derby, DE1 1DA.
1997

Dedication

This book is dedicated to the
memory of Edith and Walt.

ISBN 1 85983 080 3

Printed and bound by Butler & Tanner Ltd., Selwood Printing Works, Caxton Road, Frome,
Somerset.

Colour separations by RPS Ltd, Leicester.

Jackets and gold-blocking by Lawrence-Allen Colour Printers, Weston-super-Mare, Avon.

Contents

Acknowledgements:

Whilst it would be quite
impossible to thank everyone
who helped in the research and
writing of this book, the
authors would like to
acknowledge the special
assistance given by members of
the *Heartbeat* team — Pat
Brown, Teresa Ferlinc, David
Nightingale and Millie Hine —
plus Tim Worsnop of Yorkshire
Television and Sharon Leatham
of Granada Television.

Introduction

THERE is always a small knot of curious French people outside our country house in the Charentes. Rather like the late Harold Wilson having his photograph taken as a boy outside the door of 10 Downing Street, they take family snapshots before our gates and perhaps they, too, dream of future fame and glory.

The house is large and impressive but not a stately home like Chatsworth or, more appropriate perhaps in this case, Versailles. It is known, in French, as a *Maison de Maitre*, House of the Master, a solid manor-cum-farm typical of a prosperous countryman with, perhaps, another imposing residence in Paris.

Then, one morning, a French TV crew turned up, soon to be followed by another. The crowd outside grew larger, until there were scores of people peering and pointing their lenses at every move by the new owners of the house, a youngish English couple, their children and a tall, heavily-built man in his 60s who had known more hair in the past.

Had this been Goathland, the tiny village on the North York Moors which for some years had been the setting for one of the most successful TV series ever made in Britain, there would have been no surprise at the crowd nor the TV cameras. Since *Heartbeat* began filming there, Goathland has been awash with tourists.

Having become accustomed to being stared at as a British TV star for more than 40 years, it would have been flattering to think that these French trippers had been drawn into the depth of the countryside by Greengrass, the cantankerous curmudgeon whose fame had been partly responsible for the Maynard family becoming proud owners of this now famous *Maison de Maitre*.

But no. My somewhat time-worn features may have become familiar in a large part of the English speaking world — thanks to the overseas sales of *Heartbeat* and many other chart-topping TV series — but to these French people, I might just as well have been the Man in the Moon. Which is just as well by me because that is why I choose to spend much of my rare leisure time buried anonymously in rural France.

Instead, they were gathered outside *Maison Maynard* because one of its previous occupants has just died: President François Mitterand, whose grandmother had once owned the manor, and where he spent much of his childhood, a place which he always spoke and wrote about with the greatest affection.

As the crowds grew, I could not help but wonder what these French men, women and children were thinking: who are this rather strange English family, what chain of circumstances gave them the right — and the cash — to buy a cherished part of French history?

Whatever the conclusions they reached, however fantastic they were, I doubt very much whether they could have matched the truth. For it is a long way from the house where I spent much of my childhood, a run-down rented terrace in a small Leicestershire village in a street which was known to all and sundry as Rat Alley, thanks to the vermin as big as Jack Russell terriers, vermin which seemed to spend as much time in our kitchen as they did on the council tip which was our stinking neighbour.

The road from Rat Alley to *Maison de Maitre* has been a long one, a rollercoaster as much as a road, and it has given me both relative wealth and abject poverty, fame of the best kind and infamy in the tabloids too. It is a road littered with success and failure, with wine, women and song when the fame was hot and humiliation when it ran cold. It is also a story of great love and almost unbearable loss.

Chapter One

Rat Alley

THEY called it Rat Alley, the first home that I really knew. It wasn't too bad a place. In fact it was a fairly new terraced council house in one of those small villages on the outskirts of Leicester which had grown up around a once thriving hosiery trade. Trouble was, back in the Great Depression of the 1930s when I first became conscious of the world around me, very little thrived. And particularly not the Family Williams. The house was, and still is, approached by a lane so narrow that a single car has difficulty in negotiating it. In those days, of course, the working class — or in most cases, the non-working class, for unemployment was rife — never dreamed of owning a car. Those with bicycles were considered rather posh. And although the local council had done its best to rid the area of some of its appalling slums by building new housing, they had overlooked one key factor: they had built next to a municipal rubbish tip that covered several acres, its surface a moonscape of rotting food, discarded tins, punctured tin baths, pathetic sticks of broken furniture and millions of sodden newspapers, many of which had been recycled as wrapping for fish-and-chips — a dish much prized as a once-a-week luxury which added a square meal to our regular impoverished diet. Which is why we had rats for neighbours, thousands and thousands of rats as big as the mangy cats which scavenged on the waste. Some were so brazen that they refused to remain as simple neighbours: they wanted to come a-visiting, which is why it was no surprise to find a fat rat under the kitchen table from time to time. Dad stopped that by acquiring a half-bred Jack Russell terrier bitch called Gyp, a fearsome beast and a true-born killer.

Problem was, her fierce temper was not solely directed at rats which, admittedly, she killed in large numbers, seizing them at the back of their heads and breaking their necks with one savage shake of her head. She would snap at almost any passing ankle, too, and terrorised the gangs of youths — boys and girls — who patrolled the area looking for fights with rivals from other streets. The streets were called 'avenues' which, at the time, was a rather smart word, resonant of the tree-lined thoroughfares where the middle classes lived — not that I spent much time in such districts. It is an old joke but the saying was that any cat here with a tail was a tourist. And woe betide any tabby that did not flee at the first sight of Gyp. On balance, I suppose, she was slightly better to live with than the rats she hunted with such ferocity, but it was a close run thing.

It all sounds gruesome now, yet surprisingly enough this tiny council house in Rat Alley — official name, Hooley's Estate — was something of a step up to the Williams family. The word 'estate', now much discredited, also had pretensions, being redolent of country squires and rolling acres, but the Hooley was nearer the actuality: it reminded me of hooligan, which fitted well most of the youngsters who lived there. We had been on the move almost constantly since I was born and the only difference between us and gypsies (despite the Jack Russell's name) was that we did not sell clothes pegs, mainly because we couldn't afford the wood.

My father, Walter Charles Williams, would have thought his condition no worse and no better than millions of men in slump-ridden Britain. As a lad, with no other prospect of work, he had joined the army just after World War One, an army which had been decimated in the trenches and was crying out for even more cannon fodder. Thankfully, for too brief a time, the cannons had fallen silent. As a Leicestershire lad, he had joined the county regiment and ended up, like many thousands more, stationed at Aldershot, then considered a long way from home. It was an army that still had to learn the lessons of modern, mechanised warfare and most of its transport was still horse-drawn, so father became a horseman: not a cavalryman in some upper echelon regiment but a groom, mucker-out and general dogsbody in a unit which thought more of its horses than of its men. It was, as far as I ever knew, a service packed with little incident and absolutely no glory. He started as a private soldier and finished as a private soldier. That, I assume, must have been the army's fault, for my father had several characteristics in abundance which I am sure would be encouraged in the modern military: he had ambition, imagination, a steely determination to better himself and an unflagging capacity for hard work.

If the army had provided him with little opportunity to exploit these talents, he used his spare time to find himself the great glory of his life in the form of my mother, Edith Maud, who lived at Heath End, near Farnham, Surrey. They married from her parents' home at 5 Oak Cottages, Heath End, and there one Walter Frederick George Williams was born on October 8, 1928. Like everything I have ever done, even my debut in this world was not without a struggle. In many ways, my parents were an odd couple. Father was short, dapper and straight-backed in proper soldierly manner, a soccer player of some note whose talents were much sought after by local teams in his younger days. Mother stood half-a-head higher than him and was wide, too, a big woman in all respects. It seems I have inherited some of her size and shape — I was to grow to six feet plus — and his determination and skill with a football because I was to come within an ace of a professional soccer career. Sadly, there was no one else to share these two sets of genes. I was a big baby, over nine pounds, and it was sometimes whispered that I had been a 'difficult birth'. Whatever complications my arrival caused I was never told in detail, but my mother was never to have another baby. There are many myths surrounding the fate of the only child but I can never remember feeling lonely for the lack of brothers or sisters. Apart from anything else, the family — all three of us — was always too busy. For the other vital ingredient my parents mixed into my genes was a capacity for hard work. Even today, when I don't have to do it, work is still my greatest pleasure.

A few months after my troublesome arrival, Dad's army service came to an end. He was transferred to Glen Parva Barracks in Leicestershire to await his demob and we came too. Father was back home but I'm sure it was not a prospect that pleased him. With millions of skilled men out of work, what chance of a decent job had a former soldier who knew little except horses? For Mum, who had put the job of laundry maid on her wedding certificate, it was the beginning of years of drudgery. At one time, she was to walk seven miles there and back to work, only to earn a pittance, a journey and a day's work so hard that I remember her coming home with her legs pouring blood from the chafing caused by her two long walks.

Perhaps people were tougher then, or had fewer aspirations, for despite these odds, we were a happy family. Survival was the objective in those early years although my father had no intention of making that a lifelong career. He had ambitions and in those, my mother supported him with both her love and her labour, without complaint that I ever heard. Despite their differences in bulk, Dad was very much the head of the family. He was firm, fair, and rarely raised his voice, never mind a hand, to either me or my mother. As a youngster in those nondescript provincial villages, I had no idea that I had reason to be unhappy. All our neighbours were in much the same boat, for even those with regular jobs rarely earned more than a bare subsistence. I was a child and I loved it. Those little redbrick villages in the rolling Leicestershire countryside, with names like Wigston, South Wigston, Wigston Magna, Wigston Fields and Great Glen, surrounded by wide fields and dense woods with tall trees to climb and streams to bathe in, were my natural playground. I was not to know that one day I would leave them in triumph for the brights lights of the big city ...and return licking my wounds like a hunted fox going back to its den. The wounds have healed now, but I still live in the same area, driving almost every day through the streets and alongside the fields where I played as an urchin. The roots may be old and gnarled now, but they are deep and firm.

—oOo—

Poverty is a relative state. These days, there are official guidelines used by Government bodies which say you can still be poor and have a television set, a video and central heating. In my day, poverty was not having enough to eat, much-darned clothes on your back, no coal in the fireplace and, perhaps worst of all, no shoes on your feet. After Dad was demobbed, we had a series of dingy rented rooms and houses in the various Wigstons. After the security of the army, he must have been in deep shock when faced with the difficulties of making a living. As a laundry worker, Mum could find regular work, low paid as it was, but would always come home totally exhausted. This in itself must have been a profound insult to Dad, for he was a bantam-cock of a man with a sense of pride and duty, in particular the duty of the man of the family to be the 'provider', a word of enormous power and significance.

He would go out day after day, seeking work, and also come back tired and disconsolate. When he realised that regular employment was to be a long time coming, he set up on his own, starting little businesses to bring in the odd copper. Sometimes he worked as a tree-feller, bringing home logs which he would chop into kindling and hawk round the neighbours at a ha'penny a bundle. He sometimes found work helping out a local blacksmith, where his skill with horses came in useful. There were many, many schemes to come as he set out towards his ambition to open a little corner shop. In the meantime, I was not being of the greatest assistance. I was already developing a repu-tation for being accident and illness prone.

That had started back at Farnham when I could barely toddle. What toddling I could manage would take me out of the house and into the middle of the main road, a major route from London to the South Coast. There was little traffic in those days and those drivers were perhaps a little more considerate than today's, but this might have been a very short book indeed had luck not been on my side. But already, it seemed, I was developing into a source of aggravation for poor Mum. It was to get worse.

In the classic British war film, *The Cruel Sea*, one character has a line which was highly risqué at the time but always got a big laugh. Describing some cock-up or other, he says: "It was the biggest laugh since auntie got her tits caught in the mangle." The gag never appealed much to me because mangles played a large part in my childhood, particularly those mangles built like steam rollers with wooden rollers the size of tree trunks and cast-iron cog wheels that could have powered an ocean liner. One day when I was about three, I spotted Mum operating one such leviathan in a neighbour's backyard (we couldn't afford one of our own). I rushed in to see her, no doubt in the hope of cadging a ha'penny to buy a bull's eye, as I sometimes did when she was working in the laundry, jumping up and down to speak to her through an open window. That window is still there to this day and it is just three feet off the ground.

I tried to distract her from her work and it was quite an act. I put my hand into those ferocious cogs and they immediately chewed off the two upper digits of the middle finger of my right hand. There was blood on the washing that day. I was rushed off to Leicester Royal Infirmary where surgeons tried to stitch my finger back. Alas, it developed gangrene and had to go.

Perhaps there is some strange psychological drive created by having just nine digits, for although I was acutely conscious of it at the time, I was to meet many fellow sufferers in showbusiness: comedians Jimmy Jewell and Dave Allen, band leader Eric Delaney, and — overcoming what one would have thought to be a major disability — pianists Russ Conway and Bill McGuffy. Bill, who was to become a close friend, actually founded the Niner Club for this élite ensemble which was a way of cocking a snoot, whatever that is, at the injury. However, being scarred for life was not a good thing at my age and time, for soon I was due to go to school and I was already 'different' enough as it was. Kids hate other 'different' kids and we were already down in many neighbours' eyes as 'Southerners' — a deadly insult in the East Midlands even to this day. Now I had a finger missing, which would make me an even greater curiosity — perhaps 'freak' is a better word. I did not know that it would be shoes, or rather the lack of them, that was to be the cause of my greatest humiliation. Before, that is, I learned to joke my way into other kids' respect.

As I said earlier, poverty is relative. If you have more or less the same number of possessions as your peers, you are not poor. But the Williams family possessions in those dark days of the 1930s were limited in the extreme. I would joke later that, when the snows came, we were so poor that we could not afford a sledge so I had to slide down the hills on the kid from next door.

Of all the possessions we did not have, highest on my childhood list was shoes. When it came time to go to school, I was dispatched in a pair of size-ten men's wellies, which were not only excruciatingly uncomfortable but made me look like Jack (of Beanstalk fame) in the Giant's boots. When I complained, Dad came up with a unique solution: he acquired a pair of second-hand football boots which, at least, were roughly the right size. He removed the studs and Mum coloured them black with the black-lead polish then used on fire-grates and ranges.

Sadly, these wore well and I was forced to endure them for many months, much to the glee of the more malicious element among my fellow pupils. I was triply damned in their eyes: a Southerner with seven fingers and no shoes. Although I was growing fast, I was a sickly child (we did not know it then but one of my kidneys was already failing) but in the ways of young boys everywhere, I had established a place for myself in the pecking order of school life. The normal way was to use your fists, which was beyond me. I learned, however, that humour was a highly efficient means of defence: make people laugh and they don't punch you. It was a lesson well learned, perhaps too well learned, for I still have a reputation for fighting my corner with a wicked turn of phrase. It is a reputation that, at times, has given me more pain than I ever inflicted.

I was to be poor for a long time, then rich and poor again, but I still remember the humiliation of those gleaming black football boots. Poverty is relative, but if your mates have shoes and you don't — then you're poor.

Chapter Two

It's An Ill Wind

THE breeding habits of rabbits are of passing interest to most young-sters in their pre-puberty years because, I presume, they give some inkling of that 'birds and bees' subject. Today, such matters are taught in school in almost clinical detail but when I was a lad, the subject was only whispered about behind the bike sheds. If you were lucky, you might find a local girl who would show you hers if you would show her yours, but we had little idea how the two things actually fitted together.

As we all know, rabbits breed like, well, rabbits, at a speed which causes a great deal of consternation to people like farmers, to whom they are a major pest. For one young Leicestershire lad in those pre-war years, even this was not fast enough. So a ten-year-old Billy Williams, as I had inevitably become known, spent long periods of that difficult time persuading rabbits to become even more amorous. This, I hasten to explain, was not as a result of an over-morbid interest in sex — a subject which admittedly was to preoccupy me to considerable lengths in the decades to come — but out of pure commercial merit. The Family Williams had embarked upon yet another money-making scheme to improve our lot and this one involved breeding rabbits for their meat and fur.

At home, things were beginning to pick up. Dad eventually got a regular job as the assistant gardener to the assistant gardener to the Bishop of Leicester, and with Mum still working her fingers to the bone — almost literally — we could now pay our way without too much discomfort. Later, the advent of World War Two was, ironically, to make things even better because Dad, now too old for the army, got a job in the munitions factories. By our previous standards, the money was literally rolling in. But I had been brought up to contribute to the joint family venture and there was still extra to be made on the side, which is why I had decided to harness the sexual drive of the rabbit to further swell the coffers. We had rented a house which had a large unused garage which I stacked with cages, filled them with rabbits of both sexes and, for a while, let nature take its course. Soon, I was selling half-a-dozen rabbits a week which I skinned and butchered. The meat went to the local butcher and I sent the pelts away to be treated and made into gloves and other items of clothing. I was breaking even, perhaps making a little profit, but was on the lookout to find ways of improving production.

Then I noticed that the female rabbit is not always as friendly as she is supposed to be. The doe would sometimes say no. And despite their enviable reputation in this sphere, the bucks would sometimes be lacking at their task, so I assumed that even a rabbit can have too much of a good thing. What to do?

After some weeks of experiment, I discovered that, by tying a doe's tail forward with a length of cotton, I could get her quite frisky. The buck, watching this strange procedure at first with grave disinterest, would suddenly get excited too: perhaps he had the sudden thought that he was in danger of being made redundant. He would attack the job with renewed vigour and within a matter of months, I was selling up to 20 rabbits a week, which was quite a business for a lad (Claude Jeremiah Greengrass himself would no doubt be green with envy).

Whether or not this was a suitable occupation for a boy on the verge of adolescence I cannot say; perhaps the psychologists would have some interesting views on the subject, particularly in view of some of my behaviour in later life. But like so many of the Williams family schemes, the rabbit breeding business would be supplanted by a new venture, just as profitable and far less demanding in time if not in effort. Showbusiness was beckoning.

—oOo—

The working men's clubs of the North and Midlands of England have, over the years, built a mystique of their own. They are supposed to be all spit-and-sawdust, with non-stop darts and black pudding sandwiches interspersed, today at least, with full-frontal strippers who are hired by the pound weight rather than for talent, charm, or beauty. It is true that they have been the training ground of many of the country's top entertainers — many comics would rather have played the lions in the Rome Colosseum than some ship-wright's club in the North-East — but before and after World War Two, in the East Midlands at least, they were viewed as centres of respectability in working class districts.

Contradictory though it may seem, the club movement had among its founders many sound-thinking men who realised that the tradition of the menfolk drinking heavily in the pub while the wife and kiddies stayed at home was a dangerous threat to family life. There was, of course, a strong total abstinence movement among many religious groups, particularly the Methodists, but more liberal thinkers believed that as a working man deserved his pint and bit of fun, it would be preferable to provide them in respectable surroundings where — at certain times of the week at least — he could take his wife and children.

These times were usually centred around live entertainment, usually two performers each doing several different acts as comics, singers, conjurors, dancers, the whole gamut of a music hall bill. For many who could not afford tickets at the local music hall or the cinema, the club was the only source of entertainment apart from the radio. And as there were literally scores of such clubs in the Leicester area alone, far more than there are today, the demand for performers was high. Like most of his kind, Dad was a regular at his working men's club, where he would take a half pint of mild and smoke his Woodbines. When there were a couple of acts for a 'family show' he would sometimes take Mum and me. It was like a drug, an instant 'hit', the most exciting thing that had ever happened in my young life. But I didn't go so much to enjoy the acts as to scrutinise them, to watch the body language and the half-disguised expressions of the performers, trying to judge how much pleasure, or pain, they were gaining rather than how much pleasure they were giving to the audience. Here was a real challenge, I thought, to keep all those adults interested and involved when there were pints to sup, games to play, gossip to be exchanged. What's more, an inkling of a thought at the back of my mind said: *They get paid for this...*

Those all-too-rare visits to the working men's club were not my major contact with the world of showbusiness. This was the great era of radio and from very early childhood, I had been singing along with the likes of George Formby and Gracie Fields, the super-stars of the day. I didn't just sing. I danced and bobbed and jived, extemporising little acts for my parents and friends. My father, astute as ever, had noticed these little buds of interest sprouting. My first break came, however, in hallowed showbusiness style. One day when I was eight, we went down to the club and the booked acts had not turned up. To fill the void, the secretary called for a 'free-and-easy' which was an open invitation to anyone in the audience to put on a turn. Dad turned to me and said: "You're quite good at that singing and dancing, son. Do you fancy having a go?" Now I feel that it is very important at this stage to make one thing crystal clear. There are hundreds, perhaps thousands, of ambitious parents on the fringes of showbusiness who push their young children almost to the point of breakdown to make them into entertainers. The whole industry, and in particular Hollywood, is awash with stories of youngsters who have been forced as square pegs into round holes to become so-called 'child stars' only to have their adult lives end in a disaster of booze, drugs, broken marriages and even suicide. Those parents are perhaps driven by their own lack of success to win it through their offspring, often at the cost of destroying any chance of a normal childhood. I loath these parents and despise what they do to their children. But my father was most emphatically *not* one of this group.

He was, as I have already explained, a man with an ever-open eye for a financial opportunity. This was driven, not by greed, but by his experiences of real poverty and a determination to better himself and us. In this mix there was almost certainly a sense of guilt that during those long years of slump, he had not been able to provide the things to which he felt we were entitled. But at no time did he exploit either my mother or me. We were a family unit, one whole made up of three individuals, and because of the circumstances of the time, we were all expected to do whatever we could to benefit each other. As I have already explained, he never in his life hit me and rarely raised his voice. Instead of exploiting, he encouraged, but only when he was convinced that I was genuinely interested in whatever I was doing. This may have led to somewhat bizarre activities, like my excursion into the rabbit trade, but I had succeeded at that by a lot of hard work and observation. Dad's theme was if you want to do something, do it the best you can, work hard at it and if, after a while, interest fades, try something else. Eventually, you will find the path you wish to follow.

So at the age of eight, when he suggested I 'have a go' in that free-and-easy, he was not thinking of cash — it was an amateur night. He could not know that he was setting a spark that was to turn into an inferno. When I stepped on to my first ever 'stage' — it was in fact a plank laid over two beer crates at the South Wigston WMC — I had a sense of total delight mixed with awe and not a little fear. I banged out George Formby songs at the top of my reedy, unbroken voice and — delight of delights — got a big round of applause, the sound that to any entertainer is more potent than heroin, more necessary than meat and drink. Best of all, Dad said afterwards: "I think you've got what it takes, son." It had begun ...but it was to be a hesitant debut.

—oOo—

That first amateur night triumph did not last long for the ill wind was still blowing. The very next day, I was dragged off to an isolation hospital suffering from scarlet fever for 16 of the loneliest — and most important — weeks of my life.

Before the discovery of antibiotics, scarlet fever was one of the dread diseases that haunted Britain along with diphtheria, TB and polio. It was highly infectious and its only means of treatment were some rudimentary medicines, fresh air, bed-rest and total isolation. Throughout the country were dotted hundreds of isolation hospitals where patients waited alone for the disease to work itself out more or less in its own time (or kill, if you were one of the unlucky ones).

Procedures were stringently enforced. Any clothes that you took in with you, any comics or books, were incinerated when you left. My parents were allowed no physical contact with me whatsoever. When they came to visit, we talked through a glass screen as they do in American gangster movies on prison visits. For an eight-year-old child, who had spent his entire young life at the very heart of a close-knit family, the sense of separation was close to unbearable. My parents understood this instinctively and, with a touch of imagination verging on genius, came up with a solution.

Dad had remembered — he would always remember, he told me years later — my words after my amateur night triumph at the South Wigston Working Men's Club: "I just love it. I want to be a star, Dad." So on my second day in isolation, when Mum and Dad appeared behind their glass screen, they had big beams on their faces and a big, strangely-shaped parcel in their hands. A nurse brought it into my room a few minutes later. I tore at the string and brown-paper wrapping and, in a moment of pure joy, there lay on my narrow, iron-framed cot a ukelele, the instrument which had helped make George Formby into one of the most famous, and richest, men in Britain.

No present before or since has ever had a greater affect on my life. I was to be in solitary in that cramped room for four long months. I could have had nothing to do and boredom is a cruel state for an eight-year-old. Instead, I learned to play the ukulele. For after the instrument came batches of sheet music which, as well as the dots, also showed the various stringing positions for various chords — where the fingers should be to produce given sounds. I was fascinated and had lots of time on my hands. By the time I left that hospital, I was a musician, completely self-taught but skilful enough to compete with most of the so-called 'semi-professionals' on the club circuit. Like everything else, though, that first ukelele went into the hospital incinerator. So Dad had to buy me another one and musical instruments do not come cheap. But once again, the Family Williams was to take on new challenges. It was time to turn pro.

—oOo—

Normally, I try to avoid the use of clichés and the 'ill wind' which blows no one any good is as big a chestnut as you are ever likely to find. But in a strange way, the ill winds of my life — the winds that actually brought me quite severe health problems — may actually have done me a power of good. Losing a finger as a toddler gave me a healthy respect for moving machinery and you get quite a lot of that backstage or in television studios. Scarlet fever, combined with my father's inspired choice of a gift, gave me the opportunity to become a professional performer which means, in effect, that it dictated the pattern of my entire life. But that eight-year-old boy in solitary had by no means seen an end to his health problems.

Just as I was about to start grammar school — an unlikely event in itself, considering my total lack of interest in any lessons at school other than English — I was struck down again, this time with a life-threatening illness which necessitated the removal of my failing kidney. That was a major operation in those days and recovery from it by no means certain. Not only did I survive in some style but my single remaining, much-abused kidney has processed a great deal of Guinness and champagne since then.

It also acted, however, as a constant warning. In my day, I was to booze with the best of them in a profession where alcoholism is an everyday event no rarer than 'flu or a sore throat. Many truly great professionals have ruined their lives with booze. To do that, you must hit the spirits hard over many a long year. If you have only one kidney, spirits take a massive toll and would probably kill you from renal failure before you had time to become a dyed-in-the wool alcoholic. So when I was living it up in the night clubs or on the racecourse, I tended to stick to champagne. This concern has also led me into charitable work for several kidney research and support organisations, which has introduced me to some of the best people I have ever met. And more than half a century since my single kidney parted friends with its mate, it is still going strong although now it mainly deals with the odd half-pint of real ale at, yes, my local working men's club and pubs which I visit to listen to the visiting bands. A small beer and a lively band is now my idea of a good night out, particularly if they play my favourite country music. It was this obsession that led to a series called *Maynard's Bill* on Yorkshire Television, in which we went out searching for new musical talent in the pubs and clubs of Leeds.

At the risk of turning this tome into a medical directory, I must also point out that the loss of a kidney was not my last brush with the ill wind. At grammar school, my only triumph (apart from falling in love with one of my teachers) was to become one of the better players in the soccer team. As a result, I was spotted by a scout from Leicester City and had expectations for a career as a professional soccer player.

I played inside-right with other youngsters in the Leicester junior teams along with the likes of Don Revie, the future Leeds United and England manager, who later introduced me to one of my closest friends, Jackie Charlton, who was to go on to an extraordinary career as a World Cup winner with England in 1966 and as a very successful manager of the Republic of Ireland team. But once again, the ill wind blew, this time in the guise of a training injury.

It was what they call a 'divided cruciate ligament' which, in effect, buggers up your knee for life. Any chance of a footballing future disappeared in one crunching collision. And that, too, might have been a good thing because even if I had made the grade — which is unlikely considering the competition — footballers, unlike comics and actors, do not get the chance to continue their careers into their 70s.

One strange thing, though. A divided cruciate ligament, once irreparable, is the injury that put an end to Brian Clough's highly successful playing career. It recently hit Paul 'Gazza' Gascoigne, although modern surgery has been able to put that right. To my knowledge, this the only sporting injury that seems to spread from the knee to the mouth

Chapter Three

First Love

SO they bought me some black velvet trousers, a collection of bright silk blouses with matching sashes and, at the age of nine, I was 'in the business', a pint-sized professional who, for his first-ever date, received the sum of half-a-crown (12½ pence in modern money) from the Aylestone Working Men's Club in the sweetly-named Saffron Lane, Leicester. This does not sound much for several hours of non-stop song, dance and music from Billy Williams, 'Leicester's very own George Formby' (as I was billed), but it was a full day's pay for Dad. For a nine-year-old to be earning more than a grown man was an indication of how the working men's clubs thrived in the evenings — and how their members were exploited during the day. Mum and Dad took me everywhere by bus at first, to support me on stage and help carry my instruments and props to and fro. Later, as my bookings and payments grew, there came a series of very small, very old, very battered motor cars. After deducting our expenses, either for bus fares or later petrol, the 'profits' were ploughed back into my act. They paid for dancing lessons and bought new costumes, sheet music, and more musical instruments: a guitar and then an arcane piece known as a banjolele, a hybrid which combined some of the sounds of the banjo and the ukulele. This was George Formby's favourite instrument and his young admirer — and plagiariser — just had to have one. Such equipment does not come cheap but Dad had the sense to invest in the future. I saved some money by not needing lessons — I had a certain knack that came naturally so I was self taught on a wide range of instruments.

For Dad, these early beginnings in showbusiness were much more than just picking up some extra money for the family coffers. They gave him the chance to deal, as my manager and agent, with a group of rather severe gentlemen called entertainment secretaries (in Northern clubs, they have the grand title of concert secretary). These were the men who selected which acts should appear and insisted, even for a half-crown performance, that a legally binding contract was signed before the act was booked.

Anyone who failed to live up to the terms of that contract by being, say, a few minutes late or singing nine numbers instead of ten, could be black-balled not by just the one secretary but by scores of his peers. They had an inform-ation network that the Mafia would envy and their attitude to business was not too different either. For people called entertainment secretaries, they were un-entertaining in the extreme from the performer's point of view.

For Dad, dealing with men like this on my behalf was part game, part business. To him the money was important but, like a good poker player, he enjoyed taking on these rather dour men at their own game — and winning. He must have been good at it because our bookings continued to soar. Presumably the entertainment secretaries had decided in their collective wis-dom that I gave value for money. The bargaining and the banter involved was good for Dad and, I think, helpful in the future. After running his prized corner shop, he then became a club steward and later, with me as a partner, a successful publican. If Dad was learning the business, I was learning the trade. At one stage, I was doing as many as nine different routines, from George Formby via romantic ballads to comic songs dressed in drag. This meant nine different costumes, all of which came out of the profits, and also a series of props.

Now the evil ability of a prop — any prop — to devastate a performance on stage or screen is a constant source of conversation in showbusiness: the door that won't open to let an actor on to the stage, the door handle that comes off as he tries to get off the stage, the chairs that move of their own accord, inevitably into an actor's path (or out of his way if he is required to sit down) are legendary, worthy of a book in their own right. For me, the first of many run-ins with props came when I was working with a singer called Peggy Neilson who was rather novel in that she could sing in two different octaves, as a soprano in flowing dresses or as a tenor in a man's dinner jacket. Our finale was a cowboy number when I serenaded her with my guitar, my leg resting on a log. Now this might be difficult to believe but you don't find many logs lying around, particularly in working men's clubs. So we had to carry our own and in the pre-car days, the aggravation of dragging musical instru-ments, costume cases and a hulking great log on and off a series of buses was not my ideal way of spending an evening. I got to dislike bus conductors almost as much as I disliked entertainment secretaries.

However, there were compensations. At the age of 11 or 12, I was earning more than Dad (he only got 23 shillings a week as the assistant gardener to the assistant gardener to the Bishop of Leicester, and I was soon on 35 shillings) and we were able to scrape enough money to buy a small car, a Singer, which was about the same size as the sewing machine whose name it shares. This was considered a major breakthrough, the very height of luxury, among our fellow entertainers. As we normally went around the club circuits in pairs, it made sense for your fellow artiste to travel with you and share the petrol bill.

One dark and windy night, I was jammed in the Singer's tiny back seat, surrounded by instrument cases and props, with a girl contortionist some three or four years older than me, which is a very big gap indeed for a 12-year-old who has just come to puberty. She was, in a phrase then used in condemnation by elderly spinsters, 'experienced' and during a long drive home her hands began to explore the more intimate parts of my body despite the fact that her own father was sitting next to Dad in the front (he, presumably, was her manager, agent and, although she certainly didn't let it inhibit her, chaperone).

Then, on this dark and windy Leicestershire night, Fate took a hand. As the little Singer chugged up a long, steep hill it came to a slow, juddering halt. After some fiddling about under the bonnet (whilst my contortionist was doing much the same with my nether regions) Dad announced resignedly: "We've run out of petrol."

He took a spare gerrycan from the boot and set off with a firm stride to the nearest garage, accompanied by the girl's father. Well, it was a very small car parked on a very steep hill and the tiny back seat was crammed with musical instruments, props and the writhing bodies of two young artistes. But she was a contortionist (the work of Fate again, no doubt) and by the time the two men returned about 40 minutes later, I had been well and truly deflowered.

Now just how it happened, I have never been sure. Perhaps some examiner couldn't add up. Perhaps those intelligence tests saved me (putting the right shape in the right hole, that sort of thing). Perhaps Fate was still at it. But somehow or other, I had passed the 11-plus and one I day arrived at the gates of a very posh school indeed: Kibworth Beauchamp Grammar School.

Set in open countryside near the A6 trunk road south of Leicester, the school was founded in 1491 and the name Beauchamp (pronounced Beecham) comes from a family of land-owning Norman aristocrats who had come over with the Conqueror. It still had boarders from all parts of the county and it stood for those very English values that I had only read about: tradition, virtue, public service, self sacrifice and many more. It also had one most unusual characteristic for its time for it was co-educational. There were girls, big girls, and that was not to help my education along a great deal apart from the times when I persuaded some of them to do my homework or copy theirs.

Now for years, I had been reading about upper echelon boarding schools in comics like *Rover*, *Wizard* and *Champion*. The antics of Billy Bunter and the boys at Red Circle School in the *Hotspur* were weekly news to me and I looked upon them almost as friends. But they were fiction; they didn't exist. Yet here I was, a raggedy-arsed urchin from Rat Alley, and I was at a *real* school with *real* boys and masters and although the antics were not so extreme, they were very much in the same mould. To stray into the pages of your favourite comic and become part of your own fictional dreams is a distinctly unnerving experience for an 11-year-old boy.

The school itself was so imposing as to be frightening to a new boy, however street-wise. It was built round the original school house, a half-stone, half-weathered brick Tudor hall where the headmaster still kept his study. Much newer blocks of classrooms and laboratories had been built on with great care so as not to spoil the grounds, acres of grass and trees which even boasted a paddock. I might, in my memory's eye, be slightly exaggerating its grandeur but for a working class boy in the early days, this was not a school but a palace. And as you would expect, the palace was inhabited by a set of people different to any I had ever met before.

It is fashionable nowadays for everyone to claim to be middle class. Back in 1939 and 1940, with a terrible war just starting and Britain not doing at all well, the middle class were not the very rich or the aristocracy — they sent their children to the great public schools — but the doctors, the solicitors, the architects and the businessmen who in fact ran prosperous provincial cities like Leicester. Even in those early days, reports would come filtering back to the school of Old Boys being killed in the war. Old Boys who were nearly all officers.

As the son of a private soldier, the thought that I might one day become eligible for the officer class had never occurred to me. The thought that I would have friends who were sometimes delivered to school by large, shiny cars, despite petrol rationing, had never crossed my mind. In my world, big cars meant either a wedding or, more likely, a funeral. The gap between working class and middle class was, to me, a chasm and one that I never really tried to cross. I could have become a swot, but I was too lazy, or tried to butter up the richer children, but that went against my back-street grain. Instead, apart from enjoying myself on the football field, I became a rebel and showed no interest in lessons whatsoever — with one notable exception.

For friendship, I stuck with what I knew in the shape of one Maurice 'Modge' Freestone, who had been my mate at the old flea-ridden primary school in South Wigston and who, like me, had passed a scholarship. For some years, Modge and I vied with each other to be bottom of the class, with 'failure' being second from bottom. Why this was I cannot really explain. I am not aware of any planned, premeditated protest against our new surroundings. Finally, though, Modge got his act together and began to work, taking full advantage of the excellent education on offer to anyone with the sense to grab it. Modge went on to university and, I believe, became a lecturer and then a school headmaster in the Channel Islands.

Me? I just larked about. I would throw meat pies up and down the refectory where we had lunch (it was 'dinner' to me) and blocked the toilets by pouring chocolate pudding down them; it set harder than ferro-concrete and tasted much the same, which is why it went down the loo. Then I got banned from the school bus for necking with one of the girls, which meant a 16-mile cycle ride there and back every day until Mum came to see the headmaster and begged (successfully) for a reprieve.

On the football field, I did pretty well: I was captain of our house team and played regularly for the school First XI and I was also made welcome at one other activity: the school concert. It was rare, then, for a boy to play an instrument like the guitar (although we had more formal instrumentalists like violinists and pianists in the school orchestra) and, of course, I was already a professional entertainer. So they always found a spot for me in the concerts and would give me a decent hand afterwards, even the teachers to whom I'd given a pretty rough time. Except for one.

First love is a painful thing and I was most certainly not the first — nor would I be the last — schoolboy to fall head over heels in love with his teacher, in this case Miss Hern who taught me English with some success. With the war well under way, and most of the young male teachers away fighting it, we had a large number of young women student teachers at Kibworth Beauchamp. None matched the fire and sparkle of Miss Hern, a tiny brunette with a stunning figure, who breathed so much enthusiasm into her classes that she carried everyone along almost spellbound. It worked even with young Billy Williams, but not for some search for academic excellence.

By this time, I was 16 years old and Miss Hern was perhaps 18 or 19. Far from being the bottom of the class, I was top every year in English. The reason: I was showing off to the object of my affections. Whatever the motive, however, Miss Hern fired in me an interest and love of language which burns today. This is an attitude that I recognise because to do good work, I need the encouragement to make the best of my own talents; directors cannot tell me to act well, only help me to do so. Trying to bully me to do my job properly has just the opposite effect; I become stubborn and dig in until we come to a suitable compromise, an attitude which I strike in dealings with any member of the establishment. Even today, when I have battles with bright young directors and producers who want to change my way of working (and lose!), I remember Miss Hern. She didn't tell you what to do but helped you discover how you should do it yourself. This is the sign of a true professional, whether it be a teacher, a TV director, or a soccer coach.

There was only one other teacher at Kibworth Beauchamp who even half-inspired me: Mr Schell who taught French. Through him I learned a French poem *La Feuille* (The Leaf) which I can recite word-for-word to this day and this has proved very useful from time to time. Whilst playing foreigners, I have often whispered it as background dialogue (as The Goons used to chant, "Rhubarb, rhubarb") but that probably is not a lot to speak of after five years of expensive education.

I left grammar school without a single qualification because in those days one had to matriculate across a wide range of subjects, including mathematics, to get a certificate. In later times, I might have gained a single O-level (or even a GCSE) for English but I was never going to pass anything in maths. From this long distance, I feel that I could have, should have, done better at school. Why I didn't is probably down to laziness, rebelliousness and tedium plus the fact that I was already earning a goodish living from the clubs and thought I was going to be a professional footballer.

But when they did my *This is Your Life* on TV and couldn't find Miss Hern, I was devastated.

Chapter Four

Muriel

*I*T didn't take long for me to get my come-uppance. The 16-year-old youth with a great future on the soccer field on a Saturday afternoon and on the stage on a Saturday night became the 17-year-old with no future, thanks to my divided cruciate injury, the footballing phenomenon which, as I have explained, spreads from the knee to the mouth. Fortunately, the mouth was still functioning brilliantly and it managed to talk me into (and often out of) a series of jobs connected loosely with selling. If I wasn't selling, I was 'fiddling', which is the word we used then. With hindsight, the better word would have been 'stealing'.

Those years at the grammar school had made few dents in the basic street morality that I had learned the hard way in Rat Alley. The gist of this was that there was 'us', the poor people who had nothing, and 'them', the rich people who had everything. It was absolutely forbidden to steal from one of 'us', but to relieve 'them' of the odd little knick-knack was not just acceptable but virtually compulsory. We did not actually look upon it as stealing, more as a justifiable reordering of the economic system, a form of social justice in action. When you got a job, of course, you were still 'us', but your employers became the biggest 'them' of all. For much of my time as a worker, until a certain good influence arrived on the scene, there was often more stock in my bedroom than at the shops or warehouses where I worked. Some came from simple theft, carried out more in a sense of devilment — getting back at the boss — than for profit. Other times I did deals, often to my own detriment: I got sacked from one place because I used to do the old cleaner's work for her and split her pay. She wanted to retire and I thought I was doing her a favour. The boss, coming back one day to find me on my knees polishing the floor rather than pursuing my career as an up-and-coming salesman, sacked me on the spot. I moved from company to company, warehouses, wholesalers and shops and, back home, my stock began to grow although I cannot ever remember making much profit from it; I usually gave it away to mates or their girl friends. Then I finally got to be a salesman at Lewis's, a rather grand store in Leicester, selling electrical goods. Even there, I could not keep temptation at bay.

In the late 1940s and early 1950s, department stores in prosperous cities like Leicester still maintained an air of Edwardian grandeur. They were slightly shabby after the war years, of course, but still carried themselves with a little pomp and circumstance: managers and floor walkers would wear morning coats and striped trousers like bankers and, yes, they often wore a flower in their buttonholes. These were the sort of places where the inhabitants of Rat Alley most certainly did not shop. Although I had absolutely no qualifications, I probably got the job because I had been to the grammar school ('where' you had been rather than 'what' you had achieved was the yardstick). Eventually, I was promoted to the electrical goods department, selling household appliances, but my methods were soon to attract attention.

I had always loved the work of the market 'spielers', the stallholders who sell crockery or linens or cutlery with a combination of conjuring skills, jokes, and back-chat with the punters. The good ones could make a living on the stage any day (but they probably make more money and pay less tax as they are). It did not, however, go down too well when I introduced such tactics to Lewis's of Leicester.

"Buy a vacuum cleaner, ladies, and let it do half your work," I cried, brandishing the said appliance at shoulder height. "In fact, buy two and let them do all of it." Within the hour, I was standing before the huge desk of the store manager in his even huger office. He leaned his elbows on the desk, bowed his head and looked at me sternly through upturned eyes: "Retailing is a serious trade, Mr Williams. I believe you are a comic by night but during the day I would like you to act like a human being."

Lewis's was, by my then untutored judgment, a highly sophisticated place. Some of the staff were still on the fiddle — one man had become a local hero by stealing an entire greenhouse panel by panel from the gardening section — but these new surroundings gave me a taste for better things than petty theft. I took up blackmail. In those days, consumer electricals like vacuum cleaners and fridges were just beginning to come on the market after the war and public demand for them was insatiable. You just stood back, crossed your arms and let the ladies fight over them. Then I made a discovery: the reps for companies like Hoover who delivered these goods to the store were on a substantial commission and yet we, the counter staff, did what little selling was required. To get their commission, which could be as high as £1 12s 6d on a single cleaner (more than a day and a half's pay for me) the reps simply had to take back to their companies the guarantee tags which came with every machine, tags which we, the counter staff, had collected and filled in with the necessary details. We did the work and they got the commission.

This was an obvious case of exploitation of the workers. The sales reps, who until now I had thought of as 'us', suddenly became 'them'. They would, of course, have to pay. So I began to point out with much pouting and shaking of head that if a rep wanted one of his guarantee tags, he would have to pay for it. By this time, the rep's face would be several degrees paler and he would begin to clutch at his shirt collar as though he needed air. I had little sympathy. These guys were making small fortunes as glorified delivery boys who merely had to fill in a few forms to pick up their very handsome pay packets. There was one such character, a former RAF pilot, who had sold his entire consignment by Tuesday lunchtime of each week and spent the rest of his time either flying his private aircraft or getting falling-down drunk in all the best watering holes of the East Midlands. No, these people were definitely not 'us'.

My going rate became 50 per cent of the salesman's commission and strictly cash, of course, and very soon I had several of them at it. Hoover's and the like probably thought these guys were working for them when, at least part of the time, they were working for Billy Williams. I think the Mafia would have been proud of me (Claude Jeremiah Greengrass most certainly would have). What with my legitimate wages and my still growing earnings from the club circuit, I was beginning to do very nicely indeed, thank you very much. I believe I was on the way to a big success in the retail trade — either that or jail, which was probably more likely — but by this time, a new influence was taking hold of my life. In fact, she was to be *the* most important influence of my life although, being the bloody fool I am, it took me more than 30 years to realise it.

Enter the one and only Muriel Linnett...

—oOo—

Before climbing the dizzy heights to Lewis's, I had worked as an assistant buyer to a company of Leicester wholesalers which sold almost everything:

textiles, clothing, haberdashery and many more arcane products. Although the title seemed full of promise for future prospects, I was in fact the general dogs-body, fetching and carrying, making the tea, helping out in the storeroom. In other words, in the scale of things, I was the lowest of the low.

Then, one fateful day, in walked an elegant young woman and, for the first time since Miss Hern, I found myself obsessed with a lady who deserved the word 'class'. Ever since my first encounter with the contortionist in the back of Dad's old Singer, I had been highly active sexually. Touring the working men's clubs had given my plenty of opportunity to meet a certain type lady performer (in both senses of that word). They were nice enough girls, funny and pleasantly obliging, and for a growing youth with a few pounds in his pocket they were pretty easy prey. Alas, few of them merited the then fashionable sobriquet of 'classy', so when Muriel walked into my boss's office, where she had just become his personal assistant and office manager, my eyes lit up. She was about 5ft 7ins tall, and looked much taller in her fashionable high-heeled shoes, which were complemented always by sheer silk stockings. And she always — absolutely always — wore gloves. They were white in the summer, dark leather in the winter, and this just added to her statement of class. She walked with a straight back that showed off to the very best advan-tage her perfectly proportioned figure. My mind immediately went back to Miss Hern, the unobtainable, for there is this strange anomaly in the sexual longings of all young men: the more out of reach a woman appears to be, the more alluring she becomes.

What's more, she was two years older than me and, in effect, my boss. Although in height I towered over her, she always seemed bigger than me. When she gave me instructions for minor tasks, I could barely listen; I would just stare into her hazel eyes, take in the rich brown hair, and stutter. She took all this in her stride, because she had seen it all before. She had just finished a stint in the Wrens, the Women's Royal Naval Service, where she had served as a secretary to several senior officers and where her duties had involved pas-sing on orders from the top brass to young ratings. They, I assume, had acted in her presence in much the same way as me.

Not only was she classically beautiful but also super-efficient. She could type and take shorthand like lightning and, as an office manager, ran, as one would expect, a very tight ship. Within a few weeks, she was virtually running the company but in a subtle, understated way that flattered her boss, the man-aging director, into thinking her success was due to his influence. To a shamb-ling, tongue-tied youth like me, wise in the more crooked ways of the world but utterly unversed in the proper ways of running a legitimate business enterprise, she was truly formidable. Within days I was hopelessly, miserably in love because I could not believe in my wildest dreams (of which I had many) that she would ever return the feelings which I held for such a paragon. As often happens in my relationship with women, I was wrong. As I was to learn later, Muriel was not the upper class demigod I had first perceived but the daughter of a storeman not much more elevated in the class system than me. But her father was the careful and conscientious type who had saved his money and the family actually owned their own home, a fairly modest semi as it turned out, but theirs nevertheless. To a youth like me, who had known nothing better than rented rooms and houses, any member of the property owning classes was a world apart.

I think this became our first point of contact. Like my own family, poor as they had been, Muriel wanted to 'better herself' — once again that phrase that had haunted my childhood. How she managed to detect such ambitions in me I do not know; I suspect that at this stage, she understood my inner workings better than I did. She also possessed one other priceless asset, perhaps the greatest asset of all: she had a sense of humour and, with a character like me, that was an absolute essential.

It took me weeks to pluck up the courage to ask her out. It was months before she finally agreed, months in which she dismissed my ardent pleas with a mere twinkle of those hazel eyes. Although she had a sense of humour, it was much more subtle than mine. At first, I feel, she just dismissed me as a 'card', a young chap whose attempts to make her laugh brought some light relief into those long, routine office days. But she did take interest when I told her anecdotes about my work as an entertainer and even more when I dreamed aloud of a successful career in showbusiness. She would have probably reacted in similar vein to any young man who demonstrated ambition in any given field. But I happened to be there, I was persistent and I eventually discovered a more sophisticated humour that actually made her laugh. I wasn't a bad looking young fella, either, so eventually persistence paid and she agreed to go out with me. Trouble was, I was always broke. Whatever I earned, both at the office and in the clubs, I spent like wildfire, a trait that I learned to control many years later but not until it had caused both Muriel and me endless suffering. I should have taken her to the theatre and expensive restaurants — that's what she deserved. Instead, I took her on the rounds of the clubs I worked in so that, night after night, she endured the same acts over and over again. This constant repetition must have caused her excruciating boredom but, if so, she never said. I like to think that, even in those dreary working men's clubs, she saw in me some future promise. She never complained but supported, like Miss Hern had done earlier. When she made some little criticism of the act, she did so constructively rather than destructively, and I soon learned to take her criticisms — suggestions is a better word — seriously. As a result, my performances improved.

Much to my amazement, she finally accepted my proposal and we married at the church of St John the Baptist in Clarendon Park, Leicester, on November 5, 1949. The choice of Bonfire Night for the ceremony was not premeditated but was to prove a fateful prophesy: our marriage was to see a lot of flames, smoke and fireworks. All of them, I hasten to add, caused by me.

By this time, Mum and Dad had gone up another small step in the world and had become steward and stewardess of the nearby South Knighton Working Men's Club. They had a couple of small rooms to spare above the club and here Muriel and I set up in married life after a brief honeymoon in Bournemouth. We were, so to speak, living above the shop and it would not be the last time that we were to rely on relatives to put a roof over our heads.

During our courtship, in my constant state of penury, I had made a habit of borrowing five shillings from Muriel every Monday and paying her back on the following Friday, pay day. After a while, she grew tired of my asking and began to leave the five bob in her office drawer saying, "Take it when you want it and put it back when you can."

For some years later, when I joked about marriage in my act, as all comics tend to do, I would tell the audience this story and add the punch-line: "There came a day when I couldn't afford to return the five bob so I proposed instead. She accepted because it was the only way of getting her money back."

I have not used that gag for many a long year now. Muriel is gone and it wasn't until we had been together for 20 years or more, had many ups and downs and supported each other through them all, that I realised just how important her love was. She was kind, astute, hard-working, understanding, forgiving and, like my mother, she was to face times when she would work herself into exhaustion to keep her family together.

I still love you, Muriel, and the pain of not having you is almost too much to bear.

Chapter Five

Professional

$\mathcal{I}$NGOLDMELLS Point is a long, flat, bleak stretch of sands on the Lincoln-shire coast, where the sea rolls in brown and, when the east winds are blowing, is as cold as a frozen pork chop. In 1951, it was a long, straggling suburb of broken-down beach shacks and pre-war caravans creeping away from Skegness — Skeggie — which once advertised on railway station posters under the slogan, 'Skegness is so Bracing'. The Advertising Standards Council, had it existed then, would have had no quarrel with the description, for Skeggie is so bracing that on windy days, you need climbing crampons to stop yourself being blown off the beach.

Despite these drawbacks, Skeggie had been for most of the century the automatic seaside destination for workers and their families from East Mid-lands industrial towns and cities like Leicester, Nottingham and Derby when they took their annual one-week holiday. It was close by, there were lots of trains and buses, and, above all, it was cheap, the modern-day equivalent of Benidorm on Spain's Costa del Grot.

Las Vegas it was most certainly not. Nevertheless, this unlikely spot des-erves a monument to its shining place in the history of British showbusiness as a hot-house nursery for the breeding of soon-to-be famous entertainers. All this was thanks to the vision of one man, Billy — later Sir Billy — Butlin, who brought the holiday camp to the British masses by giving them cheap and cheerful seaside hols which, compared with the grim working lives they led in their factories and foundries, had a dash of glamour.

Billy Butlin had one brilliant idea. Working men in those days were not accustomed to controlling the family budget. They would hand their weekly pay packet to their wives, who would dole out a couple of pounds for the old man's spending money, and split the rest on housekeeping, rent, clothing and other essentials. When holiday time loomed, they were never sure how much it would cost and how they could manage to control the flow of cash so that it lasted the whole week with enough left over to pay the landlady of their boarding house.

Butlin came up with the idea of the all-in holiday where all the major items were paid for in advance: accommodation, meals, funfairs and entertainment. All the family needed when they arrived was a few quid for the odd pint (and you could still get a good pint of mild for less than a shilling) or a few ice-creams for the children. It created a whole new era at the British seaside, attracting millions of families and, incidentally, making Butlin a very rich man indeed. Once inside those gates, guarded only slightly more efficiently than those at Colditz, the punter could wander anywhere and use all the camp's facilities like a millionaire.

The camps looked more like an army barracks than a holiday paradise, with row upon row of wooden huts which went under the then posh-sounding name of 'chalets'. There were family chalets and others for single youngsters, strictly segregated by gender and, at night, patrolled by security men in an attempt to prevent bed-swapping, a mission in which they largely failed. During the day, acres of young flesh were seen to be pitted with love-bites which went under the familiar name of 'chalet rash'.

Now these youngsters, and indeed their parents, could get a few pints and visit the dance halls back home. They could even get a severe case of chalet rash in some entry in a bleak terrace of redbrick two-up and two-downs. What they could not get, however, was almost non-stop entertainment at a time when television was still rare and the variety theatres charged a pretty penny for a seat. Billy Butlin saw the provision of free entertainment as the icing on his holiday cake, the glamour which scattered a sheen of stardust upon the dismal roofs of his rows of chalets. Being the man he was, he wanted his entertainers on the cheap, which meant that no top-liner would consider such a booking, so he set up the most efficient, most demanding talent-scouting operation the industry had ever seen. The idea was to spot emerging stars before they emerged, pay them in buttons, and get first-class entertainment at knock-down prices. Although his showbusiness machine offered these youngsters very little by way of financial reward, it did dangle the biggest carrot of all: experience and, most vital of all, exposure. The ability of the Butlins operation to spot up-and-coming stars had been quickly noted by many of the top London agents and theatrical impresarios who would send their scouts around the camps to wave lush promises, contract forms, and cheque books (still thinnish cheque books, I should add) under the noses of promising young hopefuls.

Early in 1951, Muriel and I were still living with Mum and Dad above their working men's club in Leicester but there was a new addition to the family. Our son, Martin, had arrived and with a new family beginning, it was time to look to the future. I was still working at Lewis's, still doing the rounds of the local clubs and, for the first time, falling out with my agent.

Since taking over the club, Dad had been forced to give up his work as my manager-agent and I had signed with a local man, Barry Wood, who was a big fish in the relatively small working men's club pool. He was hard-working, dedicated and paid great attention to small detail. I was hard working, too — but attention to detail was not my forte. The clash came when I had bought a second-hand dinner jacket to add a little class to my act — a jacket of which I was inordinately proud — but my choice of accessories was not what you would call ideal. As ill-luck would have it, Barry showed up to watch my act on the night I wore the DJ with brown shoes.

He was incandescent. I still have the letter he wrote me, enclosing a small cheque and the sack. He was no longer prepared to handle me, he said, because in spite of every encouragement, "I am convinced that you will never make a pro because you do not take the job seriously enough. I am sorry to have to say this but it means the end of your business relations with me, at least for the present."

This was not my first set-back from sartorial considerations — I could still remember the humiliation of the black-leaded football boots at school — nor would it be the last. It came at a very bad time when I needed to increase my income rather than torpedo it. But there was, I believe, some significance in Barry's last line which said we were finished 'at least for the present'. For some reason, even though I drove him to the very edge of despair, Barry must have retained a soft spot for me. A few weeks later, he telephoned to say that Butlins were holding auditions in London to set up a concert party troupe at Skegness and advising that I go along. Like a kindly uncle, he added the warning: "The man in charge is Richard Stone and he's one of the biggest and best agents in London. Do me a favour: don't bugger him about."

Thus I became both a Butlins performer and a client of Richard Stone who was, indeed, one of the biggest and best agents in London, a man who did wonders for my later career and with whom, almost inevitably, I was to have a major fall-out (although that breach, I am pleased to say, has long since been mended).

Richard had been a colonel during the war in ENSA and the CSE, the units which had sent touring parties to all corners of the world to entertain British and Commonwealth troops, often in appalling conditions of climate, disease and danger. These touring parties had become a nursery for some of the greatest talents to grace British entertainment: Spike Milligan and Harry Secombe had got together under their auspices and went on to form The Goons. Ian Carmichael was one of Richard's proteges, soon to star in the comic film masterpiece, *I'm All Right Jack*, which made international stars of both Ian and Peter Sellers.

It was Ian Carmichael who held those London auditions for Butlins, who chose me as second assistant feed to an up-and-coming comic called Terry Scott, and who was to be our director for the summer season at Skeggie. Not a bad trio to set off for the desert wastes of the Lincolnshire coast en route to stardom.

—oOo—

The Butlins season represented a huge leap forward in my career. It meant that, for the first time, I was going away to make my living as a full-time entertainer. I was going to be a *pro*, my ambition since I first stepped on to a plank in my local working men's club at the age of eight. But it was a move not without its problems. It would mean giving up my regular job at Lewis's and, of course, my club engagements for the summer. As Butlins were offering me a measly £10 a week (with £1 deducted as commission for the Richard Stone organisation), it actually represented a substantial pay cut.

These considerations weighed heavily upon me on the train back to Leicester. We had a new baby to feed and clothe and, like all young married couples, were looking forward to getting a home of our own which meant a small fortune for all the paraphernalia of carpets, furniture and the rest as well as rent (the idea of buying a house on a mortgage seemed an unattainable dream). To accept the offer would also mean a separation of some 20 weeks from Muriel, which would be hard on a young women lodging with her in-laws, however supportive they might be, and a tot to look after.

By the time I got home, I had almost made up my mind to say no. When I told her I had been offered the job, Muriel lit up like a lamp. When I explained my doubts, her face went black. "If you are serious about a showbusiness career, you *must* go," she said with a firmness that I had rarely seen before. "It's now or never." It was one of the crucial decisions of my life and, as I grew to expect in later years, Muriel made it for me.

My job was humble enough: second assistant feed to Terry Scott, who was already something of a star with comedy sketches which ranged from mis-playing speeches from *Macbeth* to his little-boy routine dressed in a striped blazer, a school cap two sizes to small, and a treble voice that quavered like a lark with tonsillitis. A year or so later, he was to become one of the first great overnight successes of television when, in his schoolboy outfit, he stepped before the cameras and said: "I like to imitate birds. I don't sing. I don't fly. *I eat worms...*"

As the star, many of the acts were built round Terry. He had a first deputy feed in the form of the company manager, who also had a double act with his wife, and I got on stage when I could. But, under Ian Carmichael's expert direc-tion, I did many things other than comedy: I sang, tap danced, played my banjolele, took part in song-and-dance routines with the female cast.

These productions were quite lavish by the standards of the day, with expensive costumes and sets at least as good as you would find in a provincial variety theatre. Compared to my customary working men's clubs, they could have been an MGM musical. When they provided the costumes, all was well. When I had to dress myself, the familiar sartorial disaster crawled out of the woodwork and once again bit me in the backside.

By contract, I was supposed to supply my own set of white-tie-and-tails so that I could play a stretched Fred Astaire in those lavish song-and-dance routines. As usual, I dug one out in some dingy junk shop and paid a few shillings for it. It was awful, positively hideous, and looked like a cross between a malting penguin and Yogi Bear. Once again I was subject to the ridicule of my peers and I remember once waking up in a cold sweat in my chalet screaming, "I hate you, I hate you," after a nightmare in which I had gone back to my old primary school dressed in both my tatty tails and my black-leaded football boots. And the boots looked better than the suit.

The reason for this lack of elegance was the old one: lack of cash. From the £9 a week I was paid after deductions, I was sending £8 home to Muriel and, even though I only drank Vimto in those days — another point of derision from my colleagues — a quid a week was not much to spend for a 22-year-old. However, even though we were paid more than the Butlins Red Coats — as the concert troupe, we were the élite of the camp hierarchy — shortage of cash was the constant complaint of the entire company. Even Terry Scott.

These were the times when the top variety entertainers flaunted their earnings in public as symbols of their success. The great stars would be on £1,000 a week and sometimes even more. As the top-liner in our little group, Terry had given the impression that he was on £30, which to me was a source of amazement and not a little envy. As we became friends, however, the truth leaked out: he was on £13, not £30, which made me feel a great deal better. The truth had come out when Terry began to show his own indications of cash flow problems and we went into the laundry business.

There is, after any show involving 20 or so performers and half a dozen costume changes, a lot of dirty washing. The Richard Stone organisation, as we already knew to our cost, watched its pennies with a miser's eye and our laundry bill was often under critical scrutiny. One act in particular gave cause for concern, for it involved the entire cast doing a hectic dance number dressed as sailors in tropical uniform: white ducks, they were called. Terry and I smelled profit here and volunteered to wash the ducks ourselves for, it seems incredible now, ten shillings apiece. Even my years of watching Mum had not prepared me for this. After several days of experiment, we came up with the most labour-saving method: we threw the costumes into a bath of soapy water and, both stark naked, would pound them with our feet like French peasants treading grapes.

So much for the glamour of showbusiness. At that time, I was over six feet tall and thin as a rake. Terry was much smaller and, shall we say, a little on a plump side. Had anyone peered through the windows of that chalet and seen two such contrasting naked figures performing strange contortions in the bath, all hell would have broken loose. Butlins had made its name as a *family* resort and one can hardly describe such acrobatics as family entertainment.

Money, too, was causing problems with Muriel and me. We were, after all, not long married and we missed each other a great deal. I had just one day off a week and, if he could spare the time, Dad would come from Leicester on his motor bike, take me home for the night, and bring me back the following day. That was a round trip of some 150 miles or so, a long way on a hard pillion seat. On the days when Dad could not make it, I would hitch-hike there and back, which was even more exhausting because of the uncertainty of getting back in time: to miss a day's work was a sacking offence.

To give ourselves a period of normal (or should I say normal-ish) married life, I arranged for Muriel to come over to Skegness with Martin for a whole week. This, too, was strictly against the rules but love will find a way. To aid the secrecy, and to save the half-crown (12½p) entrance fee which Butlins charged as admission for non-resident guests, Muriel walked four miles along the beach with Martin in her arms to enter the camp the back way. And although it was marvellous to be reunited and spend some long nights together, the subterfuge took its toll. Martin was about six months old and, of course, he would sometimes cry. In a chalet where no baby was supposed to be and where the security men were on constant patrol, keeping him quiet became a nightmare. This was an experiment we never tried again.

If all this sounds rather dour, it was in fact a great deal of fun and, more importantly, unparalleled training for the higher reaches of showbusiness. The pay was low and the work incredibly hard, for it did not entail merely putting on a show every evening. We worked a 16-hour day because when not on stage, we were required to be out and about on the camp, judging the knobbly-knees contests, calling bingo for the pensioners, playing with the kiddies down by the swimming pool and, not infrequently, getting pushed in fully clothed.

Since I became a household name and face on television, I receive three or four letters every week from would-be entertainers and actors asking for my advice about how to get into drama school. Some of them even plead poverty and ask me to fund them through such a school. My advice to them is always the same: Forget drama school. Go to Butlins!

For the one glorious lesson I learned by those dreary sands at Ingoldmells Point was how to work an audience. That means getting them on your side, making them an integral part of the act. If you can do a long, physically exhausting show every night, and spend 12 hours during the day keeping the pensioners and toddlers happy, then you know how to work an audience. Get them on your side and they will forgive you virtually anything.

I have, over the years, met many, many actors with impeccable pedigrees, degrees from RADA and good roles in classical plays, and the vast majority of them are simply *terrified* of an audience. They do their work in their own private vacuum, pretending that the audience is not even there. The reason is that they are afraid of their fans. They even have a name for it: the Fourth Wall.

Some years later, I was to work at the Nottingham Playhouse with one of the most gifted actors of his generation, John Neville who, among many other accomplishments, had played Shakespeare and many of the other great classic roles. Like many classically trained actors, he was fascinated, almost in awe, of the stand-up comic. Whilst we played classical roles together in rep, he also begged me to teach him some stand-up routines. What began as a joke escalated until we had created a tailor-made act for him, an act so good that I eventually got him a booking at the quite famous Parkside Club in

Nottingham. We rehearsed for weeks which, after our long sessions at the Playhouse, added an extra burden to the day. All the time, I was trying to build John's confidence so that he could face a live audience, a Fourth Wall that might answer back (night club audiences do not show the same respect for their entertainers as those in the legitimate theatre). Alas, the act was never performed in public because at the last minute, John backed out. To this day, he still says he regrets 'bottling out'. And that was a reaction of a supreme professional — in his own field.

Do a couple of years at Butlins, and a few more in the working men's clubs, and you develop the courage and the confidence — usually through ignorance — to bring an audience along with you. That makes them feel involved and therefore important. In other words, make a friend of the Fourth Wall.

Chapter Six

Image

$\mathcal{O}$N today's world of entertainment, budding stars can be created as though they had been pressed into a mould, to pop out in almost any shape or style the public demands (or rather, in any style their highly-paid advisers think the public demands). Show the slightest glimmer of talent and a youngster will be snatched up by some ambitious manager who has on call a vast range of so-called experts like PR people, crimpers, photographers, fashion designers, voice and song coaches and writers. The idea is to create an instant image which will sell, much as they sell yoghourt or margarine via television ads.

Back in the early 1950s, the word 'image' had barely been invented in this context. You didn't have an image, you had an act, and you lived or died by it. The prospects for a young lad from Leicester, barely scraping a living to support his wife and family, of building a team of such advisers were unthinkable. For a start, such experts were very thin on the ground. And the costs of hiring their talents was totally beyond reach. I was lucky to have a good agent but that was it; any image that I was about the build I would have to painfully build myself from trial and error, and there were to be plenty of both. There was one other vital factor that was, thankfully, to be on my side: plain, simple good luck.

After my first season at Butlins, Skeggie, it was back to Lewis's in Leicester where I had learned to control my wilder fits of fancy and was climbing steadily up the corporate structure to become a carpet salesman, the top of the department store sales ladder because carpets are expensive and the commission on them is high. Further progress seemed unlikely, however, because

I took two weeks off at Christmas to do pantomime in the Home Counties. This was to be the first of many — panto is one of the business's great training grounds and, when one is established, a chance to return to your roots and recreate those ephemeral links with a live audience. This one, however, must have been pretty dire because I can remember virtually nothing about it. Then, the following year, I was offered another Butlins spot, again as a feed — second feed — to Terry Scott, this time on the Yorkshire coast at Filey. It was another infinitesimal step up the ladder and, although I didn't know it, my days as a carpet salesman were numbered.

At this time, Britain still maintained huge numbers of service personnel around the world. There was a full-scale shooting war in Korea, we had large armies on the Rhine in Germany, where the Russians had embarked upon the Cold War, and in many of our possessions in the Middle and Far East, where local rebellions were either under way or about to break. The Government in its wisdom had decided that it was important to keep the troops who were living under extreme tension, if not actual fire, happy. Richard Stone, as a former colonel in first ENSA and then its successor, Combined Services Entertainment, had maintained his close contacts with the armed forces and sent out regular concert parties to entertain the troops. Thanks to CSE, I was about to receive important lessons that would change forever both my public and private personae. One came in the shape of a haircut. The other in the form of showbusiness aristocracy.

I was still very much a provincial carpet-salesman from Leicester. My idea of a good meal was fish and chips and a couple of bottles of Vimto. My dress sense had barely improved from my days in Rat Alley and mixing with the working class punters at Butlins, although fun, had scarcely left me with a veneer of sophistication. Then I was booked to do a tour of British army bases in Germany in a show called *Tear 'Em Up* and for the first time I made friends with an established star, the wonderful Jon Pertwee.

Jon hailed from the showbusiness upper classes. His parents had both led successful careers in the arts, both in the theatre and as authors, and he had been brought up in that almost surreal world where men and women all called each other 'Darling', and kissed each other on the cheek, where good food and fine wines were on the menu every day. Style — *real* style — had come with his mother's milk rather than laboriously learned on the stony path which I was just beginning to tread. Jon was a patrician in every way and, because of his lifestyle, might have been expected to play plum-voiced leading men in Noel Coward light entertainments. Perhaps his looks mitigated against that, for he was angular and stick-like and his wavy hair stood on his head like candy floss (it is perhaps no surprise that later he was to become a favourite among young TV audiences worldwide playing a TV scarecrow, *Wurzel Gummidge*, and, in my opinion, the best *Dr Who*).

Whether or not he ever wanted to play those romantic leading man roles I do not know, for he never mentioned it. He was just one of those delightful people who was happy doing whatever he was doing at the time, so long as it brought in the cash to support his lavish lifestyle. In this contradictory way, he was already a major radio star for his role as a zany postman with a broad yokel accent whose catch phrase, referring to the letters he was supposed to deliver, had become part of the national vocabulary: "What's it matter so long as you tear 'em up?"

That phrase, of course, gave us the name for our touring show and off we went to Germany, the worldly-wise patrician and the pleb from the provinces he had, for some reason, decided to adopt. I had never been out of England before and, for a youth brought up during the war, the very thought of touring the old enemy, Germany, held a frisson of danger as well as the thrill of the unknown. To do so with Jon Pertwee was a revelation.

Jon is, sadly, no longer with us, but those who remember him as Wurzel Gummidge or Dr Who will no doubt be surprised that he was in real life a remarkable Romeo, naturally talented and highly successful in the mysterious arts of seduction. His life was full of judiciously selected props to support this particular piece of theatre. He changed clothes several times a day, although his favourite day-time footwear was a pair of old desert boots — chukka boots — made of soft suede and soon to become so much of a fashion craze that Clark's could not make enough of them to satisfy the home market (they exported the best and we Brits had to put up with seconds). His basement flat in Chelsea was hung with velvet drapes and had mirrors on the bedroom walls and ceiling. There was was always a bottle of champagne chilling in the fridge and, for the unsuspecting, going to the loo could be distinctly unnerving: the flat was just above a London Underground line and whenever a train passed, the whole room shook as though an earthquake had hit. When on tour, John drove an American Chevrolet convertible and towed a caravan behind which, to all effect, was a mobile facsimile of his Mayfair pad and put to much the same purpose.

Why he took a shine to me I cannot say but he began my education in good food, which knife and fork to use to eat it, and what wines to drink with it. As a man of the world, he took great delight on the German tour of taking me around the infamous Winkelstrasse in Hamburg, the 'red light' quarter where the whores sit naked in the windows showing their wares like the plaster mannequins back home in Lewis's. I was so embarrassed that I bounced a ping-pong ball as we walked along the streets, my eyes on the tarmac, my face burning. It was perhaps the biggest laugh for Jon of the entire tour.

I was so impressed by this man that I began to ape his ways. I, too, acquired a pair of chukka boots and wore them for years. I began to tidy up my wardrobe and bought myself a Crombie overcoat, then the statutory status symbol for a successful comedian, which I was yet to be. When I eventually attained those lofty heights, the first thing I did was to go out and buy myself — a Chevrolet convertible. These were perhaps the superficial lessons that I learned in my first brush with showbusiness aristocracy. There were others, deeper and much more significant. Jon taught me that success and pleasure can be created in this business by playing even the most humble of characters — so long as you play them well: an anarchic postman who tears up the letters he is supposed to deliver is an unlikely figure to become a national celebrity, yet Jon Pertwee achieved it. He also taught me that you can live life as two completely different characters, the one you play on stage — usually an oaf — and the one you live in your private life. Too many entertainers fail to make that vital differentiation, as indeed did I until the Jon Pertwee lesson finally sank in.

In the meantime, I was still plain Billy Williams. Bill Maynard was yet to be born, as ever by accident. And it was on that German tour that another piece of that complex character fell into place. Being the ignoramus I was, I had learned only one German phrase, "Eine bier, bitte," for by this time I had given up Vimto. It had served me quite well until my hair, which I wore as fashion dictated, slicked down with Brylcreem, grew too long.

Ordering a beer at the barbers was not a lot of help and I believe I must have chosen a chap whose last job had been shearing new recruits to the SS. When he finished the first cut, I looked like a haystack. I ordered more to be taken off and ended up with a crew cut. In desperation, I ordered him to brush it forward. As I peered into the mirror frowning, I realised that it did not look too bad. In fact, it looked quite good. Most important, it was *different*. One component of Bill Maynard, crew cut boy and sex symbol comic, had been born. That, in my day, is how you got *image*. By accident.

—oOo—

In the early 1950s, there was still a lot of work to be had for young comics. The variety theatres were still in existence, although soon to face their death throws. Cabaret clubs were thriving. Radio was at its peak, with top-rated situation comedy series like *Ray's a Laugh* and *Educating Archie*, and regular song-and-comedy spots like *Variety Bandbox*, which took the audio content of the variety bills and put it on the air. Dancers and jugglers were not so lucky but their time was coming: the coronation of Queen Elizabeth II in 1953 had proved an enormous fillip for television sales and this new medium, albeit in black and white on a single BBC channel, created a brave new world for our business. Problem was, there were also hundreds, perhaps thousands, of young hopefuls trying to break down the barriers and get into that big-time.

I had been nibbling round the edges for a couple of years and, thanks to Butlins and the CSE, had begun to make some contacts in the upper echelons of the business. I also had the formidable talents of the Richard Stone organisation pushing for me (ten per cent of a tenner a week was barely worth their while, after all). Television was still a dream away but it did have one useful effect on my career: by creaming off the top talent from radio, the variety theatres and the cabaret clubs, it was creating a vacuum lower down, sucking in new names to fill the empty spaces at the bottom of the bill. I was one of those who got 'Hoovered up' and things began to happen with almost unbelievable speed.

One target was radio and I made my first assault on the ether in a show called *Up & Coming* which, as the name suggests, was a talent show for newcomers. Then came bookings on *Midday Music Hall* and *Variety Playhouse* and gradually I began to develop a definite style. Most stand-up comics of the day were loud, brash and ripe with innuendo, forcing their acts down the public throat by sheer personality and quick-fire joke after joke. I am not decrying this, for I admire the skills of those who can do it because it takes a lot of style and even more courage. But this was not my way. I had developed a shy, almost bumbling, stage character who got his laughs with self-deprecating humour.

I had long since learned that you do not take the rise out of the audience — they will turn on you like lions. Instead, I took the rise out of myself, which had gone down well when I was an urchin trying to avoid a punch up in Rat Alley, and had been much appreciated at Butlins.

Although, today, it sounds excruciatingly embarrassing, I would go on stage as a callow amateur and start the act by explaining that I was new to the job and my manager (which I did not have) had told me to tell my best joke first. That way, he said, I would have them rocking in the aisles from the very first minute and the rest of the act would be a doddle. Then, God forgive me, came the first joke:

"There were these two ants running across the side of a corn flakes packet. One was out of breath so it said to its mate: 'Why all the rush?' The mate pointed at the printing on the packet and said: 'Can't you read? It says tear along the dotted line.'"

Total silence.

I would pull a long face at the audience, pout as though on the point of tears, and say plaintively: "That's the best..."

Then came a titter which, after a few more such abominations, would become a laugh and, with a bit of luck, an outright roar. I would finish with a song which, even though at the time I was also singing with bands as a sort of parallel career, I delivered hopelessly out of tune, a technique which was to be exploited by many comics later (in particular, by Les Dawson and his outrageous piano playing). Then the punch line:

"I bet you didn't know I couldn't sing."

On a good night, that brought the house down. In today's more cynical climate, it sounds so *gauche*, with no vulgarity, no sex, no satire. All performers are superstitious, to the point of obsession, about not analysing their work too deeply — we are frightened that if we discover the secret treasure it will be taken from us — but all I can say is that it worked. I talked to the audience, chatted with them, rather than hectored them. As I have already explained, I got them on my side so they would forgive me anything. Even gags which, today, make my skin shrivel.

One day, Richard Stone contacted me to say that the BBC Radio were holding auditions for supporting acts for shows like *Variety Bandbox* and *Workers' Playtime*, two popular shows which, nevertheless, were getting a little long in the tooth and would soon go under to the arch-rival, television. They were to be held in the old Paris Cinema in Regent Street, the famous shopping thoroughfare in London's West End. These were forbidding surroundings to me as I arrived off the train from Leicester, instrument cases in both hands, and fear already in my heart. The BBC had established a reputation as the world's finest broadcasting organisation during the war and, in the deity of showbusiness, represented the Temple of the Gods.

Not that I was trying to join such immortal company. Although the pay was pretty poor, I needed every penny I could muster to support the family, and radio did dangle one important carrot: national exposure. There were hundreds of hopefuls in the cinema but, as it turned out, most of them were rank amateurs hoping for better days. By this time I had developed a little polish and, to my great joy, was offered a handful of spots. Then came the problem.

As I was signing some of the contract forms, a worried looking clerk came up to me and said: "I'm sorry Mr Williams but you're going to cause us a lot of bother in the accounts office. You see, we have so many Williamses on the books — mostly chorists or musicians working for BBC Wales — that we are always getting into a bit of a muddle. The right cheques going to the wrong people, that sort of thing. It would be a great assistance to us, and I know it is asking a lot, but I wonder if you would mind ...eh ...changing your name?"

Now this is an odd sort of request to get at the end of a long day of travelling and waiting and then pushing all the limits in the audition proper. I am well aware of the Shakespeare allusion of a rose by any other name but I was not a rose, I was Billy Williams. I had been Billy Williams all my professional life, Billy Williams had got me this far in showbusiness. My wife was Muriel Williams and my son was Martin Williams. I was quite fond of the old name but, however, not too fond to change if it would boost my career. "Well, I suppose I could," I half stuttered. "But what to? I can't come up with a new identity on the spur of the moment. Could I think about it...?"

"Of course," said the clerk brightly, pushing a piece of paper with his name and telephone number into my hand. "But quick as you can, eh?"

So I walked out into the busy crowds of Regent Street, my joy at getting the bookings somewhat marred by this new conundrum. I pushed my way through the crowds, practising strange names in my head. I got to the Underground station at Piccadilly Circus with a whole range of possibilities in my head, none of them particularly striking, and decided to ring the clerk and ask for advice on the matter. Then, glancing up, I saw a sign advertising Maynard's Wine Gums.

I found a phone box, dropped my coppers into the slot, rang the clerk, and said: "How does Bill Maynard sound?"

"Just fine," he said. If I'd said 'Attilla the Hun,' he would have answered in just the same way. But a few words on a London billboard had given me a whole new persona. I suppose it could have been an advertisement for lemons or hams or turkeys, which might have made for better gags, but I was to spend the rest of my life as a fruit gum. Strange though this may seem, there was still one last part to come in the jigsaw that was to make up Bill Maynard.

About this time, I was on a cabaret tour and one of the other acts was a group of singers called the Kordites. I had taken to wearing chunky sweaters, a style that was then distinctly unfashionable. One of the Kordites, a girl called

Kay, came up to me, gave me a long look up and down, and said: "You know, Bill, you should go on stage like that. The sweater really suits you."

I was appalled. These were the days when aspiring comics wore smart suits, collars and ties, and the aforementioned Crombie overcoats. What's more, I had just bought a new gabardine suit for the princely sum of £17, which Muriel and I could barely afford. I justified the extravagance as being necessary 'for the act' — an argument that I knew Muriel would never contradict. And here was a mere slip of a lass telling me I should go on stage in a baggy *sweater*!

I thought about it for some some time. I was already aware that to progress in the cut-throat world of light entertainment you had to stand out among your peers. There were dozens of hopeful young comics, just as good as me if not better, dressed in the above uniform, their hairstyles slicked down with lavish daubs of Brylcreem. So far, the only thing that made me stand out in the crowd was the crew cut. Even when I made the decision, I was cautious; I would try it as an experiment.

I waited until one night when the theatre was almost empty and walked on stage wearing my sweater and the trousers of my gabardine suit. The precious jacket I held high on a hanger. So far I had said nothing and the audience were plainly puzzled. I took the jacket off the hanger, walked to stage front, and held it high.

"I thought I should let you know that I can afford the whole suit." Had there been more than four of them, they would have brought the house down. The last piece of the jigsaw had clicked into place. Here was a comic with a missing finger, thanks to his mum's mangle, a brushed-forward crew cut thanks to an SS barber, a brand new name thanks to a BBC clerk and a wine gum and, thanks to a crooner called Kay, a chunky sweater.

Bill Maynard had an *image* and not a public relations man in sight. I was young, self-deprecating, and different, thanks to a series of pure accidents. It was an image that within months was to propel me into a success that was almost beyond comprehension. Billy Williams, once 'Leicester's very own George Formby', had been re-formed in his own right. The press were to call me the Sweater Boy, and my style became a national fashion, taken up by other entertainers like Dave King and Val Doonican. Women of all ages were to call me all sorts of names, few of them repeatable here. I was to be a totally new phenomenon: a sex-symbol comic.

Chapter Seven

Tilting at Windmills

THE 1950s were the last years of the Age of Innocence in Britain, soon to sink under the tidal wave of drugs, sex and rock'n'roll that the 1960s — and the Pill — brought crashing in. There was, of course, sex but it was usually furtive and rarely talked about except by young men in the pub. Young couples went out together for months, perhaps years, before they actually made love, usually a brief encounter in an entry, a park or, if you were lucky enough to own or borrow one, on the back seat of a car. After a few months of these unsatisfactory clinches, the majority of couples elected for marriage so that they could at least share a bed together with parental approval, a situation which often led to disastrous marriages because divorce was rare, difficult and expensive to achieve, and a subject of considerable scandal.

Prostitution, however, flourished openly on the street corners of most of the major cities, with the girls being dragged off to court every now and then to be fined £2 — the going rate for a 'short-time' encounter — which they looked upon as paying their taxes. Of these so-called red light districts, the most celebrated in all the land were those narrow, crowded streets at the centre of the London theatreland: Soho. This wonderful, colourful, noisy district, boasted other attractions, too, like small foreign restaurants, delicatessens selling food that the average Englishmen had never seen, never mind eaten, and was beginning to sprout coffee bars selling liquid exotica like 'espresso' and 'cappuccino'. These coffee bars were soon to be the launching pads for young British singing stars like Cliff Richard and Tommy Steele, although these were much looked down upon by the habitues of Soho's many jazz clubs and pubs.

The population of Soho was the nearest you could get in the England I knew towards to the word 'cosmopolitan'. There were Italians, French, Germans, Poles, Jews from most nations of Europe, and a growing number of immigrants from what was still the British Empire: Maltese and Cypriots, Sikhs, Pakistanis and West Indians. The sounds of their music, the babble of their shouted conversations, the spicy smells of their strange foods, all mingled to give this tiny hub of West London the feel of an Eastern bazaar. They ran restaurants or shops, did manual work as cleaners and porters, or made a living somehow in the big department stores and expensive hotels of Oxford Street and Piccadilly. But most of all, Soho was known for *sex*.

The Wolfenden Report, the controversial enquiry that was to sweep the streets clean of prostitution (for a decade or so, at least), was yet to come before Government. Girls and women, from young teenagers to fading grandmothers, stood in every doorway, touting their wares to the hordes of cruising men, mostly foreign tourists, servicemen on leave, or pimply young-sters from the provinces. For those who did not want to pay for the real thing, there were dubious clip joints where pretty hostesses sold fake champagne at exorbitant prices and made assignations for later which they never kept. And there was a handful of so-called strip clubs, where the girls didn't — not all the way, that is — and any man who complained was hustled quickly on to the streets by muscular bouncers who, as likely as not, could barely speak a word of English.

All in all, this centre of mainly cheap and mostly cheerful sex was a curious destination for a provincial comic in his mid-20s, with a wife and child to support back home. What drew me there, however, was not the seedier side of Soho but its one shining light of sophisticated sex (perhaps a better word is titillation) in the shape of the renowned Windmill Theatre, London's answer to the Moulin Rouge in Paris. This tiny but always packed theatre in Great Windmill Street had flourished during the war under its famous slogan, 'We Never Closed', because its girls had never stopped dancing while the bombs were falling all around. It had become a beacon for the millions of servicemen on their way to, or the way back from, war.

By the standards of the day, The Windmill was risque in the extreme, although nowadays you can see much more on television virtually every night. The Lord Chamberlain's office still imposed theatre censorship with an iron fist and one of the many rules strictly enforced was that no naked or half-naked young women could *move* on stage. The Windmill, nevertheless, advertised moving nudes, which dragged in the rain-coated visitors by the thousand. It was, of course, something of a confidence trick. The Lord Chamberlain's rules did permit static nudes, usually tableaux aping some famous sculpture or painting, for this was *art* and therefore acceptable by the hypocritical standards of the day: art was improving, sex was dirty, or so the Lord Chamberlain seemed to say.

The Windmill was owned and run by the formidable Vivian Van Damm (or VD as he was somewhat cynically known), who to all intents and purposes was the King of Soho. He took this as the royal prerogative to bend the rules. His nudes did move but not their bodies. They struck their classical poses, topless but with their lower regions swathed in flimsy silk and lace, on turntables built into the stage. The girl stood concrete still whilst her body was revolved mechanically. There would be a fan dancing act, too, where the fan might not get into place quite fast enough to prevent the house gaining a brief glimpse of bare breasts. A pure accident, of course, as were the specially designed costumes for the chorus girls which, in almost every routine, would allow a nipple or two to pop out over the top whilst the girl danced on obliviously (or so it seemed).

If Vivian Van Damm was ever questioned about such irregularities I do not know. But I am sure he would have pleaded: "Accidents will happen, old boy!" Had the Lord Chamberlain's men been truly keen on their task, and attended a series of performances one after the other, they would no doubt have seen the same nipples pop out of the same dress at much the same time in every routine. Far from being oblivious, the girls in fact were watching the audience like hawks. They took in the nods and winks and nudges among the assembled men as par for the course but occasionally would be disturbed at activities going on under mackintoshes folded over male laps. Once off-stage, they would whisper, "Second row, third from the left," and a burly stage hand would escort some embarrassed visitor to the door, sometimes before he had chance to button his trousers.

It is perhaps a little sad, now, that the days are long gone when the sight of an illicit nipple would send young and not-so-young men into a masturbatory frenzy but we should give more credit to Van Damm's showman's brain. It was the fact that those stray nipples were technically illegal — and the audience knew that they were so — that added the exciting dash of forbidden fruits to an otherwise simplistic, almost innocent, show. Sex was like that in those days: something you shouldn't enjoy so, if you were lucky to get any, you enjoyed it all the more. I doubt if today's gynaecological strippers ever raise that sort of excitement, even with whips, chains, leather and even the odd python which seem to be *de rigeur.*

However, this was not what drew me into the frightening presence of the mighty Vivian Van Damm for the first time. I was looking for a major leap forward in my career, for VD had also woven into his famous shows a vital extra strand: stand-up comedy.

I suppose all professions have their private Everests. The barrister who takes silk to become a QC, the footballer who runs out at Wembley for the first time, the classical actor who first steps on to the stage of the Royal Shakespeare Theatre at Stratford-upon-Avon. When it came to stand-up comicry, The Windmill represented that Everest for me and my peers and for a very simple reason: the audiences were overwhelmingly male and they went to see the girls. The comics in those days were all men and their job, more or less, was to keep the audience sweet while sets were changed and the girls donned, or rather un-donned, new costumes. In Africa in the old days, young men had to prove their virility by running bare foot over hot coals. To prove the same in England in the 1950s, young comics had to make a Windmill audience laugh. For a while, I thought I would prefer the hot coals.

Very few comics survived The Windmill trial by ordeal. Those who did went on to become some of the most famous names in the business: Tony Hancock, Harry Secombe, 'Professor' Jimmy Edwards, Arthur English and George Martin and many more become national or international television stars. These names were already famous, and their Windmill prowess talked about with awe in the profession, when I received a call from the Richard Stone office saying that they had arranged a 'special' audition for me in Greater Windmill Street. Now was the time to don my crampons, pick up my ice axe, and climb my personal South Col. It was to be a disaster.

The agency had explained that 'special' meant there would only be myself and VD present. So I packed by guitar and my ukelele, got on the train to London, and finally entered the most famous stage door in English comic history. To put it politely, I had been somewhat mislead. The Windmill was a very small theatre and most of the backstage area was taken up by a large spiral staircase that winds up to the stage itself, a staircase usually aflutter with half-naked girls either casting on or casting off flimsy costumes. On this day, every rung of this stairway to fame and riches was occupied by one, and sometimes two, would-be comics awaiting anxiously their turn to be ushered into the magic presence. So much for 'special'.

After what seemed like hours, I finally walked out into the spotlights. Van Damm was out there somewhere in the unlit auditorium, an invisible but all powerful presence. I told my first joke and The Voice spoke.

"Next."

"I do impressions," I said in desperation.

"Next."

And I was off. My first attempt on Everest had ended with my walking off the cliff with barely time to scream. On the long, lonely train ride back to Leicester, I sank into a gloomy spell of introspection and self-examination which made me even more depressed. All entertainers take knock-backs like this in their careers, it comes with the job. For those who can't take rejection, it is often the end. They quit altogether and go on to lead ordinary, and for all I know happy, lives in some normal trade. The ones who stick it out need a certain thickness of skin, a blind faith in their own abilities and a large dash of luck. Anger helps, too. I very much objected to being publicly humiliated. And I was doing all right, anyway, I said to myself. In this, I was not being too over-optimistic. I had a career which was branching out in several directions: there were fairly regular variety bills and touring dates, I was singing as a crooner with some of the big bands then still in fashion, I had some radio dates and there was even some talk of down-the-bill spots in television variety. But rejection still hurts.

This from a young man who, as yet, rarely swore, drank very little and went home like a lamb to his wife and baby every night unless out on tour. This was all to end within months. Thanks, once again, to Fate, in the guise of a chance meeting.

—oOo—

As luck would have it, I soon picked up a cabaret spot in a smart London hotel. In the audience, black tie and all, was a man who was patently enjoying himself, although probably more from the booze than from my act. Afterwards, he came over and introduced himself as Ken Bandy, the publicity man at, of all places, The Windmill Theatre.

"You're good," he said. "I can arrange for you to get a special audition with Vivian Van Damm."

He was, I believe, a little taken aback by my response. He was, after all, acting with some generosity and making an offer that would have caused most young comics to drop to their knees in prayer. After a few hostile moments, he finally listened to my explanation and waved his hands in the air: "Don't worry. This time, I'll make sure it *is* special."

I really didn't want to go. The following day, I discussed it with Richard Stone who thought I was mad in wanting to turn it down (not, I hasten to add, for the last time). I still didn't want to go. But I was in London anyway. I had little to do during the day. What's more, with my gradually growing earnings I had managed to make myself a major purchase, the Crombie overcoat which was the absolutely essential status symbol for the ambitious young entertainer. It was the coat that swung the decision as much as anything. I thought I would go along just to show that I was getting on just fine without them, thank you very much.

I had, of course, been conned again. Just by chance, auditions had already been arranged for that day. When I went in the back door, the spiral staircase was jammed with hopefuls. From out front, I could here the familiar chant of, "Next! Next!" from VD, initials I was now beginning to appreciate because I was coming to look upon their owner as something of a painful disease infecting my life. I became even angrier when, as I finally reached the upper rung on the spiral, I saw that the preceding act was setting up a complex system of props which included a full set of drums.

Anne Mittell, a lady who was to become a good friend later, was production manager of The Windmill and was handling the audition backstage. Would anyone mind going on, she asked politely, while the other fellow was getting his kit set up — it would save a little time and Mr Van Damm was a very busy man. I volunteered immediately because I was so furious, anyway, and walked on to that famous stage expecting more humiliations. Let's get it over with, I thought.

I had no instruments with me. I had not bothered to prepare a routine. My only prop was that Crombie with its big belt and I opened with a line I shall always remember: "I won't be taking my coat off. I don't think I'll be staying long. I've been before."

I spoke the words with venom into the shadowy auditorium where I assumed VD was sitting. Then I waited for the inevitable, "Next!" It didn't come. Instead, I thought I detected the sound of a slight chuckle. Now, although I was still seething, this was something of a teaser. I had nothing prepared, not an idea in my head, and behind me this fellow was noisily going about setting up his props as though I didn't exist. Like any good stand-up, I used whatever came to hand, turning my anger on this unfortunate no-hoper. I began ad-libbing as the fellow went on arranging his instruments, about how long it was taking. And then I stood there in silence, my back to Van Damm, which is not what is normally expected from a comic. Behind me, the chuckle had grown to full-blown laughter. I turned, shaded my eyes against the spotlights, and could just make out Van Damm. He was shaking with laughter. Then he said:

"When can you start?"

I was dumbfounded and too stupid not to show it.

"But this is not my act," I protested. "I have a very good act but last time I came you didn't want to hear it."

He waved a dismissive arm: "Yes, I remember it. We don't want that sort of rubbish here."

And so I came to tread the most famous boards in British comedy by *not* doing my act. Just what I *was* expected to do took some time to dawn but then I realised it was so simple: I just had to talk to the audience, say virtually anything that came into my head, get them involved and therefore on my side, as I had as a child in South Wigston Working Men's Club. I had learned the true meaning of stand-up comedy: play the audience by ear, adjust the tune to their music, let them set the tempo. Then they'll forgive you anything.

This was my first real triumph, my first huge step into the big time. I was to earn £40 a week at a time when a young professional man was planning a career that would eventually pay £1,000 a year — if he got lucky and played his cards right. Even better, within the environs of the sex capital of Britain, there were many opportunities for a funny man to double and treble that money, which I was to do and more so. Whether or not this was beneficial to the one-time urchin from Rat Alley is more difficult to judge. This sudden rush of hard cash, and the fame that would come with it, were to create endless problems for this young provincial with a loving wife, a baby son and — soon — a daughter on the way. The beer days were over. The champagne days were here. With them came all the temptations of Soho, including an almost inexhaustible supply of glamorous show girls eager to be seen on the arm of a celebrity. And not just on his arm. I was young, rich, and away from home. These were the champagne days and, whatever the risks, I was going to enjoy them.

Chapter Eight

Soho Days

SO I started my first Life at the Top surrounded for most of the working day, and much of the night too, by beautiful naked women. My leisure hours, if they can be called such, were spent either playing bar billiards in The Windmill canteen or in the local cafes and pubs with a motley bunch of friends which included prostitutes and their pimps, taxi drivers and jazz musicians, the real creatures of the night. It was a strange nocturnal habitat for a 24-year-old from a poor but respectable family and it took some time before my somewhat puritanical shell began to crack. When it finally did so, it shattered into a thousand pieces.

First, let's consider the temptations. I was doing six nine-minute shows a day at The Windmill, which had two completely separate chorus lines, the 'A' company and the 'B' company, who worked a 'shift' system. When I climbed that spiral staircase to go on, these girls came down like helter-skelter riders for their quick change, hurling skimpy bits of the last costume into the air so that the whole backstage became a snow-storm of frilly bras and panties. I might well have been part of the furniture, for they spared no thought for modesty, neither theirs nor mine. And they displayed a rather startling feature which at first shocked, then fascinated, and finally seduced me. In his wisdom, the aforementioned Lord Chamberlain had decided that even the slightest show of pubic hair on stage would corrupt the public morals.

Considering the costumes these well-shaped women wore, there was only one answer to this legal stipulation: they shaved every day, an inconvenient and highly uncomfortable procedure. As a married man with a few pre-marital sorties under his belt, I was reasonably familiar with the more intimate nooks and crannies of the female form. To have a dozen or more bald pubis and well developed mammaries flashing past one's eyes many times a day was an unfair temptation to an active young man a long way from home. That, of course, was on the way up the staircase. On the way down, my spot finished and the girls going back on stage, I had no choice but to get to know these lovely creatures from all angles.

And it wasn't just at The Windmill, where the curtain came down at 11pm. Within days of being booked there, I had picked up two spots a night at the Prince of Wales Theatre just around the corner. The show was, would you believe, the *Follies Bergere*, and once again I was surrounded by naked show-girls. So I spent my later evenings in the company of naked Amazons and even that was not the end. I was also taking bookings at the Astor Club to work with the owner, Bertie Green, and his Lovelies which, as you would expect, was a girlie show. By the time that finished at 3am, I had spent 16 hours among much of the most desirable flesh in the West End. And, as is the way with showbusiness people, 3am was the time to go out to play.

Consider, too, the money. The Prince of Wales and the Astor Club were each paying me £100 a week on top of The Windmill's £40. Comparisons are difficult but this was probably the equivalent of some £250,000 a year now and there was money coming in from my radio appearances too. My one problem, apart from sending large chunks of it home to Muriel in Leicester, was finding a way to spend it. This may seem curious in a place like Soho, swamped as I was by all its garish temptations, but even Soho slept in those days. The neon went out at much the same time as we finished work and, apart from one little place called the Beaufort Club, where the food was good throughout the night and taxi drivers on the night shift drank coffee and played snooker, there was virtually no place to go.

Nor was the money going on rent. I had begun to share a grubby flat above the Beaufort Club in Lisle Street with Jimmy Curry, a jazz guitarist, and the comedian Dickie Dawson, who was later to marry Britain's answer to Marilyn Monroe, Diana Dors. This flat was probably the only non-brothel in Lisle Street and the brothels were much better kept. It was, quite simply, disgusting: cigarette ends ground into the carpets, sink perpetually full of dirty dishes and empty booze bottles, linen that cracked when you got into bed. It was also a meeting place for those other nightbirds, the jazz musicians, some of them like Ronnie Scott and Tubby Hayes, already quite famous.

This group used the flat as a dumping ground for spare instruments (when they were not at the pawnbrokers, that is) and as a convenient flop house after long night sessions. One early morning, as I staggered in, a group of them were sitting in a circle on the floor passing around from mouth to mouth what I thought at first was a cigarette. I was offered a drag and vehemently refused. It was, of course, marijuana and I would like to claim that I rejected it because of an iron-willed aversion to the dangers of drugs. In fact, I did so on purely hygienic grounds: I was not going to put something into my mouth that had been in so many others. I took an instinctive dislike to drugs there and then and it was perhaps one of the best snap decisions I ever made. Many of the talented young musicians who passed through Lisle Street went on to harder, more hateful, habits. And they have been gone long since.

Finally, in this somewhat lame explanation of why this young family man finally went off the rails, I should mention an old showbusiness myth concerning the lead comic in a variety troupe. The comic, goes the legend, is invariably a lonely man, a sad man. This is a variation on the old chestnut on the clown who wants to play Hamlet. As the lead comic is a vital part of any show, perhaps the *most* vital part, his whims must be indulged: a happy comic means a happy troupe. Keeping him happy tended to revolve round two items, booze and sex. According to tradition, the comic provided the former and the leader of the ladies' chorus, the head girl, provided the latter. In the days of the travelling music hall, on those long weekend train journeys to smoky, gritty towns in the North and Midlands, the chorus captain was expected to take on this duty for the good of the troupe.

This was an act of philanthropy which, as with all philanthropists, had a deep sense of self-interest at its core. It was a tradition that was still alive and well in Soho in 1952 and the object of the operation had the combined talent of dozens of lovely young women willing to make the necessary sacrifice. Even better for them, I suppose, was the fact that the man involved, the newly-named Bill Maynard, aged 24, stood six feet tall, had a trendy new haircut and, in a somewhat battered sort of way, was verging on the handsome. To add to a head of steam that was already building to bursting point, his wife was 100 miles away and he was spending 16 hours a day in the company of young women with all their attributes on display.

I cracked. I believe that any healthy young man in my situation would have done the same. But I still had the problem: where to go to take advantage of this cornucopia so suddenly set before me? At three in the morning, the best clubs and restaurants had long closed. My professional beauties were unlikely to be impressed by the taxi drivers in the Beaufort Club. The Lisle Street flat was out of the question, for even if any bed were not already in full use, it was

so filthy that a self-respecting sow would have refused even to cross the thres-
hold, never mind give her all.

So I got together a bundle of money and, with the lessons of my mentor Jon
Pertwee still very much in mind, went out and bought myself a left-hand-drive
Chevrolet drophead coupe, a car with a back seat bigger than many of the
brothels in Lisle Street. I finally found the right venue, too, a rather esoteric
one at that: London Airport, Heathrow. This was, of course, open all hours and
in those days before package tours brought air transport to the masses, was a
place of high adventure. At 3am, I would whiz my latest philanthropic beauty
through the deserted streets of London, zip down the A4, and take her into the
terminal where we would drink a coffee and listen to the announcements for
aircraft leaving to far away places.

Then, with our minds full of pictures of romantic beaches and swaying
palms, it was out to some secluded corner of the huge car park. I would have
a bottle of champagne in the car, once chilled but now decidedly tepid, but
who cared. These girls spent most of their working time naked and any
bashfulness had long disappeared. Their clothes came off in a flash and they
were very good, very practised, at what followed. This was Soho sex, with all
its erotic extras, and once I had tasted it I was to develop an appetite that was
to cause me, and others dear to me, a great deal of pain for years to come.

—oOo—

By now, I was a well-known figure in Soho, on speaking terms with the whores
and their pimps, the publicans and the shop-keepers, the street cleaners and
the plain-clothes detectives who were supposed to be undercover but who
were known by name (and probably by rank and serial number) by everyone
else in this cosmopolitan hotchpotch. The street life came to fascinate me, with
all its variety. Seedy it may have been but rarely sordid, as it is today. It was still
a real community, a village at the heart of a great city, and although there were
always punters to con (they were fleeced with some skill, rather than robbed
with violence), the 'locals' lived together with a cheery indifference to the ways
in which their neighbours chose to earn a living.

By this time, I suppose, I was a *star*, at least on the revue scene. But so what?
The whole village was swarming with entertainers, many of them famous
actors from the big West End theatres. They came to Soho for a drink or a meal
in places where they would be called John or Jill, not Sir. There were musicians,
writers, painters, journalists, some of them famous columnists, as famous as

the TV pundits of today. They came to Soho for its informality, for its anonymity: the blonde with the gin and tonic next to you at the bar could be either a headliner from the Haymarket Theatre or a two-pound-a-time whore, and they would chat to you just the same. When I had the time, I would sit silently just drinking it all in, absorbing every sound and sight and smell. It was good training for the actor to be.

Just walking to work was an education. It would be just before 11am, and as likely as not I had not been to bed before six, but the first girls would already be in the doorways. "Morning Bill." "Morning Mavis." "Morning Bill." "Morning Gladys." Although they knew I would never be a customer — why should I with my never-ending free supply of their particular commodity? — they would always try it on. I think I had become something of a challenge. They may even have had bets on me, a tenner for the first to bed Bill Maynard.

"Come on Bill. Give us a good start to the day."

"Sorry luv. Can't afford it."

"I'll do it cheap."

"Still can't afford it."

"How about one on the house then?"

"Sorry, luv. Late for work."

Sometimes, in between slots at The Windmill, I would slip out for a cup of coffee at a cafe where the tarts took their breaks — "Just taking the weight of my poor back, Bill." They were not all beautiful, and many were frankly far too old for the job, but they were nearly always cheerful.

Sometimes, a pimp would come into the cafe and say, "Come on girls, back to work — the punters are queuing up on The Dilly." And off they would go, grumbling good naturedly, with no more thought than a group of mill girls going back to their looms. One day, one of the pimps joined me at my table, shook his head and gave a long sigh. "Sorry about that, Bill," he smiled. "I'll have to stop these tea breaks."

To my uncritical eyes, this all seemed harmless enough. Many of the girls were on the streets to provide an upbringing for their children better than the one they themselves had received. This was the sort of decision which I had known from childhood, one which I not only understood but which I had embarked upon myself, although by slightly different means. These girls felt, too, that they were performing a useful social service: "Better 'e does it with us, luv, than go and rape some innocent young gel." Quite a lot of them, at the end of their shift, went back to their little semis in Wembley or Watford where they conducted perfectly respectable lives.

Being non-judgmental in this way was one of the lessons I learned in Soho, although there are no doubt many people who disagree with me profoundly. One of them was soon to pay me a visit: Muriel was on her way from Leicester and what she saw, I am convinced, left her in deep shock.

—oOo—

As I have already explained, Muriel was the very epitome of respectability, in the very best meaning of that word. She was not a dragon who spewed fire over anyone who strayed, however slightly, from the straight-and-narrow — she was far too intelligent and broad-minded for that — but she believed in what people then called 'standards'. Just as she was always impeccably dressed and groomed, any home she had was always impeccably maintained, not just hoovered and dusted regularly but always freshly painted, the curtains laundered, the windows and mirrors agleam.

She walked into the Lisle Street flat, held her hand over her mouth to prevent herself gagging, and walked straight out.

No surprisingly, I was suffering from terrible guilt about my treatment of my beautiful, intelligent and supportive wife, the mother of my son. She was stuck with *my* parents, not even her own, in a working men's club in Leicester while I was living the high life in the nation's capital. She had surrendered any chance of having a normal married life by opting for a would-be entertainer with a highly questionable future, and had then thrown all her considerable talents into making that future a success. She also held a steely conviction that a stable marriage and a stable family life were the only keys to lifelong fulfilment.

I had visited her in Leicester whenever I could, which was not often in view of my work schedule, and was now sending home more money than we have ever dreamed of. But frankly, those visits had bored me to the point of speechlessness, a story that must have been repeated over the centuries for the young man who leaves home and finds the bright lights. And then she came to visit me in Soho, saw a flat unfit for pigs, saw the prostitutes on the streets, the lurid photographs in the strip club windows — and, indeed, outside my place of work — and, to say the least, she was not very happy. She went back to Leicester and, to this day, I wonder how close we came then to a permanent parting. I did not deserve her, of course, and I suspect she kept the marriage going for the benefit of young Martin, a decision which many young women took in those days before a quickie divorce became the easy option. While she struggled alone with these heart-wrenching decisions, I was still enjoying the champagne life. Part of this entailed my going into a long lasting series of mood swings. Some of the time, I was plagued with the guilt, trying to make up for my behaviour with expensive presents for Muriel and Martin. The rest of the time I devoted to self-justification, telling myself that I had married too young, that I had taken on responsibilities before I was ready. I was away from home and family, I thought, not because I was enjoying myself but to further my career in everyone's interest. That familiar old phrase came back: 'You must better yourself.' These were miserable moments. But they did not last long.

Partly due to Muriel's shocked reaction, partly due to the fact that Jimmy Curry had found himself a permanent girlfriend, I decided to move out of Lisle Street. I was pondering the flat-finding problem — with so little time off, such a search was a major obstacle — when the answer was brought to me as if by angels (although not by angels is any sense of the accepted meaning of the word). Five dancers from the *Follies* were sharing a huge flat in Upper Berkeley Street and they had a spare bedroom: would I care to join them? Despite my concern about Muriel, I must have been in one of my self-justifying moods for, to borrow Mario Puzzo's timeless phrase, this was an offer I could not afford to refuse. Who could?

Perversely, sharing a flat with five of the most beautiful young women in London turned out to be more like being a boarder at a boisterous girls' school (as I imagined it) rather than the bordello of every young man's dreams. If I had thoughts of picking beauties off the shelves like a hungry child in a sweet shop, I was much mistaken. Oh yes, they walked around me in every state of dress from fur coats to stark nakedness but I was used to that anyway — it happened day in day out. I was more of a mascot than a live-in sex aid, some-one to be mothered rather than taken advantage of. They washed my clothes, cooked me good meals, and in general treated me like a kindly nephew. Muriel would never have believed it. I still can't myself.

Perhaps my protests at this monk-like existence sank home, for one night, as I lay alone in my bed, I heard whispers and giggles outside. Then the door burst open, the light flashed on, and all five leapt naked onto the bed. They had, I presume, taken a drink or three and they swarmed all over me, lips, hands and tongues delving every orifice of my body. It was the realisation of a sex maniac's wildest fantasy.

Then a voice whispered throatily in my ear: "We've come to see what you are made of."

This struck me as hilariously funny. I began to chuckle, then laugh, then roar. At first somewhat taken aback, they grasped the funny side, too, and joined in. And that's how my first and last orgy ended: five naked chorus girls and one naked comic in the same bed, laughing until the tears came. Had we been wearing socks, we would have laughed them off. But nothing else happened. Honest.

For years after this, one of my favourite gags went: I've seen so many tits and bums in my life that the only woman who interests me now must be wearing a buttoned-up boiler suit.

In Rat Alley, with my banjolele and Gyp, who took care of the rats.

That's me, first left on the middle row at Kibworth Beauchamp Grammar School.

A snappy dresser in December 1945, aged 17.

A couple of years later and even more sophisticated, with double-breasted suit and trilby.

Aged 19 and doing my stand-up at a working men's club.

Billy Williams in 1948 – 'Leicester's very own George Formby'.

Muriel and I on our wedding day.

Aged 21 and judging a beauty contest at Butlins. Also pictured are Terry Scott's first wife Thelma (left) and Hetty Braine.

With Terry Scott in *Great Scott It's Maynard*, in November 1955.

'…he Sweater Boy' sets a national trend.

Opening a garden party at Weymouth in 1956.

Surrounded by beautiful girls during a summer show at Weymouth in 1956.

tle did we know
with Tonia in the 1950s.

It's Wilhelminha and Stinka, alias Bill
Maynard and Ted Ray, in *Babes in the
Wood* on BBC TV in December 1957.

Maynard
the male model, in
the sweater I
designed to go
with the tie.

Coming to the end of my stand-up days in the 1960s.

Chapter Nine

On the Box

ONE OF my stranger traits as a young man was that, having struggled to get on to a good thing, I would immediately jump off. Whether or not this was caused by some form of subliminal desire to avoid 'type-casting' I cannot honestly say. I don't remember consciously sitting down and deciding that I must keep on changing my working style. I did, however, have an almost constant restlessness, an ever-present feeling that I had somewhere else to go, although I was never quite sure where it was. As a result, I decided to quit The Windmill, a decision that Vivian Van Damm took very hard. In fact, a few months later, he virtually begged me to go back, which was a refreshing change of affairs after our initial encounters and a great boost to my confidence. Not wanting to return, I demanded £100 a week, thinking I would be rejected. To my surprise, VD coughed up and back I went, another offer too good to refuse. That was, I believe, the highest wage ever paid to a comic at The Windmill which, although we did not know it, was already doomed. Its form of sexual titillation would not survive the full-frontal nudity of the Swinging Sixties. I went back but my mind was elsewhere. These were revolutionary times in the business. One great age was coming to a close and another was about to start. Only a few visionaries were foretelling that television would grow to dominate not only light entertainment but virtually all of family life. Even the great movie moguls of Hollywood scoffed at this new medium, dismissing it as a flash in the pan — and, as a result, came very close to extinction. For the ambitious comic in Britain, undreamed of new opportunities were unfolding.

Since the 19th century, light entertainment in Britain had been dominated by the great music halls circuits. Each generation produced a handful of headliner stars who eventually became household names, but not until after years on tour. Every small town had its music hall. The bigger cities would have two or more. It could take several years before a top performer, supported by an ever-changing cast of supporting acts, could tour the entire country. That allowed them a huge luxury: they only had to change the act every couple of years or so. Comics would, of course, throw in a few topical gags to match the latest goings on in the newspapers. Singers would learn some of the newest songs. But by and large, the act, the costumes, the props would remain basically the same until they had been staged at every major venue in the land. Apart from the pains of touring, it was a relatively easy way of earning a very good living.

The music hall had, of course, been fighting a major rival in the form of the cinema since the 1930s. Although some of the major stars like George Formby and Gracie Fields made the jump from the boards to silver screen, the two arts were different genre and lived reasonably happily side by side. Radio then made up a trio and, to some performers, it was a Godsend. Entertainers could become major stars over the airwaves and be big hits in the theatres too. People who knew them by voice only (apart from the occasional photograph in the newspapers, that is) would turn up in droves to see them in the flesh. Radio was the best advertising possible for performers going somewhere, which is why I was keen to build a name on the air.

But in these tumultuous times, even radio was about to be overshadowed. The one-eyed monster was stalking the land. And our cozy old world would soon to be gone forever.

Few showbusiness outsiders understand the pain that goes into creating a modern act. It can take years to perfect a character, as it had done for me. Writing, rewriting, and re-rewriting a script goes on for weeks and months, always in the back of the entertainer's mind. We practise these things constantly, in the bath, on the loo, in bed in the cold dawn hours when we lay awake searching for that tiny improvement, a single word, a change of emphasis, that can make a good joke into a great one. If you work with a partner, these tiny improvements have to be rehearsed time and time again. It is a process of constant upgrading, a never-ending quest, and, when you are young at least and have yet to *know* your capabilities, your only guide is gut feeling.

Then you go on television and blow the whole thing in four minutes flat.

This is the challenge of television. You can tell a joke just once, play a sketch just once, on a major TV show and it is gone forever. It will be watched by millions and those who haven't watched it will be told about it by their friends or family. Untold hours of preparation are beamed out into space in a few bats of an eyelid, never to return. If your are lucky, the show may be recorded and repeated later, although even that was rare back in the days when BBC 1 was the only show in town. That is just about acceptable: the audience know it is a repeat and if you have been good enough, they will watch you again. But repeat a joke in a new show and you are stone dead. "He's told that one before," says dad and reaches for the off switch.

I have been asked many times how you keep a television character going for months or, in Greengrass's case, for years and still keep him interesting. The best analogy I know is to compare it with a marriage: you must keep changing yourself slowly but surely or your partner will get first bored and then irritated. At first, she likes the way you stroke your nose, a little gesture I was to use in my early TV days, when you are thinking hard. By the time the honeymoon is over she is likely to rear up and snap: "I wish you would stop stroking your nose — it's beginning to get on my nerves."

For scores of old time music hall pros, who as often enough had eked out one basic act to last them an entire career, the challenges of television were simply insurmountable. They had just forgotten the habit — had they ever had it in the first place — of continuous improvement (a phrase much used now by trendy young businessmen). The old-timers perhaps tried TV a couple of times, used up all their best material, and then went back to the boards, to fade away into posterity like the music hall itself. This was sad for them, perhaps, but it did newcomers the likes of me a huge favour. As I said earlier, it created a vacuum of big names at the top and this in turn 'Hoovered' in at the bottom youngsters who could change their acts, and even their characters, fast enough to keep pace with the medium's insatiable appetite for new material.

With my background in the clubs, at Butlins, and on the revue circuit, this had become second nature. By working with the audience, I could change track almost at will, often making it up as I went along, testing the audience's reaction. I had already done several radio spots which had been reasonably well received. It was time to go On the Box.

—oOo—

Many of the BBC's early TV variety shows were cribbed from radio. One of the programmes chosen to make the transition was Henry Hall's *Face the Music*, which was performed before a live audience. Richard Stone landed me a spot and the great moment had arrived. I was so nervous that, now, I remember very little about that first time before the cameras (in view of what happened next, this could well be a case a voluntary amnesia). I did my bit, telling a few jokes and belting out a song with the ukelele, and was much helped by the presence of the audience. I thought I did pretty well and certainly none of the BBC staff complained. Then a young girl called Sally Barnes went on, a comedienne who told her gags as a charlady while she scrubbed the floor (as it happened, a BBC floor, so some of the 'in-jokes' were quite tasty for it was a new thing then to take the mickey out of the Grand Old BBC).

The following day, I bought all the newspapers and turned anxiously to the television reviews. There, to my delight, was the headline I sought: A STAR IS BORN (one would have thought the sub-editor could have thought up a less hackneyed line). With a deep intake of breath, the pride swelling within me, I began to read: "Television last night created a new star, a young comedienne called Sally Barnes..." I was not even mentioned.

—oOo—

This slap in the face did me a lot of good. I had long known that to succeed in television, you had to be 'different'. Now I was different in many ways: I was younger than many of the established comedians of the day, I had my trendy crew cut and I had my sweaters. But, to use a truism, television is above all a visual medium and I sat down to think of ways of giving my act more visual content. This led me to break one of our business's oldest taboos: never work with children or animals.

As a father, I had begun to incorporate into the act that chestnut of a song, *My Son, My Son, You're Everything To Me*, only I turned it into a joke. The cloying sentimentality became almost a satire on family life. For a time, I even thought of bringing young Martin on stage with me but realised that this might rebound against the humour: one could lampoon wives and, in particular, mothers-in-law — this was virtually *de rigeur* — but to target one's real-life baby was probably pushing the anti-family line too far. And anyway, I doubt Muriel would have approved. So one day I picked up the phone to speak to Chipperfield's Circus. It was, at first, a dreadful mistake.

I was appearing in another live show, *Garrison Theatre*, at an RAF base in the Midlands. The object of the call was to see if I could hire a chimpanzee for the night. They said yes, but only under very strict conditions. The animal must be brought to the studio in a heated vehicle by a trained member of the Chipperfield staff who must remain on hand at all times. It must be kept warm in the studios and kept fed and watered. And after the show, it must be taken home immediately in the same luxurious transport. OK, I said, how much? Thirty pounds, they said, which staggered me for I was only getting £18 for the appearance. Nothing ventured, nothing gained, I thought, and made the deal. What I had in mind, televisually, was going to be very different indeed. Fortunately, the great television-loving public were never to know just how different…

It started badly and got a great deal worse. Chimpanzees may seem cuddly, kindly creatures, but they are in fact immensely strong — they could kill a man in a bare-knuckle fight — and some of them are also subject to violent temper tantrums. When my particular chimp arrived, it was accompanied, to my surprise, by a girl who seemed to be in her late teens. She was also in tears, which was not surprising because her dress had been ripped almost to pieces and blood was oozing from a series of bites and scratches that covered her arms and neck. The chimp glared at me like a cobra about to strike.

"What the hell happened?" I asked, my heart going cold. "I don't know," snuffled the girl. "She just went berserk. I've never seen her in a mood like this."

This was a situation which called for a cool head as well as a cold heart. I had invested hard cash in this deal and spent a lot of time preparing the act, an act which, I was convinced, was to make me into a TV star. Yet it all depended on a simian psychopath which, as far as I knew, could launch into another deadly assault at any minute. With me as the target. I was already wise enough to know that, should the beast attack me on television –*live* television, no less — the viewers would be ringing the RSPCA in their thousands (there is, unfortunately, no body called the Royal Society for the Prevention of Cruelty to Comics, which is a great shame because it would be a very busy organisation). No, if anything happened out there, if I were to be covered with blood and bites, it would be *my* fault, not the chimp's. In this animal-loving nation of ours, I could see no future for a comic with a bent for monkey bashing.

Whilst the unfortunate handler was given first aid, I did what I could in the couple of hours before show-time to make friends with the beast. I offered her bananas, which she rejected with contempt. I tried to stroke and and pat her, only to see those huge teeth bared and pointed at my flesh. If this is a lady monkey, I thought in dismay, what would a male be like? When the band was stirring and the MC was clearing his throat, I began evasive action. My Windmill training came into play: I would play the scene as though the son in the song were there. I would talk my way through it, playing it by ear. Then, at the end, I would explain that there should have been a chimpanzee on stage but it had refused to act with me in case I stole the show. It was thin, pitiably thin, but what alternative was there?

I had forgotten, of course, that I was dealing with a pro. This was a trained circus monkey, to whom bright lights and fanfares were meat and drink. Like many a temperamental actress before her, she metaphorphosised from a hard, snarling, complaining bitch into a demure young *lady*, all big smiles and fluttering eyelashes. Must be something to do with the hormones, I suppose.

I went on and did the first part of my act. I could see her off stage, holding hands with her handler as though they were bosom friends. Then I began my song: "My, son, my son, you're everything to me..."

Somehow I staggered through it, dreading of the explanation I was about to make. I held out my hand in one despairing gesture ...and out she came into the lights, mincing like a young girl in a Butlins beauty contest. She took my outstretched hand, looked up at me ecstatically, and turned to the studio audience. Then, I swear, she *bowed*! The outburst of applause, the shrieks, the laughs, the banging of feet, went off like an explosion. I was startled but the chimp was totally shocked (perhaps in the Big Top, applause gets more widely diffused and therefore does not have the intensity of a cramped TV set).

The result was that she leapt into my arms and cuddled her head under my chin, no doubt to shield her ears from the din. Whatever the reason, it was the KO punch to an already groggy audience. They were out for the count, the air full of more sighs than the Soho brothels on Cup Final Night. The producer and cameraman, God bless their souls, were professionals, too, and realised here was a shot unique in those early TV days. They pulled us into tight close-up, just Maynard and the monkey embracing like lovers.

It took an age for the hullabaloo to die down. Then I was able to deliver one of the most devastating punch-lines of my career. Clearing my throat, I said huskily:

"Ladies and Gentlemen, I have an important announcement to make about our young friend here..."

A puzzled silence, the odd uncertain chuckle.

"I'm afraid to say that this is not my son..."

Laughter.

"She is in fact ...my daughter!"

Near riot.

Even today, with all the computer-driven technology of a modern television studio, with all the skills and generations of experience among animal trainers, it would be a superlative shot. In 1953, when studio technicians were still inventing much of their craft as they went along, it was sheer magic. And, at the risk of repeating myself once too often, it went out *live*

To quote the SAS motto in an unusual context, 'Who Dares Wins'. I had chosen to break one of the hallowed rules of showbusiness in a reckless throw of the dice. Only now do I realise just how great that gamble had been, to go on stage live with a temperamental and potentially dangerous animal I had only just met. Today, very few professionals would even contemplate such a scene. Those foolish enough to do so would get to know the animal over a period of weeks, if not months, and the number of takes needed to get that final cuddle would, I'll bet, run into dozens at least. And it's odds on they would not get the same result.

That chimpanzee could have killed me, physically as well as professionally. Instead, she made me into a star. A national star. I had become the legendary overnight success in almost 20 years in showbusiness with just three minutes work. Such is the power of television. In my glee over such success, I was yet to learn that the power of television can also rob an individual human being of any chance of ever again leading a normal life. The gains are enormous but the losses eventually take their toll.

Chapter Ten

Fame

T HE DOUBLE ACT has a long and honourable place in the history of comedy. In an extreme sort of way, Punch and Judy were a classic of the genre, because when they were brought to England by Italian puppeteers in Tudor times, they introduced an element of violence and cruelty into humour. That streak of violence, with one character trying to dominate the other, is a classic component of the double act: Oliver Hardy always bullied Stan Laurel, Bud Abbott was regularly vicious with Lou Costello. As a device, the double act has several advantages over a single stand-up comic: its allows the partners to go about their act reacting with each other, rather than directly with the audience, who can watch and listen as eavesdroppers surreptitiously enjoying someone else's family spat, a Peeping Tom view of the world that gives a certain vicarious pleasure. Additionally, because the good guy, usually the funny guy, always wins through in the end, the act has a certain morality of its own which appeals to the underdog in all of us. But although I first won national fame as part of a duo of comics, Terry Scott and Bill Maynard were *never* a double act. We were parcelled off together by the Richard Stone organisation and sold as a package to the BBC, and for that I shall be eternally grateful. As Terry and I had been good friends for years — good enough to do our Butlins laundry together in the nude, which is as about close as two heterosexual men can ever get — working together was a pleasure as well as the vehicle which took us finally to the top rung of the showbusiness ladder.

But despite *Great Scott It's Maynard,* the hit TV show we created together in 1955 and 1956, we were never a double act.

From the very beginning, when the programme was first proposed by the

Stone agency, we had very firm ideas about how it should play. BBC producers, our joint agent, the press and, I suspect, many millions of television viewers, thought we would develop into a double act that might have rivalled Morecambe and Wise (two struggling newcomers at the time) in popular longevity. Not only was I against this idea — more so than Terry, I believe, although when we started he was still considered to be the bigger name of the two — but I also wanted to create something very different, a bespoke show specially tailored for television rather than a simple series of variety acts lifted straight from music hall and plonked before the cameras off the peg. Additionally, both Terry and I had honed successful individual acts and had no intention of diluting them into one watered-down compromise: that would have been a rare case of the sum of the whole being worth considerably less than the two halves.

The answer we arrived at, with the help of a good director and a team of five writers, was a *themed* comedy show which, today, seems so utterly obvious but which in those days was something of a breakthrough. This was not a situation comedy, a comedy play in its own right, but a judicious mix of acts and sketches all following the same general theme: one night we would send up the ballet, next time the Wild West or Shakespeare. This allowed Terry and I to do individual spots while not working together, something that true double acts always find difficult (witness later how Eric Morecambe would always have to intervene when Ernie Wise was trying to do one of his 'serious' bits).

Also very new was our method of introducing these shows. Until now, as in theatre and radio variety, most programmes had been introduced by a dinner-jacketed MC who also acted as link man between the acts. Terry and I introduced the show together, he in a dressing gown trying desperately, and failing hopelessly, to play a Noel Coward lookalike, and me, crew cut, sweater and all, parrying his sophistication with my mickey-taking, self-deprecating humour. Hardly the stuff of revolution, it seems now, but we actually became that much misused cliché, an *overnight success*. The show hit some nerve among the viewing public, satisfying the ever-present demand for something new. Our viewing figures soared and I even created a catch-phrase that entered the national vocabulary and stayed there for the best part of a decade, which is one of the most satisfying achievements any comic can boast.

In one sketch sending up the Roman Empire, I was playing a Jewish Julius Caesar being greeted by the Roman crowds after returning home from one of his many triumphs. I was introduced as: "Mighty Caesar."

(Cheers)

"Commander of the Legions."

(Cheers)

"King of All Rome."

(Cheers)

"Ruler of the World."

(Cheers)

Then the camera cut to close up. I put on my self-deprecating grin and spoke into the camera: "When you're in, you're in."

It was this five-syllable phrase which, I think, finally brought home to me the overwhelming power of this frightening new medium. This was the time when Harold Macmillan was at 10 Downing Street and the country was enjoying its first boom of prosperity after the long war years and the austerity which followed. Macmillan himself was to cash in on the mood with his famous political slogan, "You've never had it so good." Also still in common usage was the old forces phrase, "Fuck you Jack, I'm all right," which was to be adapted for the title of the famous Boulting Brothers film starring Peter Sellers and my old friend Ian Carmichael. Perhaps some bright young psychology student will one of these days get a large grant to study just why some comic catch-phrases click to fire the public imagination while others disappear without trace. This is a puzzle that never ceases to bewilder stand-up comedians for, make no mistake, they spend most of their working lives searching for one that will be forever theirs. As it happens, most of them are created by accident, as was mine. They are the ones which reflect the mood of the time and these were times when many working people in Britain were beginning to grab some of the riches of a booming economy for the first time in a way their parents had never known. *When you're in, you're in*, hit this vein and entered the language. For years, I could never go anywhere without it being shouted at me, by people in the street or in the pub, by taxi drivers and shop assistants. It what a somewhat chilling thought that television can do this in a fraction of a second.

Great Scott It's Maynard was to top the TV variety bill for two years but it would be unfair to claim all the credit for Terry and myself. We had a great supporting team that included established revue performers like Pat Coombes and Marie Benson and two youngster who were to go on to greater things: the glamour was provided in the (wonderful) shape of Shirley Eaton, a bubbly blonde still in her late 'teens, who was later to achieve world fame as the James Bond girl murdered by Goldfinger by covering her from head to toe in gold paint. Our Scottish character actor, Ian McNaughton, was to become one of the key creative figures in modern comedy as a director of the *Monty Python* series. And then, of course, there were the writers.

For a comic who had sweated over his own lines for years, practising them alone in the bath or *ad nauseum* on bored family and friends, working with professional writers was at first an enormous luxury. Finding the line in the first place is the difficult bit. Delivering it, once you have served a decent apprenticeship in the trade, comes as second nature: your *character* does it rather than you. So here we had a team which, I thought at first, did all the hard work for you. Once again, I was wrong.

TV writers, like the jazz musicians of my Soho days, tend to be an anarchical bunch. They have a talent which they cannot explain and which, like comics, they do not discuss and dare not analyse too deeply in case it gets lost in the process. One just cannot sit down and think up jokes. You have to gather funny situations from everyday life, by ear-wigging in pubs or on the Underground. You pick them up from newspapers or books, or something your wife has said to you, or an item that you may have seen on TV or heard on the radio. You squirrel away these little nuggets in some inner file and, if you are lucky as well as talented, they will pop out again in some newly-created surroundings and be funny. In the best writing teams, someone sug-gests the surroundings — ie, the basis for a sketch — and after a long process of bouncing these ideas around, the dross is shaken out and the nuggets lie gleaming on the surface. On *Great Scott It's Maynard,* we had a basic team of five writers and Terry and I worked with them closely. With all these varied talents in play, and given the anarchical nature of the people involved, this was a novel experience for some of the older members of the BBC hierarchy who were accustomed to an orderly sort of life. One of them didn't last long: Johnny Speight, from whom I had once bought gags at The Windmill for ten shillings a time, left early on, not for any lack of humour but because he was something of a rebel and that did not gel too well with the given way of doing things. Whoever took against Johnny must have suffered serious trauma a few years later, when he was back as the feted creator of Alf Garnett in *'Till Death Do Us Part.* It was perhaps because Johnny, too, had known his days in the wilderness that he was later to figure as a crucial figure in my life when I was also eating the bitter fruits of humiliation.

But there are writers and writers. In the legitimate theatre, a playwright will burn the candle at both ends, working day and night alone to create his masterpiece. Certainly, during rehearsals, he might co-operate with the director, changing a line of dialogue here, a scene there, but by and large his work is done when the curtain finally goes up. Actors are not usually trained to question their lines (although there are some exceptions to this rule) and, with luck, speak them much as the writer had intended. In the production of television comedy, this is totally different: writers and performers work as a team and, this business being what it is, there are often some pretty hefty egos on show. There is also a dichotomy in play, too, between the people who put lines on paper and those who have to speak them before the camera. Something that is quite hilarious on paper can become the proverbial lead balloon when spoken. For the comic, the joke must be much more than merely funny. It must have a certain rhythm to it, so that it flows towards the punch line with a natural smoothness. Only then can the comic make full use of those essential skills, delivery and, crucially, *timing*.

It was in this key area that I began to build a reputation that I still carry today. Our writers were some of the best in the land — the success of the show testified to that — but there were times when I felt that I was being left high and dry. I recall rehearsing one sketch for a Christmas show when, opening as ever with Terry in his dressing gown and me in my sweater, I was drawing up a list of Christmas presents I yearned for but was hardly likely to receive.

"How do you spell voluptuous?" I asked Terry. Terry ignored me and walked off to change for the rest of the show, leaving me alone. In front of camera. With nothing to say. Now this breaks a fundamental rule of comedy in that a performer must always have a last line before making his exit. Not to have one leaves both him and the audience in the air, a situation which in the theatre leaves a nervous silence hanging over the stage, a silence which destroys any atmosphere you have struggled to create in the build-up.

"This is no good," I protested. "I need an exit line."

Consternation. Terry came back and began to think with a furrowed brow. The writers gathered round. There was a muttered conference, a few feeble suggestions, then one of the writers, Lou Schwartz, suggested: "How about, 'Has anyone got a long buff envelope?" Everyone laughed: Terry, the writers, the director, the technicians. Even me. But then I thought about it and shook my head: "It might be funny to us but what does it mean? We have to make it clear to an old lady watching in Wigan or Winchester. And I'm the poor sod who's got to say it," I retorted testily.

Lou looked somewhat abashed and added lamely: "It's Goons humour, that's all."

Goons humour it probably was but, as I pointed out somewhat angrily, we were not The Goons and our audience was not a *Goon Show* audience. They had attracted a huge radio following and were undoubtedly one of the greatest-ever creations of British comedy. But their genius was never successful transferred to television or the stage. They played to a radio audience attuned to their uniquely surreal humour. We were creating our own brand of television comedy, our own identity in a world of many imitators, and one of my growing ambitions, one that is still alive and nagging me today, is that we should be accessible to the old ladies of Wigan and Winchester.

It took three days to settle that row, which may seem a long time for a line of dialogue which would last for less than three seconds. However, all my previous experience before live and often highly critical audiences told me that now was the time to dig in. Those highly-paid writers were among the cream of their profession but when it came to the wire, I was prepared to back my own instincts against theirs when it came to the delivery of a punch line. It still happens, from time to time, when I feel that certain lines in *Heartbeat* should be changed. There are some who look upon me as being difficult, the archetypal temperamental star. I deny this, although I do admit that I no longer worry about winning popularity contests. Good writers actually welcome my contribution, for they have faith in the years of backbreaking experience I have put in. I should know, they say. Others take is as a professional affront but perhaps this is as it has always been. Every generation goes out to learn its own lessons, dismissing the advice of older heads as antiquated tosh. I am quite sure who loses by this attitude and it most certainly is not me.

As it happened, during those three days of deadlock over my TV Christmas list, the newspapers had been full of the marriage of Marilyn Monroe and Arthur Miller, the celebrated playwright. It was an odd union, the beautiful blonde with a reputation for playing brainless bimbos and the tall, aesthetic intellectual. Even then, the newspapers were speculating on just how long such a marriage could last (with great accuracy, as it turned out) but here was a news topic that would have been read about and discussed in virtually every home in the land.

Eventually, I came up with a bit of business (the technical term for what actors do with their hands whilst on stage) with my list. I looked at the list, looked at the camera, and said: "You know, if I really got what I wanted for Christmas, Arthur Miller would be furious."

It was most certainly not the greatest exit line in showbusiness history but it got me off with a laugh, which was the object of the exercise. This is something that can sometimes be overlooked when creative people take themselves too seriously. All the vast expense of making television, all the script meetings and rewrites, all the rehearsals and the set design and the hours in make-up, all the skills of highly-paid technicians and their hugely complex equipment, should be directed to one end only: the enjoyment of the viewer. There are people in television who seem to feel that all this elaborate technology, all this hard work by skilled and talented people, was created to act as a mirror for their own egos, the most flattering theatre for narcissism ever created by science and art.

Me, I think of that old lady in Wigan or Winchester.

Chapter Eleven

Sex Symbol

T HE bookings, the money and, although I don't feel too proud of it now, the women started to roll in at a rate that one could scarcely believe. For the remainder of the 1950s, the pace of my life was so fast that I could barely keep up with it. Almost without my realising it, I had split into two separate characters, a sort of showbusiness schizophrenic, with two totally divorced lives. It was not, I hasten to point out, a mental illness in a clinical sense, more of a man being drunk on his own success, bewildered at what was happening to him but never having the time nor the inclination to sit down and think about the problems his behaviour was causing. This was success and I set out to enjoy every minute of it, grabbing any sensation on offer with both hands and to hell with the consequences.

First, the money. In the days when the BBC had a television monopoly, the corporate purse was watched over by a set of Scrooges who worked on the principal that to appear on television, if not actually an honour, was most certainly the best advertisement that any entertainer could have for his craft. You went on television to build a name, they said, and therefore you should not expect huge fees as well. Your reaped the rewards of the fame *they* made possible, elsewhere. So while every viewer in the country no doubt thought that I was earning hundreds, if not thousands, of pounds per appearance, in fact I started *Great Scott It's Maynard* on a miserly £40. Even when this was increased to £60, this was still less than half I had been picking up in my Soho days.

They were, however, correct in reading the business. With television stardom came an avalanche of bookings, for summer shows at major venues, for touring variety, for personal appearances, for spots at the most exclusive revue clubs and hotels. It was just a matter of picking the plums, taking the best and fitting them as best we could into a diary and rejecting the rest. For Bill Maynard was now top of the bill and the rewards were barely conceivable: at one stage, I was earning £1,000 a week at a time when, as I have already pointed out, a professional man thought £1,000 a year was a worthy reward for a long and successful career. Again, comparisons are difficult but in those pre-inflation days it was probably worth £1 million at today's prices. And along with the money came all the other trappings: the best suites in the bests hotels, the best table and the best champagne in the very best restaurants, the fast cars and the even faster women.

All this time, of course, I was a married man with a son and, soon to arrive, Jane, who was born in 1954. While the more sensible side of me was in control, Billy Williams, Family Man, took these responsibilities seriously. With a little help from me, Dad and Mum had now moved on to a back-street pub, The Bower, on the west side of Leicester, and I had the top floor furnished and decorated in the most expensive 'contemporary' style we could find. The family now had a secure and extremely comfortable home and this allowed the 'other me' to feel I was doing my familial duty. It was so splendid that, one week when I was appearing in Nottingham, I took one of the acts home, an up-and-coming singer called Tommy Steele. He gazed at the flat open-mouthed and said in his broad Cockney: "Blimey, Bill, you've broke me dream. I hope that I can have a place like this one day!" He went on to do rather well, young Tom.

Leicester was still home base but I saw little of it because I was almost constantly on tour, filling theatres throughout the country with such success that the impresario Bernard Delfont, who was no fool when it comes to spotting a showbusiness winner, took a full page advertisement in the trade press thanking me for my efforts. Muriel watched most of these developments as an outsider, reading about her husband's antics in the national newspapers much as her neighbours did. It was time, I decided, to involve her more in the business and she became my manager-secretary and began to handle the mountains of correspondence that came piling in, literally by the sackful. That was to be an experience for both of us for, thanks to the power of television, I had become a new species: the TV sex symbol.

There had, of course, been Hollywood heart-throbs for many years, from Valentino onwards, and they had entire departments to handle their fan mail. But these were actors on the silver screen based on the other side of the world, unattainable except as huge images on the screen down at the local Odeon. I was a comic, a funny man, expected to make ladies laugh, not swoon, yet things did not work out that way. Again, this might be an interesting research project for some ambitious psychologist: just why does a certain type of woman fall helplessly, and often erotically, in love with the image of a man she has never met, flickering on the TV screen in the corner of her sitting room? I have pondered this question for years, and have never come up with a satisfactory answer, but I tend to believe it is the intimacy of the medium which triggers the situation. As a regular visitor into people's homes, you become accepted as one of the family, a friend, almost a confidante. As Muriel and I were now to learn, many women in the land were dreaming of turning that mythical friendship into a flesh-and-blood affair.

I remember one of those first days when the avalanche of mail began to hurtle down the mountainside. I walked into the room and Muriel was going through my mail looking ashen-faced. She shook her head, handed me a sheaf of letters, and said: "I just don't know *how* women can bring themselves to put this sort of thing down on paper." I began to read and, despite years spent working among the strippers and the whores of Soho, even I was shocked. Many of the letters explained how these women would sit naked to watch my act on television, fantasising that I was there in the room with them. Some of them masturbated while they watched and described in intimate detail what they wanted me to do to them. For this group, the fantasy was the foreplay and writing to me in such explicit terms was the climax. This, I can only believe, is the sort of vicarious pleasure that makes male flashers expose themselves in public. But there was another group to whom fantasy was not enough: they wanted the real thing and were prepared to go to almost any lengths to get it.

Of all the thousands of letters that Muriel read on my behalf, the most shocking of all came from a 17-year-old girl who described herself as a doctor's daughter. Written on expensive paper in an immaculate hand, this missive did indeed give off an air of high respectability. Until you studied the contents. They explained that she had never had sex but wanted to lose her virginity to a very special man. She had also recently inherited £17,000. Would I be prepared to deflower her and, if so, the £17,000 was mine! Should I agree, I was to fondle my right ear during my next show.

This letter presented a couple of problems. The first was that I regularly fondled my ear in between gags: this was one of my trademark bits of 'business'. So I hope that girl is still not waiting for me to knock on her front door (not that she will be a girl, anymore, and most hopefully not a virgin).

The second was more serious and I could see this in the strange way Muriel looked at me after I had read the letter. For the first time, I believe, she was beginning to grasp just how different were Billy Williams, husband and father, and Bill Maynard, travelling comic and TV star. If some young girl were to offer a substantial fortune for sex with a man she had never met, how did the women behave who actually knew me? And, my business being what it was, those women tended to be glamorous and *available*, given the fact that we shared the same hotels during our almost constant tours.

Now Muriel, as I have explained at length, was no fool. Nor was she the doormat type, happy to be walked over. She was, in many ways, much tougher-minded than me, much more focussed on the family and the future. Even in the days before my name and photograph were featuring regularly in the national press, often with a lovely young co-star at my side, she must have had her suspicions about the girls who surrounded me at The Windmill and other revue clubs. Now she was being subjected, day by day, to a non-stop avalanche of near-pornography. As if that were not enough, she was soon to discover that being married to a new breed of sex symbol could be physically dangerous too.

—oOo—

Even though I was a major star, I was still taking most dates the BBC offered, partly out of gratitude but perhaps with another reason in mind. I may have had some inkling that it was all too good to be true, that one day the bubble would burst and it would be back to Billy Williams at the South Wigston Working Men's Club (which, in fact, was not too far from the truth). Also, when a date was not too far from home, I would stay the night in Leicester and take Muriel with me to the venue. Thus one day we set out to do a *Workers' Playtime* spot for BBC Radio at a factory in the West Riding of Yorkshire.

Perhaps it was some long-delayed reaction to my infant school black-leaded football boots but I had taken to dressing with considerable flamboyance, playing the big star in public. I did my act in my sweaters, of course, for that was my trade mark. I still wore the compulsory Crombie overcoats. But I had discovered a taste for outrageous hats, the flashier the better, which, given my six-foot frame, made me stand out in any crowd (it was a habit that was to get my into trouble more than once). On this day somewhere near Wakefield, I had chosen a large straw hat for my radio performance which took place at lunchtime in the work's canteen. The show had gone well and the audience, mainly young factory girls, had gone berserk in a way that I had never seen before. Then, as I made my way out of the factory to the car park, I took a wrong turn and walked out into the open air.

"It's him."

"Isn't he lovely."

"I just love that hat."

"Yeah — let's get his hat."

Blinking in the sunlight after stepping out from the dingy corridor, I realised that I had come into the main factory yard. This was packed with scores, perhaps a hundred or more, of the young girls who had just given me such a good reception. But now, all thought of going back to work had gone and they came bearing down on me like a stampede of long-horned cattle in a Western movie. Suddenly, I was surrounded by these girls, tearing at my clothes, snatching at my straw hat and clothing, even grabbing locks of hair. I was laughing, trying to fend them off with a smile and a joke. I did not laugh for long.

This, remember, was before The Beatles, when the custom of young fans mobbing their idols became so dangerous that police forces developed new tactics for protecting celebrities from serious injury and perhaps even worse. It was, of course, completely new to me and it took me a few dangerous minutes to realise that I could be in serious trouble. I was a big, fit fella and these were only young lasses. But there were dozens of them and their hands were ripping at anything they could reach: my sleeves, my jacket and, with some force, the front of my pants. Most of all, they wanted my hat and in their efforts to grab the major prize, the initial humour turned into a form of mob frenzy. Within minutes, the hat had been pulled down over my eyes, my head popping out through the top like a jack-in-the-box. Even then, I thought this was quite funny. But when the topless brim was pulled down round my neck, and frenzied hands were tugging at it from both sides, I began to choke.

I suddenly realised that I was in real danger. I could either be strangled, which was indeed imminent, and had I gone down I would have been trampled underfoot. Many of these girls were wearing murderous stiletto-heeled shoes, the sort which were then banned in most dance halls because they could actually punch holes into the floorboards. What they would have done to the prostrate form of Bill Maynard can only be a matter of conjecture but it would have undoubtedly been painful in the extreme. Faced with two highly unpleasant alternatives, I did the only thing I could: I began to lash out, as first pushing, then slapping and, as a genuine fear began to overtake me, punching my weight. The screams of girlish laughter turned into howls of outrage and they began to punch and kick back. Then a flying wedge of factory security guards and male workers punched its way through the wheeling throng and I was rushed off to my car with the angry protests still ringing in my ears.

Among my new bodyguard was the factory personnel officer, a woman close to tears with anxiety, who started a non-stop stream of apology: "I'm sorry, Mr Maynard. So sorry. I don't know what came over them. They turned into a bunch of savages. I've never seen anything like it..."

Neither had I. But I was not listening to this shame-faced litany. I was staring at Muriel, standing by the open door of the car in the visitors' car park, her eyes full of what can only be described as sheer terror. Not many wives, thankfully, are subjected to the sight of their husband on the point of being torn to shreds by a rampaging mob. For that mob to be made up of howling girls gripped by some form of mass hysteria only added to the inexplicability of it all. We accelerated out of the car park as though we were leaving the front grid of a Grand Prix but drove home in near silence. Once she had ascertained that I had not been seriously injured, Muriel fell into a sombre mood of deep thought.

Now it is always dangerous to speculate on what one's spouse is thinking in such moods but I will hazard a guess: "How did I get into a situation in which my husband can face serious injury or worse at the hands of a mob of screaming girls? *Just what is it that has changed Billy Williams into a sex symbol?*"

—oOo—

The answer, of course, is fame. And fame is one of the great ironies of showbusiness. It is the holy grail that all hopeful entertainers cherish, a quest which only a rare few ever complete. It is the great galvaniser, the bringer of wealth and influence. The irony is that for many who achieve it, it turns out to be a poison chalice. Nice, ordinary folk can turn into monsters overnight when fame arrives. They can be prepared to sacrifice everything at its altar: family, friends, peace of mind. They often feel that fame is the only real happiness when, in fact, it can make happiness in the true meaning of the word almost impossible. It came to me with such bewildering speed that, for the first time round at least, I never really learned to cope. Had it not been for Muriel, I would never have regained my composure and learned how to handle it with reasonable skill. Now, I must say, I quite enjoy it because it allows me to make friends with people very quickly and takes me to places and parts of society that young Billy Williams could never have entered. But in the beginning, although I enjoyed the trappings with relish, fame was a pain.

For a start, I soon discovered that I could no longer go into a pub for quiet drink. For in any bar there would always be some man who, half drunk or worse, wanted to drag me into a fight. The reasons for this are many: first, to hang a famous scalp on the belt is a powerful incentive for a certain type of hooligan — "Guess who I belted last night?" Or he doesn't like your act, an opinion to which he is quite entitled although I prefer my critics to use words, not fists. Or the sex thing again: "My wife won't cook my dinner when your on TV because she thinks you're fucking fabulous," — thwack! Even today, elderly chaps come up to me and say, "You're all right now, mate, but if I could have got my hands on you back in the 1950s, I would have killed you."

You get the same in the street or the shops. People stop you and demand autographs, which I am usually happy to give unless, as rarely happens, they become aggressive. To the lad from Rat Alley, all this was deeply disturbing once the novelty of the situation had worn thin. With my background, the thought of becoming a snob was completely alien. Even when I was to join the Rolls-Royce and racehorse set, I never attempted to hide my humble beginnings. People either liked me as I was or they didn't, and it made little difference to me. Sheer circumstance drove me into another world, the world of luxury hotels and expensive restaurants, for at least there I could get a little peace and quiet: most well-to-do people feel that toadying up to a celebrity is demeaning so they leave you alone. But in all worlds there are exceptions to the rule and I was to make sensational headlines for the first time in unusual surroundings, at a grand Masonic ball that was the highlight of the Glasgow social scene. Once again, my choice in headgear was the spark that lit the flames.

Glasgow once had an unenviable reputation as the toughest city in Britain, a place of razor gangs, sectarian violence between Protestant and Catholic, and the infamous Gorbals slums. For entertainers, the Glasgow Empire was renowned as the toughest venue on the top music hall circuit, a nightmare of a theatre where Scots audiences full of whisky and patriotic fervour chewed up English comics and spat them out in half-pound cans. In real life, Glasgow was two cities, the one just mentioned and the other an enormously prosperous society of merchants, ship owners, lawyers and engineering millionaires, the people who had earned Glasgow the title of the 'Second City of the Empire' in Victorian times. These were the grandees who made up the guests at the annual Masonic ball, along with the High Sheriff and the Chief Constable and similar local luminaries. The very fact that an English comic starring at the Empire Theatre was invited along as guest of honour was an indicator of just how high I had climbed on the social ladder.

I went along with Marie Benson of the *Great Scott It's Maynard* troupe on my arm. She was dressed in a stunning evening gown, I was in a brand new dinner jacket and, to top off this splendid ensemble, I chose a large, flamboyant fedora. The hazardous lesson of my Yorkshire straw hat had not sunk in and, as I have already said, there are always exceptions in any society, however polite.

One of these was a pushy young wife with a rather large husband. Even as we made our entrance to the immense foyer, she took an instant liking to my headgear, as had those young factory girls in West Yorkshire. She asked me to give her the hat as a souvenir and I declined as politely as I could. Marie took charge of the situation and we duly handed hat and coat in at the cloak room. Sadly, this young women pestered us several times during the evening, which was particularly unpleasant in such surroundings, and by the time the evening was over I was thoroughly peeved by her attentions. These are the sort of times when fame can be a burden.

Came the end, when the High Sheriff and the Chief Constable had left (wisely for the latter, as it turned out) Marie and I went to collect our coats and, surprise surprise, my hat was missing. The cloak room attendant apologised profusely saying that a young lady had said she was picking it up for me. And then came our friend, dancing across the foyer with my hat on her head. Marie, sensing trouble, stepped between us and tried to smooth the situation. I said the women could keep the hat but it was to no avail. She turned abusive and it was now my turn to step in because I did not want the evening to climax with an all-female brawl. It didn't...

At this point, the husband chose to make his entrance. Misreading the situation, thinking I was chatting up his wife, he took a swing at me but fortunately missed. I had had more than enough and lashed out with a haymaker that left him stretched out on the thick foyer carpet while his wife went into hysterics. Then someone dialled 999 to get rid of my assailant. The police could not have been far away — in view of the Chief Constable's recent presence, they could have been outside on the pavement — because when they arrived I was still standing over the semi-conscious body.

This could have been a scene straight out of a Max Sennet two-reeler, a sort of Keystone MacCops. Here it was, the great social gathering of the Glasgow season, men in evening dress, women in elegant gowns, and a groaning Scotsman spreadeagled on the plush carpet. Whether or not any nationalistic feelings came into play I do not know, but to the police it looked simple: there was a Scotsman lying on the floor and an Englishman standing over him. The

Scotsman's wife was sobbing bitterly and, worse still, the Englishman and his partner were *theatricals*.

Brushing aside any explanations from Marie, me and the cloakroom staff, I was thrown into a Black Maria and dragged off to Glasgow Central police station.

There I was charged with assault, told to pick up a straw mattress, taken to a cell, and banged up for the night, a tall, dinner-suited Sassenach alone in a cell usually occupied by Sauchiehall Street drunks. I was livid at the injustice of it all. My evening had been ruined by constant pestering and I had lashed out in self-defence. Yet I was the one in the cell.

I pressed a button in the wall, hoping to summon my jailer. Instead, the toilet flushed. It was the first time I had seen such a mechanism, installed presumably to prevent the cell's regular occupants from tearing the handle or chain away from the plumbing. Even more angry, I began to bang on the heavy metal door, demanding attention at the top of my voice. Eventually, a little spy-hole opened and I could see a single spiteful eye peering at me. The Max Sennet routine, Act II:

"I want to see a lawyer."

"Ye canna."

Slam.

More hammering on the door, more shouting. The peephole reopens.

"I want bail."

"Ye canna."

Slam. Hammering. Shouting. Peephole opens.

"In that case, could I have a coat hanger for my suit…"

Slam.

Being late at night, the story did not break in the Glasgow papers until the following day. The day after that, Muriel was sipping her cup of morning tea in our luxury flat above the pub in Leicester when huge headlines leaped out of the morning papers: 'MAYNARD IN JAIL,' and 'TV STAR ON ASSAULT CHARGES.' And there were photographs of me, in a now thoroughly dishevelled dinner jacket but still wearing that flamboyant hat, being released from Glasgow Central nick.

As it happened, explanations were made and the charges dropped so, thankfully, I did not have to stand trial. This, however, was not a lot of consolation to Muriel, nor was it the last time that headlines involving her husband would disturb her morning cuppa. A new force had entered our life, the ultimate penalty of fame: the tabloid press.

Early in 1997, as chance would have, I was to be thrown into a cell in *Heartbeat* by Derek Fowlds, the evil Sergeant Blaketon. Now as a man of some experience in these matters, this called for a script conference. And, yes, the scene was played virtually word for word from Glasgow Central except that I did not make my final request a coat hanger (not the sort of item which would overly concern Greengrass). Instead, it ended with my asking for a cup of cocoa. All great art, say the critics, comes from real life. Here was the proof. But I feel there are easier ways of doing the research.

Chapter Twelve

Ticking Time Bomb

ONCE again, having worked my way on to a very good thing indeed, it was time to get off. On the face of it, I had almost anything a man could want: wealth, fame, and, thanks to Muriel, a loving family. Jane had arrived on the scene in 1954 and the Family Maynard had most certainly moved up in the world. One of the few sensible things I did with the money that was rolling in was to buy a house at Fleet in Hampshire, not far from my birthplace. It was not a stately home but, nevertheless, a rather smart modern place with a nice garden and three cars in the drive. These varied over the years, for I bought and sold motors like an auto maniac, but there was usually a flashy American beast used when I was on tour, a two-seater sports car for cutting a dash on the country lanes of Hampshire when I was at home, and a small saloon for Muriel's shopping expeditions.

Muriel, a natural home-maker, set about furnishing with great care and taste, buying a piece here, another there, and planting the garden with shrubs and flowers chosen with similar skill. Whether or not she liked the cocktail cabinet I installed I would not like to say, for I was constantly entertaining at home and our household bills were running at £100 a week, much of which went on drink. We became part of the local social scene, for fame drags people to you like iron filings to a magnet. Whether or not they actually like you is often hard to judge.

This matter of fast friendships can become a problem when you are in the public eye. They might like being seen with you, or of boasting that they had been to your house for a meal or drinks, but that is another matter. There are many people in showbusiness who, despite years of fame, still truly trust only the friends they made before they became rich and famous. Trouble is, those old friends can themselves be put off by all the flashy, sometimes trashy, behaviour of the newly rich. One is left with the classic dilemma: do they want to be with me because I am me or because of my money? At this time, however, I did not bother to waste time on such speculation: I was loud, brash, and threw money around with total disdain. Muriel accepted all this with her usual stoicism. She had a nice home, the first home of her own in her entire life, and two children on which she doted. When they were old enough, they went away as boarders to expensive prep schools which, we assumed, would mould them for the major public schools which we expected them to attend. This was partly due to my own fantasies about boarding school life, nurtured by the stories I had read in my boyhood comics, and partly due to a fierce desire to give the children a better start in life than I had enjoyed. There was, however, another more sinister reason, the flip side of the coin of fame. All children have this innate sense of wanting to be the same as their school-mates, to be part of a tight-knit group. In semi-rural Hampshire, this was not possible when your father was on the television night after night. Martin, who had gone off to the local village school, started coming home with black eyes, cuts and grazes, his shoes scuffed and his clothes torn. For some time, he would not admit what was happening but enquiries at the school revealed the truth: other boys were ganging up on him because of his famous father and he was pluckily taking them on.

Apparently, he held his own pretty well when it came to fisticuffs but he was, of course, hopelessly outnumbered. Like all mothers, Muriel was dis-traught at the idea of her children going away to boarding school but we reasoned that, in the company of children from other financially successful families, the envy factor which led to Martin's playground brawls would be absent. So as the 1950s came to an end, Martin went off to St Paul's School at Burgh-le-Marsh in Lincolnshire and, three years later, Jane went to Morcott Hall School near Uppingham. Fortunately, I paid most of their school fees in advance...

With such domestic problems solved — or so I thought — I felt free to indulge in the life of the big star. The champagne kept flowing, the leading ladies were dutifully bedded — for some reason, I felt I was under compulsion to do this, almost as a matter of honour — and I began to gamble heavily, on horses, on greyhounds, on cards. Whether I won or lost scarcely seemed to matter — I could always give the money tree another shake and the fivers could come floating down. This was a serious act of self-delusion, for after years of steadily climbing the ladder of success, my grip on the top rung was becoming increasingly precarious. The Bill Maynard self-destruct time bomb was beginning to tick. Sadly, I was too preoccupied with success to listen.

—oOo—

The cracks first began to appear in *Great Scott It's Maynard*. There was no personal animosity between Terry and I and we were to remain close friends for many years. But as I have explained, we had been packaged together for the show by Richard Stone wheeling and dealing and we both considered ourselves to be individual artistes. Trouble was, Terry would walk into a room and someone would say: "Hello Terry. Where's Bill?"

When I walked in, it was: "Hello Bill. Where's Terry?"

I began to find this particularly irritating — more so, I think, than Terry who at that time was a more level-headed and sensitive character than me. And I was also feeling that the show had passed its peak and was in danger of becoming repetitive. It may well have been one of the first truly innovative shows of the new medium of television but the medium itself was changing at lightning speed and I thought there were new possibilities to explore. In this quest for new ideas, I had taken to flying to America, to watch their television and take in some of the comedy shows in New York clubs and theatres. On one of those trips, I had been excited by a new piece of TV technology which allowed the screen to dissolve in a series of wavy lines between scenes which gave the viewer a sense of passing place and time. This, I believed, had great possibilities for comedy.

When I finally announced that there would be no further *Great Scott It's Maynard* shows, a lot of people were not best pleased, including Terry, who would have been happy to carry on. Both Richard Stone and the BBC took it badly but I already had the great idea (or so I thought) of what should replace it — a show called *Mostly Maynard*. I was to star in it alone, of course, and we were to build on the 'themed' structure which Terry and I had developed. But instead of various sketches being linked by a piece of on-screen patter, I was to wander from one to the other as if moving through time and space. This was to be accomplished by the dissolve machine that had so impressed me in New York.

That was the first problem: those machines were very expensive and the BBC did not have one. Other problems began to flow thick and fast. I had hoped that the talented director of *Great Scott It's Maynard*, Duncan Wood, would be assigned to the new show but instead he went off to direct *Hancock's Half Hour*. Duncan's assistant, Phil Barker, and I had established a close working relationship so I asked for him. For the first time, I ran into the BBC brick wall: they had their way of doing things and you challenged them at your peril. Phil could not possibly do the job, old boy, I was told; he is only an assistant director and an assistant could not possibly be given control of an important new comedy series. Nevertheless, just a few weeks later he was given the *Bernard Braden Show*. Perhaps this was pure coincidence and Phil had served his time as an assistant and was ready for promotion. Perhaps someone already had a knife out for me. If so, it would not be the last time...

The director I was given was an extremely pleasant and competent chap but we disagreed vehemently on my idea of linking the sketches using the American slow dissolve gadget. He won that argument with ease because not only did the BBC not have one, they also had no intention of buying one. This shot huge holes in my vision for the show and although we cobbled together a compromise on the links, they simply did not work. This destroyed the entire cohesion. Months or planning and work had created a disaster.

One tabloid television critic wrote the next day: "The crash you heard at 8.30 last night was not a clap of thunder but the sound of the new Bill Maynard show falling flat on its face." It was perhaps the most damning one line of criticism I have ever endured and, as I discovered later, it might not have been entirely due to my *on-screen* performance. As it happened, I had been 'looking after' the critic's girlfriend and he may have discovered the fact. Whether or not this affected his professional judgment is, however, unlikely because sadly most of the other critics took the same line. Here we had a crisis. And the BBC had an answer to it: sheer panic.

There was a series of meetings — inquests is probably a better word — and in the end the blame fell on my scriptwriter, Eric Merriman, a man in whom I had total confidence at that time. We had worked together for a long time and when his original scripts had their first readings, everyone, including the director, had fallen about with laughter. However, these things were quickly forgotten in the face of the hostile reviews. It was suggested that I should change the writer. I refused. The matter went to the Head of Comedy, who said I *must* change the writer. Again, I refused. I was too stubborn to realise that I was putting my future, and the future of my family, in severe jeopardy.

Just what caused me to take on the big guns of the television world was an accumulation of reasons, some good, some bad. For a start, I had a burning feeling of injustice at the way Eric Merriman was being treated. He had struggled to do his best when the available technology was against him and he, in my opinion, was being cast as the scapegoat. I also had this inherent dislike of being bullied, something that no doubt that went back to my sickly childhood. But I was also big-headed and arrogant, with offers pouring in every day from major theatres and cabaret. As I have said before, the fees I received from the BBC were peanuts compared with the huge sums I was being offered to appear live. I could do without television, I decided.

The BBC fought back. They called Richard Stone and said unless I agreed to change writers, the series would be axed after six shows. Richard Stone, with considerably more business acumen than I was displaying, took their side. Without television exposure, he explained, the other dates would dry up too. By this time, I had decided that there was an enormous point of principle at stake here. Again, I refused. This time, I was making a near-fatal error.

Richard had been a key player in my success. With a mixture of encouragement, experience and knowledge, he had pushed me slowly but surely up the greasy pole. But the row with the BBC was not our only difference at the time. In my ever-restless way, I had decided to achieve another ambition, one I had secretly cherished from my boyhood years watching the stars of the silver screen in the flea pits of Leicester. I was tired of being a comic. Like a million star-struck youngsters across the Western World, I decided that I was going to be a film star.

The difference was that 99.9 per cent of those youngsters soon drop their dream and take proper jobs. The few who actually make it to the fringes of the film world usually have little to lose, and lose what there is anyway. Me, living the life of a millionaire, a dual life with family on one side and wine, women and song on the other, I had everything to lose. This, of course, to the pig-headed young man I was, meant little. So with little regret I waved a frosty goodbye to the BBC. I knew what I was doing, or so I thought. I would start at the bottom all over again. If I were to become a film star, I would have to learn their craft. It was time to become a proper act-oor!

—oOo—

The clown who wants to play Hamlet is perhaps the oldest showbusiness chestnut of them all. I don't think I was bitten by this particular bug from some obscure romantic leanings, rather out of my life-long restlessness. As an adolescent, I had moved from one money-making scheme to another, quickly losing interest in one when overtaken by the excitement and challenge of another. This was a process I repeated over and over again. It had been the same in showbusiness, using one little success as a springboard to the next, then getting quickly bored as I had at The Windmill, despite my hefty pay packets and the well-endowed ladies who I looked upon as my rightful fringe benefits.

This grasshopper mentality had long been a source of puzzlement to Richard Stone who, by this time, was no doubt hoping that I would grow out of it when all the trappings of success became mine. He was wrong, poor Richard. For months I had been telling him that I wanted to be an actor. For months he had prevaricated, thinking no doubt that it was a passing phase. Then, one day when I was appearing in variety in Aberdeen, I telephoned him and said: "Find me a play or I will quit the agency."

This ultimatum was something he could not ignore, inadvisable though he thought it was. A couple of days later he rang back and said he had found me a play called *You Too Can Have a Body*, a comedy thriller by a writer I had never heard of, Fred Robinson. Did I want it?

"I don't know. Is it any good?"

"Do you want it?"

"Shouldn't I see the script first?"

"You asked for a play, I've got you a play. Do you want it or not?"

"Oh all right then."

Thus I came to the legitimate, or at least semi-legitimate theatre, as an actoor. What I did not know, but have long suspected, was that Richard Stone had cast around for the worst play his considerable network could unearth. His reasoning, I believe, was that if I had one disastrous flop I would give up all this silly theatrical nonsense and go back to what I was good at: being a comic. Once again, he was wrong, but not before considerable effort had been expended to prove him so.

When I finally received the script of *You Too Can Have a Body*, I knew I had been conned. This did not please me, although I guessed at the ultimately honourable motive behind it, because the play was simply awful. For me to appear in such rubbish would be to invite a career disaster of major proportions and I had no desire for a repeat experience of the *Mostly Maynard* TV series. However, I had agreed and we were due to open at the Connaught Theatre, Worthing, in a matter of weeks. What to do?

The obvious decision was to go to the font, the writer Fred Robinson. When I finally got his number, his first words were not encouraging: he had been so disappointed with the play that he had given up writing and gone back to his proper job. This gave me the opportunity I was seeking because, as I knew to my cost, suggesting changes to some writers can be like suggesting a rewrite of the Ten Commandments. Would he mind if I added some of my own lines to make it more acceptable — at least to me? I was, after all, a professional comic and had a good idea of what makes people laugh. Fred, who was later to become a close friend over our collaboration, seemed delighted that I should bother to take such an interest. Go ahead, he said.

We set to work and by the time the curtain went up in Worthing, we had a smash hit on our hands. This may have dismayed Richard Stone but word got round like lightning. On the third night, Tom Arnold, a theatrical impresario of almost legendary status, came on the phone and asked if we could take it to the West End. This did not thrill me as much as it might because I had intended to make my West End debut as a serious actor, rather than the star of a somewhat lightweight farce. But Richard Stone began to twist my arm, too, and so did Eric Merriman.

So off we went to the Victoria Palace, opening in the middle of a bus strike which prevented many Londoners getting into the West End. Despite this, we did reasonably well at the box office and I had cause for some satisfaction: I had my name in lights for the first time not as a comedian but as a comic actor, and that is simultaneously one of the narrowest and one of the broadest divisions in showbusiness. All truly great actors love to play comedy. Great actors will also admit that playing comedy requires a deft touch which is one of the profession's most difficult skills to acquire. I was by no means a great actor at this time but I had demonstrated before some of the world's most critical theatregoers that I had *the touch*. That was another important step forwards. Or backwards, depending how you look upon it.

The major achievement of *You Too Can Have a Body* — apart from relaunching Fred Robinson's writing career for he was to go on to create successful TV series — was that it attracted the attention of some of the bigger provincial repertory companies. Was I prepared to take the play on a rep tour?

Now repertory theatre holds a very special place in my heart. It is the cradle of the English stage, which in turn is the cradle of the world stage. Rep brings on fine young actors, writers and directors, often in appalling conditions. The pay is abysmal, the hours long and hard, and the theatrical digs financially viable to penniless actors in many provincial towns and cities are often cold, damp and dismal. Only people with a true love of the theatre survive this baptism of fire.

The reason for the dismal financial rewards available is not necessarily the result of penny-pinching managements. Most repertory theatres, even the famous ones, live in a state of constant financial crisis: pay the actors or the electricity bill, which is most important? Seeing themselves as they do, as the moral guardians of 'true' theatre, the reps regularly present new and challenging drama well received by the critics and the theatre-going *cognoscenti*. Sadly, plays like this do not always put bums on seats and with box office income so desperately needed, this presents hugely difficult decisions to their managements: do we go popular and pay the bills or stay high-brow and let the theatre go dark (ie, close forever).

To balance this tightrope, most managements compromise. They will do Shakespeare or Shaw one week and put on a popular show like a musical or a comedy the next (plus, of course, pantomime at Christmas). These lighter entertainments build a bigger box office and subsidise the weightier work.

At the time of my minor success in the West End, I was well aware of this situation. When the offers came in to tour *You Too Can Have a Body*, it struck me that here was an opportunity to advance my acting ambitions. I would do the comedy for one week, I said, if I could appear in a straight role in a serious play of my choice the next. The bait was snapped up and off I went to tour the reps.

This was, of course, a highly unusual step for a famous comedian. And the money, it goes without saying, was washers compared with my variety and cabaret earnings. Richard Stone, smelling disaster on the wind, advised strongly against it. But I would have my way. Coming, as it did, soon after the BBC debacle, this was the parting of the ways for seven long years.

My desire to become an act-oor had lost me my most important adviser although not a friend; Richard and I maintained a strong bond throughout the separation. It also cost me all the expert back-up of the Richard Stone organisation, in particular its accountants who, until this point, had kept a close track of my enormous earnings, ensuring that my tax bills were paid on time. I had sown the seeds of disaster but I was completely oblivious to the fact. The champagne days, unbeknown to me, were coming to an end.

Chapter Thirteen

The Slippery Slope

TELEVISION can and does make stars overnight. The fact that most of them have been in the business for years if not decades gives rise to wry little jokes like: "It took me 17 years to become an overnight success." Although this can be a cause for resentment among those who never make the top of the bill, the fact of the matter is that those 17 years serve only to get the artiste before the cameras. Once there, the performer makes or breaks his or her career in the ensuing few minutes. This is the overwhelming power of the little box sitting in the corner of millions of living rooms throughout the land. If TV makes overnight successes, it does not create overnight failures. The British viewing public, God bless it, forms very close attachments with its TV idols. They become almost one of the family and are remembered for years after they have disappeared from the screen, like Old Auntie Gladys who you see only at Christmas but is still always there. This was a blessing for me as I stood unawares at the top of the slippery slope, for it was to take me some years before I descended into comparative obscurity, years that took me into the Swinging Sixties on a wave of booze, gambling and female ladies of the opposite sex.

I was still a major star at the beginning of that wild decade, despite my exile from TV, and that allowed me to chose my roles, alternating periods in rep at £50 a week with highly lucrative bookings for variety and cabaret, so I continued to squander money like a maniac. Horse-racing in particular became a passion and while on tour, I would visit local courses and soon began to build up a big-spending circle of friends among owners, bookies and jockeys. This, I am sure, added further to Muriel's sense of foreboding about my lifestyle.

With the children away at school, Muriel now spent more time with me on the road. This did at least keep me out of other women's beds but I knew instinctively that she would have preferred to be back at home, painting and decorating or pottering about in the garden. I have memories of one racing day in Newcastle which, even today, makes me shrivel with embarrassment. I had been given a tip on a horse named, very appropriately, Turmoil in the Pitman's Grand National at Newcastle and I dragged Muriel along to see him run. I placed a £100 bet and went to the bar where the champagne began to flow. There we met an elegantly dressed, well-spoken man, probably one of the owners. When I told him of my bet, he was totally dismissive: "Not a chance old boy." So on went my first side-bet: if Turmoil won, I would buy the champagne; if his horse won, he would do similar.

Turmoil, after fading early on, picked up and won in a canter. I was jubilant and the flow of champagne became a torrent for him and his large party. During the celebrations, I learned that our newly-acquired friend was holding a poker school that night. "Great, love a game of poker," I said, rejecting Muriel's plea that I shouldn't invite myself to other people's private parties. My reluctant host apologised, saying that he was throwing a dinner party first and there was only enough pheasant for his invited guests. "Don't worry mate," I said. "We'll have a cheese sandwich."

There was, of course, a considerable gap between the end of racing and my self-invited poker party, so I dragged an increasingly belligerent Muriel off to the local dog racing track. That wasn't yet open, so we went to a nearby pub and I continued to drink heavily, getting involved in a game of darts with some Geordie lads who themselves were bound for the track. They, too, had a tip and to their astonishment I told them to put on a bet for me — and handed them £200. They, themselves, had managed to scrape up a fiver for their stake.

I drove them to the track in my Studebaker, which further added to their sense of awe and disbelief, and dropped them off while I went to find somewhere to park, a process which in my befuddled state took a good deal of time. This was, of course, in pre-breathalyser days but I was most certainly in no condition to drive and I shudder to think what my alcohol count must have been. By the time I got to the track, the important race was over — and my Geordie friends handed me something like £1,000 in winnings. I doubt whether they would have earned that much for a year's hard work so I had little choice and, once again, the drinks were on me.

By the time that session was over — the third of the day — Muriel was no doubt hoping that I had forgotten my poker date. But by this time I was flying high, convinced that my Midas touch was immortal. I was also so drunk that she realised that argument was pointless. So off we went again, this time, thankfully, with Muriel driving, into the countryside to the address we had been given somewhat reluctantly. After a long search, we came to a large house at the beginning of a long gravel drive. I got out, hammered on the door, and said to the somewhat surprised man who answered it: "OK. We're here. Where's the cards?"

The man looked me up and down somewhat sniffily and said frostily: "You are at the lodge, sir. You must want the manor house at the end of the drive."

It was not a house, not even a mansion, but more of a stately home, with a huge flight of steps running up to a magnificent portico door. I hammered the huge door knocker and we were eventuality let into a film-set: antique furniture in a huge entrance hall, corridors hung with paintings leading off into the wings. Muriel stiffened with horror but I was far too drunk to notice. Our host greeted us as though we were perfectly normal guests and so we sat down to cards. I lost, I believe, something like £37, but to be frank the later memories of that evening are somewhat misted, and not just by the passage of time.

I awoke the following day, lying in my sweaty pants and vest, on a vast bed in an even vaster bedroom, complete with marble-panelled bathroom. Muriel was in her petticoat and we did not even have a toothbrush between us. Then there came a polite knock on the door and a servant served us breakfast in bed on silver trays.

Even I, brash, flash and vulgar as I then was, realised that the humiliation I had poured upon my long-suffering wife was unforgivable. That she did forgive me was a miracle. But even this was not enough to end my fascination with the Sport of Kings. And I was glad that Muriel was not there on a later occasion, when things were going very, very wrong, and I tried to gamble myself out of the financial hole I had dug for myself and my family.

It was some years later and I was working in Torquay alongside the Beverley Sisters, then the most famous female singers in Britain, and we had become friendly with the owner of a nightclub in Paignton. With little to do during the day, we would pass the afternoons watching racing on television in the club. It was then I tried my 'system': to double up on favourite after favourite until I made the big killing. As anyone in his right mind knows, this is not a system but financial suicide but, of course, my mind wasn't exactly right in those days. I persevered through every race in a two-day meeting and by the middle of the afternoon of the second day, I was £1,200 in debt to the betting shop across the road — outside which, fortuitously, I parked my last prized possession, my Studebaker car. My debt was less than one day's winnings on that strange, drunken day in Newcastle, but times had changed — this was £1,200 I did not have. Bent on one desperate last fling, I sauntered with false confidence into the bookies and put £800 to win on a horse owned by the Queen Mother, Bali Hai III. The bookie looked distinctly uneasy: "You're already into me for quite a lot, Bill. I think I should have something on account."

It was time to bluff my way through. I stuck my thumb over my shoulder and said, "You've seen my car out there. It cost me 3,000 quid. Take that as security." He agreed with a hard, suspicious look. People with hard cash don't bet their cars. Back over the road in the club, I watched Bali Hai, ridden by Harry Carr, being overtaken a couple of furlongs from home. It was, I thought, the end, not just for the Studebaker but for almost everything I owned. Unable to bear the tension, I rushed to the loo and was violently sick. I was on my knees, throat full of bile, eyes full of tears, head down the lavatory, when there came a knock on the door. Joy Beverley, the leader of the group, announced in an excited voice: "Bali Hai has won." That was the day that Harry Carr became my patron saint.

It should have been a triumph. Instead, because the odds were very short, I picked up something like £47 for the non-existent £2,000 I had bet on the meeting. For under £50 I had put my entire family at risk. So much for the Sport of Kings.

—oOo—

But it wasn't just the betting and the booze. The non-stop stream of women passing through my life had put my marriage to Muriel under intense strain for some years. The family was the one sheet anchor in my stormy life. Without it, Bill Maynard, fading star, would have gone on to the rocks and, most likely, would have been wrecked for life. Just why I did it is hard to explain. Why Muriel put up with it will remain one of the great mysteries. However, having had long lonely years to ponder over it, I think I have some idea...

My own behaviour sometimes puzzled even me. It perhaps sprang from my childhood in Rat Alley, when to have nothing was the norm and to dream of having everything was all I could do. 'Everything' included pretty women. There was my arrogance, too, which allowed me boundless self-justification: I had worked hard and I deserved whatever I could get. Then, of course, were the somewhat elastic rules towards morality common in my chosen trade: casual affairs are the norm in showbusiness, particularly among touring companies, when there are long, empty days with little to do but drink or have sex. Drinking was considered the worse of these two activities: to go stage drunk has always been considered grossly unprofessional (although, admittedly, there were some big-name stars who made a career out of it, their stardom protecting them from complaints from mere directors or theatre managers). I always considered myself to be an arch-professional, so heavy drinking *before* a show was out. And a long way from home, that left the alternative.

At the end of almost every tour, couples will have been formed and the parting is usually marked with declarations of undying love. Most of the time, they never communicate again, never mind meet. Young people seem to do same thing these days with holiday romances. I had such flings with many of my leading ladies and sometimes they were very intense — while they lasted. One of them involved a ravishing young Belgian singer called Tonia Bern, who went on to marry the doomed speed-ace Donald Campbell. Tonia was to come back into my life much later in highly unusual circumstances but for the most part, when an affair was over, you remained good friends but nothing more. In showbusiness, where flamboyance is the norm, sex is merely an extension of friendship, the offering of a pleasant gift, rather than a commitment of affection. As many of my gifts came exquisitely wrapped, I accepted them with gratitude.

The problem is that outsiders, and in particular the popular press, don't see things in quite the same light. Sex scandals are their meat and drink and the bigger the celebrity, the bigger the story. For years, Muriel had been opening the papers to see pictures of me with pretty women on my arm. Much more seriously, I had been cited in two divorce cases, which gave the press a field day. My sexual prowess was at one stage a national talking point, so much so that one day a women's magazine telephoned me to ask what advice I would give to a woman who suspected her husband was having an affair.

"She'd better assume he is," I retorted. "I know very few married men who aren't."

This, I suppose, summed up rather well my attitude to extra-marital sex: it was a bit of a fun, almost a joke, but nothing of great import. Had I been more sensitive, I should have realised just how wounded Muriel felt about newspaper and magazine reports like this. But just like me, Muriel had two sides: caring wife and mother and long-suffering wife of a big star with a bigger head.

When another magazine asked her how she felt about other women fancying her husband, she put on her public face and replied: "If other women didn't fancy him, I probably wouldn't myself."

I was extortionately proud of this quip, telling all my friends about it, even keeping the clipping for some time. From my distant view now I realise that, despite this show of public indifference, she was hurting badly underneath. But she was a tough lady. She had, after all, served in the Wrens and had worked with sailors for some years. She knew what men got up to when they were out and about on their own. But that, of course, was men in general, not her particular man, the father of her children. I was too insensitive, or perhaps too selfish, perhaps even both, to recognise this crucial difference. But the time was coming when I was about to push that insensitivity too far, to the very brink of disaster.

—oOo—

As Richard Stone had so wisely prophesied, a prolonged absence from television was beginning to eat into my public popularity. The 1960s ushered in a flood of new stars, pop musicians, actors, and comedians. Independent television was well established, breaking the stranglehold monopoly of the BBC, and throughout the land failing theatres had been converted in bingo halls or supermarkets. Television had fundamentally changed the British way of life and I was out in the cold. Slowly but remorselessly, my variety bookings began to dry up. I was still busy in rep, which is what I enjoyed, but £50 a week covered only half the household bills down in Hampshire. The answer was to go abroad.

In those days, it took a couple of years for television shows to filter down to Australia (now, *Heartbeat* runs a matter of a few weeks behind). I was still a name Down Under, so off I went to sunny Oz with the promise of a few TV appearances and some cabaret club dates. The tour was supposed to last for three weeks but I actually stayed for five months. One of the reasons was that I fell in love with the Australians, an open, tough, cheerful people with a sense of humour that greatly appealed to me (and, fortunately, mine seemed to appeal to them). Here I met and became friendly with an American entertainer, Paul Desmond, who was to be an important piece in the jigsaw of my later life. Here, too, is where I almost dragged my sheet anchor of a marriage because I fell for yet another woman.

I was appearing at a night club called The Embers in Melbourne where, unlike poor Paul Desmond who had preceded me, I was drawing big crowds. I was also making regular TV appearances on a show called *In Melbourne Tonight,* just chatting and telling a few of my self-deprecating gags, so I had become something of a local celebrity. Then I walked into the star dressing room one evening and standing before my mirror was a stunning red head in a fur coat. Now it is not done to invade the star's dressing room without an invitation so I put on the best BBC accent I could muster and said: "Good evening, madam. Could I help you in any way?"

She turned to reveal a Rita Hayworth face and figure and said in slurred Oz: "An' 'oo the feckin' 'ell are yew, darlin'?"

I shall not name this lady. Suffice it to say she was a jazz singer, a drinker with a formidable capacity, and had a temperament as fiery as her red hair. Her language was foul, her manners were worse, yet on stage she was simply electrifying. This was the sort of character that the Australians loved. And I fell for her too, hook line and sinker. After years of casual or semi-casual affairs, when I had kept some sort of control over my emotions if not over my body, I launched into a wild affair.

It was like a great incandescent flash. I knew it could not last because the two of us were so intense that we would have burned ourselves to ashes. Whilst it did last, however, I wanted to keep it going so I pulled every string I could to get more work in Australia, even presenting *You Too Can Have a Body* on television with a cast of part-time actors who, during the day, were car mechanics and truck drivers. This being Australia, it got rave reviews.

I was so besotted that, for a while, I thought of divorce. Back home, Muriel was getting more and more suspicious as I made excuse after excuse to extend the tour. I even planned little speeches, offering Muriel the divorce she so richly deserved. In these, I did at least have the courage to take the blame. Then, inevitably, this great flame of an affair burned itself out; we had used up all the fuel we had and the fire simply went out. She did me one great favour, that wild Australian redhead. After her, I knew that there could be no more other women. I had finally realised at last that Muriel was the only woman I could spend the rest of my life with. Perhaps I had finally grown up. I packed with eager anticipation, looking forward once again to home, wife and children. Unfortunately, my redhead was to do me one disservice, too. I arrived home to an unexpectedly hostile reception which was explained when Muriel handed me a huge joke card. "From a friend of yours, I believe," she said icily. Inside, my jazz singing maniac had written in explicit detail just what parts of me she was missing.

This, I thought, was the end. I began one of my carefully rehearsed speeches. Muriel cut me off with the only swear word she ever used: "Bollocks!"

I could barely believe that she was prepared to forgive and forget yet again. I told her that I was prepared to do anything to make it up to her. She replied with an icy stare: "In that case, just stop doing *it*."

And I did.

Chapter Fourteen

The Axe Falls

THE lull before the storm is a time which fascinates sailors, farmers and many people who enjoy the outdoors, a period of intense calm when everything seems brighter, more peaceful. I was allowed this wonderful time for a couple of years in the 1960s although, unlike sailors and countrymen, I didn't have the nouse to know that the storm was coming. This is the time when I became an act-oor, as the word was pronounced by old time leading men trained to throw the voice so that every syllable could be heard by the poor people up in 'the gods'.

Until now, due to persistence, good fortune and, I hope, a certain amount of talent, my career had risen in a steady upwards graph with a few startling peaks thrown in for good measure. I thoroughly expected that those peaks would continue ever upwards until I achieved my final target: movie star. To do this, I was prepared to take a few years out to learn the acting craft. I did not know that this time out would run to the best part of a decade and that by indulging myself, I was to precipitate a crisis which would nearly destroy my family. This, of course, is written with hindsight. Those balmy days in rep was one of the most fulfilling and exciting periods of my life. I was thoroughly enjoying myself and, in my arrogance, believed that Providence would look after me and mine.

For a few years, when my name was still fresh in the public mind, I had some good roles in touring companies which, because I was a name player, were able to raise £150 or £200 a week, still very good pay indeed for the times. I appeared, at first, mainly in light comedies like *The Chiltern Hundreds*, playing Lord Lister, a role made famous in the cinema by A.E. Matthews, but

I had a longing for 'real acting' — the great classics. In the meantime, our household bills were running at £100 a week and the children were away at expensive schools. Our savings began to decline but, despite Muriel's growing fears, I refused to pay heed — after all, I could always do a couple of highly paid variety and cabaret tours and refill the coffers. It took me several long years to realise that the name Bill Maynard was no longer on the public lips.

As my popularity dwindled, so did the bookings and so did the earnings. But I was still enjoying myself because, eventually, I had found a permanent billet at the old Nottingham Playhouse, performing the entire range of acting roles from the classics down to panto with John Neville, one of the truly inspirational actors, directors and theatre managers of the last half of the 20th century. Under his guidance, the Nottingham Playhouse created something of a new phenomenon, a major centre of theatrical excellence outside London. First nights in Nottingham were regularly attended by the leading London critics and we drew our audiences from all over the Midlands and the North.

Despite these great successes, the Playhouse was still a repertory company and, as such, conditions in it were strictly controlled by Equity, the actors' trade union, and this set my maximum pay: £50 a week. Charles Dickens' immortal Mr Micawber had laid down the ground rules a century earlier: "Annual income £20, annual expenditure £19s 6d, result happiness. Annual income £20, annual expenditure £20 0s 6d, result misery." I was never much of a fan of the Micawber view of life but his vision of misery would have been pure joy to me. Sixpence may well have been a lot of money in Victorian times, and I realise that the quotation was only used metaphorically, but it still represented a quarter of one per cent of the equation. Here was me earning less than *half* of our weekly housekeeping bills, never mind school fees and the rest, and I still had my own digs in Nottingham to pay. And, damn it, I was still enjoying myself!

The axe fell in 1962 when the Inland Revenue presented me with an enormous tax bill for my earnings during the years since I had left the Richard Stone organisation and, more crucially, its showbusiness tax experts who had so carefully kept my affairs in order. What's more, they wanted the money six months previously, for in my total contempt for all things worldly, I had never bothered to keep accounts of my huge earnings, nor of the expenditure I could have legitimately charged against them. The Family Maynard had finally hit the brick wall I had been driving towards at full speed.

I drove down to Hampshire like a whipped dog, fully expecting — and fully deserving — another sound thrashing from Muriel. There, in our nice new house in Fleet, with the garden finally laid out and the squirrels running up and down in the trees, we sat down and finally faced the calamity of our situation. Muriel was, of course, furious but, to my surprise, not bitter. On the return from my final wild fling in Australia, we had patched up our differences over other women. I had stuck to my word in that regard, but here was a far graver crisis. Or so I thought. Now, perhaps for the first time in our married life, I began to appreciate just how much steel had gone into that woman's erect backbone.

First to go were the cars, my beloved American Studebaker, the swish Austin Healey 100 sports car, which would be worth a small fortunate as a collector's item today. Even Muriel's Standard 10 had to go, which made shopping and other little errands a nightmare in a rural area. The cars were followed by the furs and jewellery which I had bought Muriel in the good days. I suspect she did not regret this half as much as me, because I had bought many of these expensive trinkets out of a sense of guilt created by my extra-marital activities, a sort of consolation prize for the faithful wife back at home, and I think she suspected this too. They went with virtually no regrets, almost with a sense of 'Good Riddance', for they represented a lifestyle which Muriel had never much appreciated, a lifestyle that, patently, was now gone for good. Much worse was to follow.

Then came the people to the house looking over our furniture, the antiques and the glassware and the silver that Muriel had collected with an expert eye. I was away working while much of this was going on, although I did haul some of the better pieces around the local antiques dealers, and Muriel had to put up with these intrusions on her own, take the sidelong glances from these people who were picking over the corpse of her home. Human nature being what it is, the rich and the famous are always subject to a great deal of envy. When you fall from that lofty perch there are many people who cannot resist the temptation to gloat. There was more humiliation to come, The house would have to go, too — Muriel's first-ever home of her own, the house she had chosen and cherished, the house she had decorated and furnished with years of loving care. The loss of the garden, where she had spent thousands of long hours alone while her errant husband was living the fast life in all corners of the globe, must have been almost too much to bear. But bear it she did, like a Trojan, for already she was planning a new life.

Fortunately, the children were still away at school and their fees had been paid in advance until the end of the year. They, at least, were reasonably cocooned from the initial shock, shielded from the sight of their home being scavenged by strangers. But when everything was gone, and the Maynards owned little more than the clothes we stood up in, the debt still stood at £17,000, almost six years' pay at Nottingham Playhouse rates and even that was not to last too long. Again comparisons are invidious, but £17,000 would be worth something like £250,000 at today's prices. For a couple who are virtually penniless, that is a massive sum of money.

I had taken what free advice I could from friends and their solution was quite simple: "Go bankrupt. That way, you can walk away from your debts — the Inland Revenue can afford it and you've paid them enough in the past." This was in fact very true, at least while I had been with Richard Stone and his careful accountants, and I felt a certain attraction to the idea. That was a mistake, for despite all the pain of those dreadful months, this was the first time that Muriel came close to cracking. She turned on me like a tigress.

"I will not be married to a bankrupt, Bill," she glared, her eyes glazed over with tears. "We will pay off this debt if it is the last thing we ever do. I can take just so much humiliation — but I will not be married to a bankrupt."

And that was that. Any accountant will tell you that it was in fact the wrong decision. Today, people go bankrupt at the drop of a hat, starting up in business again the following day. But darling Muriel was made of sterner stuff. She came from a humble but respectable home. She was prepared, however reluctantly, to put up with the antics of a drinker, a gambler and a womaniser in the interest of keeping her family together. But under no circumstances was she prepared to live with a *bankrupt*. The easy option was out, thanks to her pride. Thoroughly abashed by this show of steely determination from a woman whose incredible strengths I was only just beginning to understand, I set off to follow her along the road to financial probity.

It was to be a very long, very hard road...

—oOo—

The Inland Revenue, having received something like three-quarters of their demand, agreed to allow me to work off the rest on an instalment basis. I think that this was more down to prudence than compassion because a man who is driven too far may simply give up the ghost and stop work. Going on the dole would never repay HM Inspector of Taxes, nor would it support my family, and I still had work to do. But we were homeless, virtually penniless, and a long way from my place of work in Nottingham. What to do?

All our worldly possessions packed into just four tea chests: a few books, mainly joke books which were legally defined as 'the tools of my trade', our cooking utensils, and our clothes. These we dragged back to Leicester. Here, at least, we had family connections and we were close enough to Nottingham for me to make my tedious way by public transport to the Playhouse and we moved in temporarily with Muriel's Auntie Elsie. I was back in an East Midlands council house after leaving a similar establishment in Rat Alley all those years before — although, I hasten to add, Aunt Elsie kept it spotlessly clean and comfortable and there was no council tip across the road. This meant there were no rats, but we weren't even the tenants. To be lodging in a council house while your children are away at expensive private schools has its ironies, no doubt, but it is a distinctly uncomfortable situation. For Martin and Jane were still unaware of the disaster which had befallen their parents.

To keep them in ignorance had been a decision taken, not from cowardice, but because of Muriel's insistence that their young and totally innocent lives should suffer as little disruption as humanly possible. This was a bit like continuing to serve them tea during an earthquake, the house falling around their ears while the polite chatter continues, but it was something Muriel was determined to achieve. What mattered most, although plans for a full public school education were now out of the question, was that they should still have a home of their own. For Muriel, that meant buying a new house, not renting one. For me, this seemed an almost impossible ambition.

With my agreement to pay the Inland Revenue by instalments now in place, I was able to put a little money aside by launching into a frenzy of work. I could still get to the theatre in Nottingham by bus and I was still able to get a few late night bookings on the night-club circuit. This would sometimes mean working 18 hour days, rehearsing a play in the morning, doing a mat-inee in the afternoon, a second performance at night, and then going off to do a cabaret turn until 2am. This was as bad as the old days in Soho, except that the money was nowhere as good because my financial problems were well known in the business and club owners who may once have paid me hundreds would now offer £20 or £30. With the deadline of the children's return from school looming, I took what I could and still got humiliated into the bargain (sometimes I would get paid at the bar after the show, the owner doling out a few fivers in front of the late night drunks who knew only too well that, a few years before, I could earn in a week what they got in a year).

Muriel was contributing, too, having gone back to work as a secretary and a receptionist, working long hours for something like £8 a week, less than I had once spent on a single bottle of champagne. To get there, she had to queue for buses in the pouring rain which, for a lady who had recently had three cars at her disposal, must have given her much time to reflect on our changed circumstances. But never once did she complain; she had her little plan.

Little by little we scraped together some £300, of which we were inordinately proud and protective, and slowly some real perspective was beginning to shape in my blinkered head. It took weeks and months to scrape together this tiny sum, with both of us working to the point of exhaustion, yet I had comparatively recently wagered sums like that on a single horse or greyhound — and had not been overly put out if it lost. Now, as our little nest grew, I was seeing financial sense for the first time in my adult life. The goal we were seeking, a home for our children, was the archetypal dream shared by almost every young couple in the civilised world, a normal, decent, praise-worthy ambition for which they suffer, scrimp and save at a time in their young lives when they could be out enjoying themselves. I had been given that dream a hundredfold — and had thrown it all away.

For £300 was still not enough. When we could, we spent the time house hunting but everything we saw was either too expensive or in an awful state of disrepair. We could neither afford the cash for professional craftsmen nor the time to do the work ourselves. And the days were ticking away at Auntie Elsie's council house, the time when the children would make their dreaded return from a world of privilege which, we assumed, they would never see again.

Then came the only stroke of luck in this sorry mess I had created. Muriel had a cousin who, with her husband, had decided to put their little semi-detached house in Sapcote, Leicestershire, on the market — they, lucky things, were moving to something bigger and better. It was a very ordinary house indeed, small lounge and dining kitchen downstairs, two bedrooms, a box room, and a bathroom above.

It was an ordinary house in an ordinary red-brick village, with a small council estate across the road. The village was, however, set in rolling open countryside and, best of all, the little house had gardens, a small plot at the front, a much bigger one behind. Muriel set her heart on it straight away. At first, her cousin laughed. She did not understand the depth of our money troubles and she assumed we were joking: "You don't want a tiny little place like this, not with all the money you've got!" If only they knew — even this was stretching us to the very limit and perhaps a bit beyond. It took days of cajoling before they understood we were serious, and days more of negotiation with surveyors, lawyers and the building society; we were to get that symbol of middle class life, a mortgage! Even the building society had seemed bewildered, but thankfully my earnings at the Playhouse were regular and Muriel had her job, too. So they gave us the loan.

Like any young working class couple with aspirations, we moved into our little semi for the princely sum of £2,600. Our precious £300 just covered the deposit and the solicitor's fees. The mortgage did the rest. Trouble was, we didn't have a stick of furniture, only our tea chests. And the kids were coming home. On the day we moved in, praising the generosity of her cousin who had thrown in the fitted carpet in the lounge free, Muriel and I embraced in our empty little house and both of us shed a tear.

She looked up at me, smiled, and then the steel came back on display: "I don't care what happens from now on, Bill, but I'm never never going to leave this house. You can make your way back to the top, and I have faith that you will, but however much money you earn and however famous you get, I am not going to go through these last few months again. We're here, now, and here I intend to stay!"

She was prophetically right on all counts. This was only her second home but it was the last home she would ever have. Here, together, we began to build our real life. The past might never have happened. The future had begun. It was to bring more tragedy but also endless pleasure and pride. Now, when the urge takes me, I can go to visit the French manor house which I helped my son Martin to buy, the house where the late President Mitterand spent much of his youth. I can go, too, to daughter Jane's luxuriously converted farmhouse in Leicestershire. Or, when up in Yorkshire filming *Heartbeat*, I can stay with any of the dozens of friends I have made in what they call the County of Broad Acres.

But most weekends, I return to my semi in Sapcote. I spend my time there alone with the memories of Muriel all around me. I have not changed the decorations she chose. Apart from a few antiques I have collected, I still use the furniture she chose. And, in the gardens front and back, I am still among the flowers, shrubs and trees she selected with such care and which she planted and nurtured with her own hands. The sheet anchor was back in place and it still holds firm to this day. Every day in the tabloid press you read stories of famous people who cannot handle success. Whether they are film stars, pop musicians or sportsmen, they get into fights, into the divorce courts, into rehabilitation clinics for drink or drug abuse. Let me say from bitter personal experience that handling success is easy — when compared to handling failure. I learned how to do that with the help of a wonderful wife, two children who understood when many would have rebelled, and a semi in Sapcote. They are the real things life: all the rest is glitter. Fool's Gold.

Chapter Fifteen

Long, Lean Years

AND so the children came home. By this time, Martin was 13 and Jane ten and, apart from breaking the bad news to Muriel a few months before, this was the most difficult moment of my life so far. Our plans for them had been full of hope, their futures seemingly secure, and for the majority of their young lives they had lived in considerable luxury. They had been given all the things that I had never had back in Rat Alley and of that I had been very proud. Now, if anything, they were worse off than I had ever been. Although my childhood had seen much deprivation, it had always been reasonably secure as my own father clawed his way slowly but steadily up the ladder to prosperity. Now my own youngsters were facing not merely insecurity but total turmoil.

As the man of the house, as the 'provider' to use another much-flaunted phrase, I had failed. What's more, I had done so in public, which to most children should have been totally unforgivable. They would now have to face the flak at the council schools they were bound to attend, putting up with the playground humiliation which I was beginning to take in the clubs. I was at least an adult (or at least, I was growing into one belatedly but very, very quickly) and children can be particularly cruel among their peers. So I awaited their return with growing dread.

I need not have worried. They were even more supportive than I had ever thought possible. Martin looked around our little bare semi, shook his head, and said: "It's not too bad at all, Dad. Just one thing: where do we sleep?" This, of course, was a problem. We did not have a stick of furniture, not even a settee never mind beds. The upper rooms did not even have carpets. And the house was as cold as it was bare, for even had we had the luxury of electric fires, which we didn't, we could not afford to run up large heating bills: we had a mortgage and the Inland Revenue to pay off. The solution was simple in that it was the only one we could think of: we slept on the lounge carpet in the few blankets we had managed to salvage, Muriel and I in the alcove on one side of the fireplace, Martin and Jane in the other alcove. At least that way we could benefit from the heat of the coal fire.

Now this, I must admit, was a highly unusual arrangement for two children who, despite their young years, were already somewhat sophisticated, thanks to the few years of private education we had managed to provide. Martin, for instance, could already drive a car, having been taught in the school grounds and given an exact replica of the legal driving test years before he was old enough to apply for a provisional driving licence. Now, he was camping out with his sister and parents in the family home. I suppose for a time this was something of an adventure but both Muriel and I expected a backlash, the sort of tantrums or sulking to which many children are prone. It never came. Instead, the children threw themselves into the task of rebuilding the Maynard family fortunes with gusto and great good humour. It was almost as though they were were enjoying themselves.

Both of them took any spare-time jobs they could fit in with school hours. Martin delivered potatoes, hulking huge sacks from the back of an ancient lorry and carrying them to people's back doors. Jane took a paper round, although she was several years too young to do so legally. Muriel, as well as her daytime office jobs, took on any evening work that came her way: typing, dressmaking, even delivering leaflets, out on foot in all weathers, winter and summer alike. It was straight back to the days in Rat Alley, with every member of the family doing his or her bit to make ends meet. We had become a family of stationary gypsies. And, like the gypsies, we finally became a tight-knit unit facing the outside world back to back.

The theme of families uniting and finding true happiness in the face of adversity is by no means new; it has been used for centuries in literature and the theatre. I will not, pretend, however, that those early days in Sapcote were a series of cartwheels of joy. They were, in fact, very tough indeed, for when and if there was any spare money, the Inland Revenue had first call and the mortgage came second. Normal household requirements like beds, and eventually a few chairs to sit on, were third and it took many, many months before we could stop camping out in our alcoves.

It would have been an unusual way of life for any family, but for one which had known such wealth so recently, it was positively extraordinary. Yet it worked. In those difficult years, we became not just inter-dependent but also good friends. When I look back at the good times in my life, it is not to the champagne days that I turn, but to this long hard struggle in Sapcote. Unbelievable though it may sound, Muriel and I launched upon, if not exactly a second honeymoon, most certainly a second marriage. We just happened to be married to the same partners — the same but, in my case at least, very new.

For a start, we were together for longer periods than we had known for years. I had stuck by my word to give up philandering even before the axe fell. We had so little money in our pockets that a rare night out consisted of a trip, on foot, to the village working men's club — yet another full turn of the wheel. And even here, I had to become a professional sportsman in an effort to buy myself a glass of beer. In my part of Leicestershire there is a centuries-old pub game known as cheese skittles. The aim is to flatten as many skittles as possible using not a ball but a flat wooden 'cheese' rather like an ice hockey puck. I had played it since I was a boy. Now I turned pro and, when I was not working, practised for hours alone. I would challenge all-comers at sixpence a game. This was not a lot but beer was still less than two shillings a pint. Here was a man who had once put £200 on a greyhound, training for hours to win a tanner at cheese skittles. It meant, however, that Muriel and I usually drank free. He had taken some hard knocks, the Bill Maynard of those days, but the Rat Alley hustler in him was still alive and well.

While Muriel and I were falling back in love again — a deep, mutually supportive love that was to last the rest of our lifetime together — we were also making steadfast friends among the straight-forward, down-to-earth folk in the little villages of Leicestershire where we had spent our childhoods. It was not easy at first because in my arrogant days in the big-time I had trampled on many a toe. I remember one working chap, who I had known for years, treating me with considerable coolness when we started going back to the local pub. He watched us for weeks but never made any attempt to make conversation. Then, one evening, I asked him why he was being so distant. He smiled grudgingly and said, "If y' wants the truth, Bill, y'wus a big-headed bastard in the days when y'was famous. Y'got my back right up." I accepted the rebuke, then asked: "And now?" He shook his head and laughed: "You're not too bad, now I suppose. But we'll have to see 'ow you turn out."

There were many little incidents like this, all of which helped accelerate the progress of Bill Maynard, erstwhile star, into the ultimate accolade of my part of the world, 'a decent bloke'. I feel I must have turned out fairly well, even though I am once again back at the top. When I'm home in Sapcote, the locals treat me exactly as one of them. They take the mickey out of me all the time, when I'm standing in a queue at the newspaper shop, in the street or at the pub. And I chide them back and no one would dream of taking offence. Those early, anxious days in Sapcote gave me back a loving wife, two great children, and friendships that have lasted the test of time. Such prizes are worth the price of a lot of hardship.

—oOo—

During this long period of readjustment and entrenchment in Sapcote, the Nottingham Playhouse had been the pivot of my working life but not the be-all and end-all. I took summer tours when I could, and night club dates whenever they were offered, anything to bring in some extra cash. In the main, however, the Playhouse was the major source of my income and an important training ground for my theatrical skills. At Nottingham, I worked with two men who were to leave indelible marks on my career, the director Frank Dunlop, and, as I have already mentioned, the actor-director John Neville, who had an impeccable background in Shakespeare and other classical roles.

By chance, Frank had been brought up in Wigston, but about as far from Rat Alley as it is possible to get in the village, and had also attended Kibworth Grammar School. People will no doubt feel that here was a case of the old school tie at work because it was Frank who first persuaded me to go to Nottingham. I like to think the opposite, because of all his theatrical skills, his greatest was *daring*: he had a great knack for unusual casting which often, pre-opening, had the critics agog with pained complaints that often verged on ridicule. Just as often, after opening night, he had the same critics eating their own words (a meal which, I can assure the reader, they find indigestible in the extreme).

It was Frank who cast me, much to the puzzlement of the critics, in *The Taming of the Shrew*, the wonderful Shakespearean knock-about comedy which, with its vitriolic dissection of the war between the sexes, and in particular of the antics of dominant women, had a certain controversial piquancy at a time when the Womens' Lib movement was getting under way. As a former stand-up comic turned act-oor, it was a play I loved but I was also somewhat in awe of the other members of the cast: John Neville, fresh from Shakespearian triumphs at the Old Vic, then the London home of Shakespeare, as Petruchio; and Joan Heal, one of the finest actresses of the age, as the turbulent Kate. Other parts were taken by two future television stars, Anne Stallybrass, of *The Onedin Line*, and Ronald Magill, who was to create the cantankerous Amos Brearly in *Emmerdale Farm*.

This was formidable company in which to flex your theatrical wings and, turning up as I did in an ancient tracksuit, I expected to be treated with coolness, if not downright contempt, by these long-standing pros. I could not have been more wrong. The Playhouse was then a small, intimate theatre in a converted cinema, where space was in critically short supply. Dressing-room space was so scarce that I had to share one with two other actors, including the 'star' John Neville, and it was so small that if one of us had to change, the other two had to wait outside. Perhaps they expected someone like me, who had been accustomed to star dressing rooms in famous London theatres, would complain but the thought never crossed my mind. I was enchanted to be in such a company and they figuratively clasped me to the communal bosom like a long lost friend. Here was real theatre, just as I had expected it to be, bursting with talent, determined to be not just good but brilliant, and swept along on a wave of good humoured banter.

It was glorious, too, to be stationary in the same city for long runs, for Nottingham is not unlike its East Midlands sister Leicester so I felt 'at home' both at work and, after the enforced move back to Sapcote, when I actually was at home too. Astonishingly, I soon created a superb working relationship with John Neville, one of the outstanding classical actors of the day. To outsiders, we must have seemed like chalk and cheese. In fact, despite our widely divergent backgrounds, we had many interests in common and one of those was stand-up comedy. As I wrote earlier, we even created a stand-up comedy act for John, with me rehearsing him and even getting him a booking at the Parkside Club in Nottingham. Sadly, he bottled-out, a decision he says he still regrets to this day.

This relationship was encouraged by Frank Dunlop, who liked the way John and I sparked off against each other. As he was always ready to exploit the unusual, knowing full-well that the educated Playhouse audience would be aware of our different backgrounds, he let us have our heads knowing that the *double entendre* would not be lost. This led to the almost revolutionary incident of a stand-up comic improving the immortal words of The Bard.

In *The Taming of the Shrew*, Petruchio and Grumio are master and servant but also, we decided, good friends, a relationship which Shakespeare himself does not make overly clear. In most performances, they are played in the straight master/servant mode and this subtlety does not come through. After studying and playing the roles together for several performances, John and I came to a simple conclusion: Petruchio and Grumio are in fact intended to be a double act and we decided to play it that way.

The two have one scene when they are trying to gain entrance to a house. Petruchio orders Grumio to 'knock' and the servant asks whom should he knock. "Knock the door or I'll knock your pate," says the Master. This is supposed to be funny, and perhaps it was in Tudor times when it was written, but in our opinion the line came over more as a threat than a jest and therefore failed to communicate the true feelings of friendship between the two characters. We overcame this difficulty by the use of a piece of pure comic 'business' borrowed from Laurel and Hardy.

Instead of going on stage together, John would enter first and then call for me. Instead of entering, I would throw on stage a bundle of clothing perhaps five feet in diameter. Then went another bundle, then a third. All this time, John would stare at the audience and give them a quizzical shrug. Then I would make my entry by falling down a flight of stairs. This established that we were a comedy couple, to be enjoyed and laughed at, and the audience loved it. In another bit of comic business, I would further embarrass John by carrying a feather duster on stage and brush him down whenever he made a speech which met with my approval.

Audiences had not seen much Shakespeare like this and absolutely adored the slapstick touch.

It was not all laughter at the Nottingham Playhouse, however. As one would expect, I enjoyed the comedy but my *raison d'etre* at the time was to learn to craft of serious acting. As I became better established and my range widened, I was to tackle much more challenging roles, like Inspector Truscott in Joe Orton's savage attack on police corruption, *Loot*. I became Frank Harris, the lascivious one-time editor of the *Daily Mail*, to John Neville's George Bernard Shaw in *The Bashful Genius*. Other favourite roles included Davies in Harold Pinter's, *The Caretaker,* and Elwood P. Dowd in *Harvey*, all challenging parts which gave me great satisfaction. Of the modern 'kitchen sink' drama which was sweeping the country, I remember with particular clarity playing Archie Rice, John Osborne's doomed music hall comic in *The Entertainer,* a role so sought after that Sir Laurence Olivier did the film version. For me, this was a subject so close to my heart that every performance left me totally drained: a case, perhaps, of life imitating art.

These were wonderful roles played out in a great company. With my life finding some sort of stability in Sapcote, these years at Nottingham Playhouse were some of the best of my life. But, as ever, times were beginning to change. Progress was afoot but not for Bill Maynard.

The Nottingham Playhouse had, under Frank Dunlop and later John Neville, become a national institution, the shining light of provincial theatre. But, as I have pointed out, it had a very small, cramped auditorium in a former cinema. With success came the demand for a better building and so the brand new Nottingham Playhouse was built at the cost of several million pounds. It was a stunning building, with every piece of theatrical gadgetry that a director could desire. We even had sturdy doors to our dressing rooms, instead of curtains at the old place, and behind those doors the rot began to set in.

When things are going well, a repertory company is a wonderful place to work, full of enthusiasm and talent and laughter. When things begin to go wrong, the first victim is morale among the players and unhappy players tend to put on unhappy plays. Sensing that things were changing, and not for the better, I took a break from the company and went off to Canterbury to do a comedy which is now considered something of a modern classic of the genre, *Semi-Detached* by David Turner. In the meantime, the great move took place up in Nottingham and the tiny Playhouse company was swelled by a horde of newcomers. *Semi-Detached* was doing enormous business and Frank asked me if I was prepared to return to Nottingham and play it for two weeks, to be followed by a demanding role in a newly-translated Spanish classic, *The Mayor of Zalamea* by Calderon de la Barca, the playwright known as the Spanish Shakespeare. The comedy was a smash hit, playing to full houses for its entire run, and I was asked to become a permanent member of the company once more. This did not go down too well among the new arrivals, who complained that 'certain people' — ie, me! — were introducing the wrong sort of drama to the theatre, which should, they said, be concentrating on heavier fare. Eventually, this led to a packed meeting where the newcomers put their complaints. I was not impressed.

"The best thing that could happen here," I said angrily, "would be to take away all those dressing room doors and go back to curtains. For once you get three or four actors behind closed doors, the belly-aching starts."

I won my point, temporarily at least, but the moaning went on. Frank Dunlop became more and more depressed and I was worried that the stress might make him ill. "If you're that unhappy, Frank," I advised, "you should get out." To my surprise, he sat down and wrote out his resignation there and then. This left me a little stunned — I had not expected instant action — but when my contract ran out I, too, quit. Months later, I met Frank again in London and said I was sorry if I had forced him into a hasty decision. He smiled and we toured the West End where, at theatre after theatre, he pointed up to the bright lights of shows he had produced. He had no less than five running simultaneously.

"Don't ever apologise again," he said. "You did me one of the greatest favours of my life."

Once again, it was the end of an era. I still value those Nottingham days, and still maintain many of the friendships that I made there. But, much later, I was to discover that, from a career point of view, they were wasted years. This sounds a very harsh thing to say, but I had gone into rep and put everything I had at risk by labouring under a delusion. That was the belief that to be a screen actor, whether on film or on television, one has to be a trained on the stage. This, I know now, is complete rubbish.

True, an old fashioned theatrical training gives one certain skills. It teaches self-discipline, to learn the lines and turn up on time night after night, even when the theatre is half empty and those who are there in the audience are half asleep. To rekindle a good performance night after night, when even the cast are getting bored, demands real dedication and determination to fight the odds. To do so in rep, while rehearsing next week's play in the mornings, presenting several matinees and six evening productions a week, demands sheer physical staying power. All these are wonderful attributes. For the stage actor.

For film or television, they are largely wasted assets. A classic drama school exercise is to get the same young actor to play a part in which his or her character ages from being a teenager to an octogenarian. Now, if television wants an octogenarian — or at least, a very old actor — the casting department just picks up the phone and orders one; there are plenty about only too delighted to be working (If they want an elderly, cantankerous, hard-drinking curmudgeon, they usually ring me!).

In the same way, much of the time spent at drama school in teaching people to imitate various regional accents is wasted time: if a director wants an actor with, say, a Geordie accent, he just picks up the phone and casts someone of that ilk. All that time spent learning how to learn lines is wasted, too. In film or TV, a take generally lasts a couple of minutes, if not seconds, and almost anyone you picked up off the street could learn one line in a few minutes. The same goes for gestures and facial expressions, which must be dramatic on stage so that the people in 'the gods' register them. Before the cameras, the skill is just the opposite: the smaller the gesture, the more subtle the expression, the more effective it is on screen.

It is no surprise to me that many of the long-lasting favourites on British television, like *Coronation Street* stars Betty Driver, Bill Waddington, and Liz Dawn, come from a music hall or cabaret background. They do not use the camera as the Fourth Wall, that phrase used by many stage actors for their audiences, but interact with it, as they are forced to do with smaller, more intimate gatherings. As they say, to act in television you only have to learn the lines and not fall over the furniture (or, in my case, the other actors!).

As ever, at Nottingham Playhouse, I had learned a lesson, or rather a non-lesson, the hard way. But I would not have missed the experience for the world!

Chapter Sixteen

Rock Bottom

EFORE, during and after my years at Nottingham, I had always taken time off to do any touring shows that came my way, or summer shows in seaside resorts when the repertory season, by tradition, closed down for the holiday months. In the beginning, when I still had a big name in the public mind, I topped the bill at the major resorts. But as I hurtled down the slippery slope, I found myself in contact for the first time with the nether world of the theatre, the small, badly financed companies with casts of has-beens or bright young things with high hopes but precious little experience. Worst of all, I began to meet the amateurs or the downright charlatans of theatre management, whose idea was to put on a show with a shoe-string budget, pay themselves whatever slender profits there were, and to hell with the rest — even if it meant the cast's wages going unpaid.

In my heyday, I wouldn't have touched such companies with a ten-foot pole. Now, desperate for income, I had no such choice. I took whatever was offered and that led to years of summer misery. For the holiday makers who paid to see such shows, they were supposed to be one of the highlights of the year. For the miserable, underpaid and sometimes unpaid entertainers trying so hard to live up to the trippers' expectations, those summer months often passed in a blur of gloom and guilt. Our appointed task was to help these people enjoy their precious holidays. As often as not, despite our game efforts, we were failing. Josef Stalin probably had happier workers in his salt mines.

There was one such show at Seaton in Devon which, on first examination, seemed a better prospect than most. The pay and conditions seemed good and the company principles seemed bright and enthusiastic. First the wage packets stopped coming. Then the principles disappeared, owing me hundreds of pounds. For me this was a major setback but for the girls in the chorus line it was a disaster. They did not even have enough money to pay their rail fares home. We negotiated with the theatre management and arranged to hire the place for an extra week and the rest of us worked for free. After paying the rent and other incidentals, that week's work raised just enough profit to send the girls home. But I went home penniless which, in our situation was a pitiful waste of the season. As it turned out, those tour principles were complete charlatans and were eventually 'blacked' by Equity so, hopefully (but by no means necessarily) we were the last company to suffer at their hands. That thought gives me a little consolation now but, of course, I never got my money.

Times were hard and were to get harder. Once I joined a small, experimental theatre company to do a strange little play on the fringe at the famous Edinburgh Festival. Here, there was no management to collect the money. We did this and all the other duties ourselves, running the box office, supplying our own props, even sweeping the floor of our so-called theatre, a small community centre which had a makeshift stage and, thankfully, a kitchen. We did not merely act in this place. We lived there, too, because we could not afford digs. We huddled on stacker chairs in sleeping bags and cooked what we could afford in the kitchen. Our only source of income was what was left from our ticket sales after we had paid the rent and I remember that this was once just £4 for the entire company of half a dozen players. Here I benefited from a remarkable act of charity from my son Martin. He knew things were tight but I doubt if he ever realised just how tight. One day, he sent me a pound from the money he had earned from his potato round assuming, no doubt, that I would go out and have a couple of pints. Our problem, however, was not drink but food; we were actually on the verge of malnutrition. With that precious pound, I bought some scraps of beef, some vegetables, and we cooked a hearty stew that gave us all the one filling meal of the entire festival. As I enjoyed this repast, I found myself reflecting that on a previous visit to Scotland, a few miles away in Glasgow, I had once been a guest of honour at the grand Masonic ball. At least, during that hungry Edinburgh Festival, I did not end up in jail!

Then there were tatty touring companies, which just about managed to pay the cast but had precious little left over for such vital extras as props. Why one of them chose to tour a play called *Plaza Suite* I shall never know because it was supposed to be set in the Plaza Hotel, New York, one of the most famous and expensive hotels in the world. To create an atmosphere which might at least half-persuade the audience that this was a world of privilege and luxury demanded, naturally enough, an opulent set — one can only go so far in asking people to suspend their disbelief. We didn't even have a carpet and that, strangely enough, set me a-thinking about one of an actor's most important attributes: his feet.

To an outsider, it would appear that an actor's most important feature is his face, followed closely by his build: tall, square shouldered and athletic looking for the leading man. For a leading lady, this applies even more: hair, face and figure are expected to be ravishing. If you are blessed with a reasonable bounty of the above, you are on the road to success but by no means there. We all know handsome actors and beautiful actresses who, despite their looks, never make the grade. To the public, that means simply that they cannot act. To the professionals, it means that they cannot *create a character*. This is the key to a successful acting career and many actors have different ways of setting about the task. For me and for many others this means starting with the feet. Get the feet right and the stance follows; when the stance is there, the visual character is established and convincing. So here I was in *Plaza Suite*, asking the audience to believe that I was a rich American staying in a famous hotel, and we didn't have a carpet. Every time I walked on stage, I clattered across the bare boards like a tin-can being kicked down the street. This not the sort of atmosphere were we so desperately trying to create so we talked to the management. No success — the cupboard was bare and there was absolutely no chance of buying a carpet, not even a second-hand one which, at least, would have deadened the noise.

I toyed with the idea of going on-stage bare foot but that was impossible: it would have been visible to people in the circle and although *Plaza Suite* does have many funny lines, this was not the sort of laugh we were seeking. In my penniless state, I had only one pair of shoes with soft rubber soles and they were suede. And in my research for the part, only homosexuals in America wore suede shoes at the time and my character was certainly not of that persuasion. In desperation, I discovered that if I scrunched up my toes inside my shoes, I was forced to walk like a cat, putting each foot into place so lightly that it made not a sound. So that's how I played it for several long weeks, in an agony most of the time and fearful that I might develop at any minute a sudden attack of cramp that would have me rolling on the stage. This, I might add, is not conducive to the convincing portrayal of a rich, successful American businessmen seeking his pleasures in the lap of luxury.

Painful as this was at the time, it now sounds amusing and there are hundreds, perhaps thousands, of similar anecdotes told by actors who had been through the agonies of the tour circuit. But it does, I feel, raise some important points about my state of mind at the time. If not actually down and out, I was approaching rock bottom and, given the treatment which was being doled out to me and my fellow professionals, I might have been excused for saying, "To Hell with it," and clattering on to the stage to raise a cheap laugh. Perhaps, with my background, the audience may have accepted it as a welcome piece of ad-lib clowning. But to have done so would have damaged the dramatic quality of the play and, even in my sorry state, that would have been unforgivable.

Whatever went wrong, however bad things became, I always clung to my sense of professionalism, a desire to give the audience value for the money they had spent at the box office. It was a rigid rule that, eventually, was to stand me in good stead. But sometimes, even when I was really in no position to take stands on points of principle, I continued to do so. This often annoyed my fellow players and, more injuriously from my point of view, theatre managements. Despite my new way of life, there were some things I could not change.

The crunch for my touring career came with what in fact should have been a prime booking. The money, some £65 per week, was ludicrously low but the part was good and the venue better: I was hired to play the great character part of Justice Squeezum in the musical, *Lock Up Your Daughters*, for a summer season in Bournemouth, one of the prime resorts on the summer show circuit. It was also a rare chance to give the family something of a summer holiday for, with the children off school, I arranged for Muriel and them to join me. The money barely paid for our digs but, as usual, the family got stuck in to make it work: Jane got a job in a haberdashery shop, even though she was only 13, and Martin worked in a fish and chip bar so we got free fish and chips every night. A change, they say, is as good as a rest. If only the management of the show had been as supportive and professional as my family.

Lock Up Your Daughters was to bring out the best and the worst in Bill Maynard. It was, as I said, a great part in a very good show and I threw myself into it with enthusiasm. Being a musical, it would, I hoped, add another string to my already well-endowed bow and perhaps halt the decline in my career. But the problems began almost immediately. There is a long tradition in showbusiness of taking on names successful in one field and putting them on to the boards to see if they can become successful in this business, too. The star status of these rookie performers is supposed to put bums on seats and sometimes it works. However, to be fair to both the audience and the professionals on the bill, these people are essentially amateurs and need careful help and guidance. Otherwise, they can destroy an entire production, however good the professionals around them.

Apart from pantomime, summer shows are often the testing ground for such big-name amateurs and in this awful summer in Bournemouth, a major part had been given to a lovely and pleasant young girl, whose claim to fame was that she was a former Miss World. She was a super creature off stage but, unfortunately, there was another fly in this malodorous ointment: a young producer who, although well connected in the business, was also a newcomer. He was also a close friend of our former beauty queen. It was to prove a disastrous mix.

What the poor girl needed on stage was careful direction, detailed explanations of what she was expected to do and why. She did not get it. As I said, off stage she was marvellous. On stage, during rehearsals, she was simply hopeless although she was trying desperately to do her best. Rehearsals dragged on and on and, if anything, her performances got worse. All the pros were muttering and moaning and a mutiny was building. In the end, I was the one who finally lost patience and roared: "Get this amateur off the stage." I apologised to her immediately, explaining that it was not her fault, but the damage had been done. This, of course, did not go down well with the management. A director who had been assigned to add the professional touch took one look and left in a hurry. And the young producer took over. I should have walked out then, but I needed the money and the family were enjoying their working holiday on the South Coast.

I soldiered on for about three weeks but, more and more, I realised that we were giving our audiences poor value for their money, putting a damper on their hard-earned holidays rather than providing an extra spark of magic. The reviews had, of course, been awful but I had long learned to live with that in my touring company days. However, I was about to receive a piece of personal criticism from a most unexpected source, one of the most wounding *critiques* of my career.

One night as I walked wearily from the stage door, I spotted a couple who seemed vaguely familiar. I stopped to chat and they introduced themselves. They were Alton Douglas, a former band leader, and his wife Jo who, unbeknown to me, had been following my career for years. So much so that I had become something of a role model and Alton had given up music to try a career as a comic (God help him). Now this was very flattering because they went on to explain that, every year, they found out where I was performing and would take part of their summer holidays to come to see my show. By this time, I was positively glowing: fans like this are gold dust, shining nuggets in what can often be (and was at this time) a very barren landscape. Then came the knee in the groin.

"I don't like to say this, Bill," said Alton dolefully, "but this show is rubbish. You're letting yourself down even by being in it." I almost went down with the pain of it. Let the critics have their malicious way, by all means, and grin and bare it. But here was a once-adoring couple who had gone to the trouble of arranging their summer holidays to fit in with my schedule, who had travelled thousands of miles over the years to see me perform, and for £65 a week I was letting them down. I went home that night in one of the blackest depressions I have ever known and I lay awake brooding until the cold light of dawn began to grey the curtains. Later that day, I stood myself before before our young producer/acting director and presented my ultimatum: "Either she goes or I do."

Guess who won?

—oOo—

Once again, the Family Maynard hit the road back to Leicester, tails between our legs. We had, by this time, managed to buy a small car but we did not have enough money to buy petrol. Muriel, thanks to her financial prudence, had been judged reliable enough to acquire a Barclaycard but, until that day, we had never dared use it. To our amazement and total relief, the garages accepted it and we got back home …on credit.

It may seem to the reader that I had been justified in walking out on *Lock Up Your Daughters*. It might be that I had done the right thing in standing up for a vital point of principle, even though I still have regrets that a nice young woman had become the pawn in a vicious game of theatre politics. But there was a much more serious side to my actions because I had committed one of the cardinal sins on my trade: I had broken my contract. The theatre, and the provincial theatre in particular, has been a fragile world since actors first began to tread the boards. Putting together a working company for any play is always a tortuous business and when the production in question is big musical like *Lock Up Your Daughters* it is extremely complex. To walk out throws the whole process into jeopardy so, once you have signed on the dotted line, you are expected to endure, however painful the process may be.

To make things worse, my departure had once again attracted a storm of national publicity. A bust-up between a beauty queen and a once-famous comic was absolutely irresistible to the popular press. Once again my name was in the public eye but this time, however, the reasons were all wrong. Adverse *personal* publicity one can withstand (in fact, it can actually be beneficial by putting bums on seats). Adverse *professional* publicity is much more damaging because it is read and squirrelled away by people who matter, people with very long memories indeed. These are the impresarios, the theatre owners, the producers and the directors who, unless you are a major star, have the ultimate control over your destiny. I was no longer a major star and I had already built a reputation for being *difficult*, which is the word that mediocrities often use of people who know better but refuse to compromise.

Now, I had committed the heinous crime of breaking a legally binding contract. The fact that I had done so for the very best professional reason — ie, in the interests of the theatre-going public — was of no account. Once again, I had shot myself in the foot at a time when I needed every hour of work I could find — you can't get much worse, financially, than being unable to afford your petrol money home. I had paid a huge price to go into the theatre, and my family had paid even more, but now that investment had proved worthless except for one valuable lesson: I have never since signed a contract without first meeting the people involved and deciding if I can establish a good working relationship. It was not a great consolation.

Through an explosive mixture of extravagance, arrogance, pigheadedness and professional pride, I had finally hit rock bottom.

Chapter Seventeen

Humiliation

A ND so the bookings in the good theatres and cabaret clubs began to dry
up…

I had, I suppose, been riding for a fall but when it came, it was harder, more
bone-breaking than I had ever thought possible. This was worse than simply
starting over again, at least worse than when I started out the first time,
because now I had two children, a mortgage, and the Inland Revenue to support. I could not spend all my time playing cheese skittles for sixpence a game
and there seemed only one way forward, one which I dreaded, but one which
I finally knew I would have to accept: I must swallow my pride and go back to
the working men's clubs.

In some ways, this was not as bad as it sounds. In the late 1960s and
early 1970s, the WMC movement enjoyed a huge boom. By pooling
resources and using their combined muscle to deal with the big breweries,
the clubs were able to buy beer significantly cheaper than the pubs and pass
those savings on to their customers (in North-East England, a federation of
local WMCs actually owned their own brewery whose beer, incidentally, is
sold in the bars at the House of Commons). The clubs were also able to
borrow money from the breweries and fund massive expansion
programmes so that the premises, now attracting almost as many women
as men, became family entertainment complexes, decorated and furnished
in some considerable, if rather brash style, rather like the major cinemas at
the height of the film-going boom. It was a time of relatively high
employment, when working men and women had spare cash in their

pockets, and in their millions they chose to spend a lot of it at their local clubs.

Not all this money went on beer and bingo. With their kitties awash with cash, some of the clubs began to hire top-class entertainers from both sides of the Atlantic: 'Satchmo', the legendary Louis Armstrong, made a much-publicised tour which included several WMC dates, as did Johnny Ray, at one time the world's most famous crooner with one of the biggest-selling hit records of all time, *Cry*. In many ways, the clubs had taken over the live entertainment role of the by now largely defunct music hall with one grave exception: the artistes they hired were in many places only a secondary attraction to the beer and the bingo, something to keep the wives and kids happy while the men got on with their traditional pastimes of darts, billiards and, of course, booze. This meant that dressing room facilities for performers, if they existed at all, were grotesquely inadequate. There was no such thing as a stage door, so one had to walk through the crowded bars to get to the stage which, apart from the heckling you regularly received before you even started your act, did little to create the 'magic' that a stage performance is supposed to create.

Then there were the concert secretaries, the committee members whose job it was to hire and pay the artistes. In their working lives, many of these were active, sometimes militant, trade unionists but, with several honourable exceptions, they would treat performers with more disdain than the Victorian mill-owners of legend. They dished out treatment to paid professionals which, had they themselves been the recipients at work, would have led to instant strike action. But they paid the piper and they called the tune. One old friend of mine, Dickie Valentine, a top-line singer who had once appeared with the Ted Heath band, was appalled to arrive at a club and find his contract and £1,000 cheque pinned to the notice board for all to see. When he protested, the entertainment secretary explained that no one would have believed how much he was being paid for a week's work without seeing the evidence!

To add to these problems, public behaviour had changed. Back in my days as 'Leicester's very own George Formby' WMC audiences, brought up on a diet of amateur or at best semi-pro entertainment, had the decency to listen with respect to the performers who had come to entertain them. Apart from anything else, they probably did not have the spare cash in their pockets to get rip-roaring drunk before the entertainment started. We were the gratefully-received bonus to add to three or four halves of beer carefully nurtured to last the entire evening. All this changed in the Swinging Sixties. By the time we went on at around 10pm in some of the more notorious clubs, many of the customers were already well on their way to being totally smashed and they gave you two choices: they either completely ignored you, which is perhaps the worst fate that any entertainer can suffer; or they heckled throughout, shouting abuse and often obscenities. As I have said, there were exceptions. There were clubs which did their level best to give the entertainers reasonable conditions and a decent audience, sometimes in face of huge difficulties raised by their own members. I remember one such club where, the previous week, even the aforesaid Johnny Ray had been drowned out by the noise from a disinterested audience, and he had been famous for the power he poured into his voice. On one stage, I had to cup a hand to my ear to hear what I myself was saying; the audience couldn't catch a word. At another, I complained to the concert secretary and he almost burst into tears. "I do my best but they never give us a chance," he choked. "This job will be the death of me. My wife's already left me because of it and, to be frank, I can't even blame her..."

I stepped back into this world with the utmost reluctance but there was no choice: I needed the money and, for doing a 'double' — appearing at a WMC earlier in the evening and then going on to a late night cabaret club — I could earn £350 a week. That was a great deal of money for a man in my desperate financial circumstances. I earned that money with blood, sweat and sometimes tears, for the humiliations grew and grew. In this respect, I was worse off than many of the acts I appeared alongside, for I bore the greatest stigma of my trade: in many eyes I was a 'has-been'.

The fact that it is better to be a has-been than a never-was does not occur to a certain type of person. They give you no credit that you, unlike them, had once had the guts to fight your way to the top. The fact that you are no longer there gives them, those who have never been nor ever will be any type of success, the chance to grind your face in the mud. I wrote earlier that, sometimes, I would be paid out in fivers in the bar after the show before a crowd of drunks or semi-drunks who would use the situation as a chance to pour out the bile. At other places in the early days of my return to the WMCs, I was even refused entry at the door to several clubs because I did not have a membership card. But even the humiliations can have their funny side, given the benefit of hindsight. I remember one particularly gruesome Sunday in the North-East, where the WMC is the very heart of working class life and audiences are usually generous. Just before I went on stage, I spotted seven soberly dressed middle-aged men at the bar. As I began my act, they carried their pints to a long trestle table at the very foot of the stage, sat down and folded their arms. I tried a gag. Nothing. Another. Again nothing. After a few minutes, the Sinister Seven each downed his pint and another seven were brought to the table by the steward. They'll brighten up after a couple of pints, I thought. I was wrong.

They just sat there, like a hanging jury in a Western movie, determined to lynch the defendant whatever his case. I was becoming more and more un-nerved because behind them, the rest of the audience were enjoying them-selves — apart from the Sinister Seven, I was having a good day. And still the pints came, so swift that by the time my 45 minutes was over, the round had done the complete circuit: 49 pints had been served and 49 had been dis-patched. But still not a flicker of a smile. I bowed out to a burst applause from the rest of the enthusiastic audience and went to change. When I returned to the bar for my money, the Sinister Seven were all there but now they were laughing and chatting eagerly among themselves (which is perhaps what one would expect after at least seven pints of lethally strong Geordie beer).

One of them grabbed my arm, grinned from ear to ear, and said: "Well done, lad. That's the best show we've had for months."

"Ay," said an other, thumping me hard on the back. "T'was great."

"Way-ay," said a third. "You must have a drink w'us."

I was dumbstruck: "But I didn't get a snigger out of any one of you, never mind a laugh."

Once again, they burst into peals of laughter, slapping their sides, grabbing at each other's arms to prevent themselves going down. Then the leader, tears in eyes, explained: "Dunna worry, bonny lad. We have a bet every Sunday. First one to laugh at the comic buys the beer. All the beer…"

And they cracked up again. As I said earlier, there should be a Royal Society for the Prevention of Cruelty to Comics. Torquemada and all his bestial comrades at the Spanish Inquisition could not have invented a more exquisite torture. If only they had told me first, I would have joined in the fun. I might even have joined the bet myself and bought the drinks had I failed to raise a laugh …and it would have been one of the wagers that in all my life I would have been most anxious to win. But I laughed with them in the end, the dour bastards. The humiliations were coming thick and fast but there was still time to laugh. I was paying off my debts and not just to the Inland Revenue.

—oOo—

Not all my friends deserted me. I already had the support of a great family.

And a handful of friends from the champagne days continued to welcome my company as though nothing had changed. It had, of course, and dramatically so, but there were certain people in my life who did everything they could to shield me from the worst effects of being penniless and they did it with such tact that I could barely notice the effort. Barely.

One of these was Frank Worthington, who I met when he was a star Leicester City soccer player and who went on to a long playing career in which, as the joke goes, he had more clubs than Nick Faldo. Frank was like me in many ways. He had glorious individual skills on the field, one of the great ball players of his generation, but off the field he did not like being organised and pushed around by people who, in terms of talent, were several divisions below. Like me, Frank was to have his brushes with the popular press, but he pushed them aside and was much loved by players and fans alike for his scintillating displays on the pitch. When I was at the nadir of my fame, Frank was at his peak. While others who had known me in the champagne days shunned my company, Frank would phone me and take me out for a quiet drink — with him paying, of course, but without him ever making the fact obvious. Today, Frank has built another career as one of the best, and highest-paid, after-dinner speakers in the country.

Another such stalwart was Johnny Greenaway, the outstanding jockey, with whom I had become close friends in my horse-racing days. Johnny was still riding the winners and was very much a super-star at the race tracks, and when he was riding would take with him a large following of personal friends. Now Johnny knew that I was broke. He also knew that I was getting fewer and fewer bookings and this left me bored as well as frustrated. Muriel was out at work all day (for her pitiful £9 a week as a secretary) and hanging around the house in Sapcote all day, waiting for the phone to ring when it so rarely did, was driving me to the point of a nervous breakdown. At one stage, I developed blinding headaches, a form of migraine which my doctor put down to stress: the stress of *not* working. To this day, when some right wing politician starts mouthing off against idle people living it up on the dole, I feel a burning anger; for people who want to work, for people who *love* to work, enforced idleness is the worst punishment of all.

Realising this, but never once actually mentioning it, Johnny would invite me along with his party to the races. At first I was reluctant to go, embarrassed that, once there, I would not be able to play the big-spending character whose role I had once so relished. But Johnny cajoled and said I would be useful. For a start, I was lucky for him. And he needed someone to look after his friends while he was on the track; he would regularly have five or six races a day, which meant there was no time for socialising. So along I went, determined to make myself useful. I would often drive him to the track, and make sure his party were well entertained with food and drink while he was at work. I got fed and watered, too, of course, but it all went on Johnny's account. Looking back, this could seem like some form of charity, the still rich and famous looking after the lame duck. But I am sure this was not so (and had I suspected it, I should never have gone because my pride, although severely dented, was still alive if not too well). I think that both Frank Worthington and Johnny Greenaway acted in this way because they were professional sportsmen and, as such, knew only too well that their own careers were limited by the simple process of aging — if they were lucky enough to survive that long without some form of crippling injury. In this way, top sportsmen and entertainers have a great deal in common. They live on the tightrope and know they can fall any minute. There is a mutual bond among we tightrope artistes, perhaps similar to that felt by soldiers at war. Looking after a wounded comrade becomes, not charity, but *de rigeur*. I thank them both for that support.

I was getting support, too, from another old friend: Richard Stone. Even during our long years of professional divorce, we had remained in social contact and, just before I left Nottingham Playhouse I had re-signed with the agency. Not that this did me much good for several years, because as a faded star even the Stone magic could not get me too many good parts. But he tried his best and, eventually, he landed me a part in pantomime at the London Palladium, no less. I thought it was the start of the long road back. In fact, the humiliation was about to plumb the depths.

There is a well-known phrase in the theatre called *giving notes*, an industrial term used by directors, which means giving advice on a performance in rehearsals. While this is under way, the director's secretary takes notes of these tips and later types them up for the benefit of the cast, hence the expression. Unfortunately, I tend do the same for newcomers in the interests of a better all-round performance from the entire cast.

In typical Richard Stone fashion, I had been signed for the Palladium as part of a package deal with one of the agency's rising new stars who had already made a big name on television because of his unusual high-pitched voice and individualistic personality. But this young performer was very much a newcomer to the stage — until recently, he had been a clerk in impresario Lew Grade's office, which meant one of his jobs was taking the wage packets round to pay the performers in various Grade productions, including me. And,

Richard Stone had explained to me, he was very nervous of doing pantomime. My job, said Richard, was to hold his hand.

"I don't want you to shout at him or take the piss out of him," said Richard gravely. "Most of all, I don't want you to hit him." This, I am sad to say, was something I did from time to time at this stage of my career. Perhaps I should have read some sort of warning into this. But I didn't. It started badly and was to get worse. When I arrived in London for the first talk-through — a pre-rehearsal process in which everyone tosses in ideas to be discussed, adopted or rejected — I saw the bill poster. The pantomime was *Robin Hood*, with Edward Woodward of *Callan* TV fame in the lead role and our rising star as second lead. I searched the bill for my name and there it was, right down at the bottom, in type so small that if a fly had landed on it my name would have been obliterated.

In pantomime, there must always be a joke routine which runs throughout the performance, a sort of natural break between major scenes. At the talk-through, the newcomer asked if we could have one and the producer, Bert Knight, said the best one he had seen involved a prop plant left outside the curtain which needed to be protected by the audience — if anyone approached it, the kids would scream: "Leave it alone!" It was a piece of business I knew well from dozens of pantomimes, so I began to talk us through it: the prop vine grows up the side of the proscenium arch, starting as a little weed in a bucket and, hauled up by a string backstage, it eventually reaches the top of the arch. Every now and then, someone — usually me — goes out to water it from an empty watering can with the gag to the kids: "You've heard of dry ice — well this is dry water." And the vine grows a couple more feet. When the vine eventually reaches the top of the arch in the grand finale, I would discover a pile of Pascal fruit sweets around its base, the 'fruits' which the cast throw to the delighted children in the audience, an archetypal piece of panto business.

Almost everyone laughed. Some of them even clapped. But not our rising star. He shook his head and said: "I think we can find something funnier than that."

Coming from the clerk who had once brought me my wages, this took me aback more than somewhat. I was doing my best to help. Everyone else had enjoyed it. But here was the most in-experienced member of the cast rejecting it. What's more, he was a *television star*, a medium I had rejected voluntarily thanks to my own folly. That meeting broke up with a sense of bad feeling and, as rehearsals progressed, a definite feeling of animosity began to grow. Back home in Sapcote, I would fulminate night after night. "I'll kill him, I'll bloody kill him," I would rage. Muriel, every ready with the oil to pour on troubled waters, would sooth me and say, "You have every right to be upset, Bill, but you *did* make a promise to Richard."

I was now beginning to realise that Richard Stone, in his warning, had in fact been giving me some telling advice. I do not know what caused our new-comer to act this way but, on reflection, it was probably simple insecurity. As a newly-minted star, and Number Two on the bill, he had everything to lose from a poor performance at the London Palladium. He, too, was on the tightrope and was unsure of his grip. I should have known this, and understood it better than most, but by this time I was getting very tired indeed on my diet of daily humiliation. Then I snapped...

One day, just before opening night, the gentlemen in question came up to me and made some suggestions of how I should change my performance. This newcomer, damn it, was *giving me notes*! I waited until he finished and then coined a new phrase: "If you give me one more note, I'm going to turn you into a mural."

He stepped back, hands raised in genuine alarm: "I don't know what you mean."

"I'm not surprised," I said. "What I mean is that if you don't stop giving me notes, I'm going to put you all over that fucking wall..."

I had broken my promise to Richard Stone but, in fact, I had for once done exactly the right thing for the young performer was completely unaware that his behaviour had been causing me distress. After a couple of days, he knocked on my dressing room door and asked if we could have a chat. He wanted to know what he had been doing wrong.

I told him, of course, in no uncertain terms and, to give him his due, he marked my advice down as a serious and important lesson in theatrical eti-quette. We struck up, if not a friendship, at least a truce. One evening he took me as his guest to an important Variety Club of Great Britain boxing dinner where one of the top table guests gave me a wave: Sir Bernard (later Lord) Del-font, another of Britain's legendary showbusiness tycoons, who I'd known well in my champagne days.

Minutes later, a waiter came to me and whispered, "Lord Delfont would like you to join him at the top table."

I looked at my colleague, who was plainly crestfallen, and told the waiter: "Thank his Lordship very much but would you tell him I am here as my friend's guest." The waiter went off with the message, bowed his head to talk to the impressario, and then returned: "In that case, would both of you like to join Sir Bernard?"

Needless to say, we took up the invitation and had a marvellous evening because, as so often happens after a spat, the 'newcomer' and I became close friends. When he later became a producer, he even invited me to join one of his foreign tours.

"I'll work *for* you," I said with a smile, "but not *with* you."

For me, that was a sweet evening with Sir Bernard. But not sweet enough to eradicate the bitter taste of humiliation that I choked on most days of the week. For this was the time when I came closest to cracking, when for the first time since I was was a boy that I seriously considered quitting showbusiness for good. This was a time when a small advertisement appeared in several of the up-market newspapers on America's East Coast. It read: 'English Shakespearian Actor and Wife seek posts as Butler/Cook/Housekeeper. References supplied. Please write to Box Number...'

During my trips to America in earlier days, I had seen how wealthy Americans lived. I knew that there was a desperate rivalry to engage the best — or at least, the most status promoting — domestic staff. I knew that the rich regularly poached good staff from their friends by offering better terms. And, having made my way below stairs at several parties, I knew that the staff often lived better than their employers, taking the finest cuts of food and the very best of the wines before deigning to serve their masters and mistresses. To play an English butler would be a doddle after years on the boards.

Muriel and I had talked it over and decided we liked the idea. It would give us a secure life, plenty of time together, and a farewell to the stress and humiliation of life at the bottom of the showbusiness pile. Our advertisement produced a gush of replies and we agreed to take up an appointment in the beautiful New England state of New Hampshire.

Our airline tickets were booked, our bags practically packed. There would have been no Bill Maynard as Greengrass, or the Gaffer, or Selwyn Froggitt. Then the phone rang...

Chapter Eighteen

Movies

THE call came from Richard Stone and if there was any single moment in my life when a lifeline was thrown to a drowning man, this was it. After years of struggling to stay afloat, I was, by 1968, on the verge of floundering, drowning with me any thoughts of a future in my chosen career. But even then, the lifeline needed an extra twist from Lady Luck and a chance encounter with an old friend. Writers, great writers, were about to make a grand entrance into my life.

Richard told me that they were making a full-length cinema film of 'Till Death Do Us Part', Johnny Speight's creation which had at first shocked and then enchanted the British television audience with its portrayal of working class life in London's East End. In the series, Warren Mitchell portrayed one of the greatest individual characters ever thrown up by television, the foul-mouthed fascist bigot Alf Garnett who broke virtually every rule in the BBC book with diatribes against blacks, whom he called 'coons', women — he called his long-suffering wife, Dandy Nichols, a 'silly old moo' — Labour politicians, Northerners and, in particular, his son-in-law Anthony Booth, who became known to the world as a 'Scouse ghet'. There is a certain piquancy to this today, 30 years later, because Anthony's real-life daughter, Cherie, a leading barrister, is in fact Mrs Tony Blair. In those days, however, the Handbook of Political Correctness had not yet been written. Had it been so, its authors would have died from apoplexy at Alf Garnett's antics.

For the film, Richard Stone explained, they were casting Alf's next-door-neighbour, Bert, who was also to be a victim of the bigot's vitriolic tongue. He had put my name forward for the part and I was due to report to Thelma

Graves, who was doing the casting at the famous Shepperton Studios, set in the London suburbs close to Heathrow Airport. It was a good part, the fifth lead, said Richard, and what's more it paid £1,000 for some eight weeks' work, a sum grand enough to ward off financial disaster for another few months. So off I went on the laborious journey to Shepperton by bus and train. The moment I walked into Thelma Grave's office, her face fell.

I knew instantly that something was wrong but just what it was I could not guess. Thelma, clearly embarrassed, talked around in circles for a few minutes and then blurted it out: "I'm sorry Bill, I didn't realise you were so tall. You see, in this part Warren is supposed to totally dominate the poor neighbour, to completely overpower him. Trouble is, you would tower over him physically and that would make the relationship very difficult to sustain…"

Her voice petered out. My heart sank, for here I was, drinking in the Last Chance Saloon, and someone had taken my whisky away. There was, she said, another part available but it was only one day's work.

At that moment, the door opened and a man walked in and began to talk to Thelma. Then he realised who I was.

"Hello, Bill," he said. "What are you doing here?"

I smiled broadly, for here was Johnny Speight, the man with whom, years ago in the Soho days, I had spent hours in the cafe next to The Windmill, surrounded by tarts, taxi drivers and pimps, as he sold me gags at ten shillings a time. Money which, at the time, he desperately needed, money that to me was less than washers. Now he was the best-known and probably the best-paid writer in British television. And I was the nobody from Sapcote, Leicestershire. When the tables are turned in my life, it happens not with a mere crash but with an earthquake.

Thelma Graves began to explain: "Mr Maynard actually came for the part of Bert but I was explaining to him that he is somewhat on the large size. We were looking for someone smaller, someone Alf can dominate."

Johnny shook his head: "No, he's perfect. Give him the part."

And he walked out again. So much for casting — and thank you, John.

Had Johnny Speight not needed to see Thelma Graves at that particular moment, I would have spent the rest of my days serving champagne and caviar to rich Americans. Instead, I was to start yet another new career in the movies although, I must admit, not as the sex symbol leading man of my earlier dreams. There is a moral to the story, too. Lord Northcliffe, the millionaire newspaper magnate, it is reported, was once travelling up in a lift with one of his leading editors. Northcliffe nodded to the young boy controlling the lift and said to the journalist: "Be nice to him on the way up. You might meet him on the way down."

When I was on the way up, I made a reputation in some quarters of being a big-headed, arrogant, self-centred oaf. But I must have played the good guy to some people because on my way down — indeed, at the very bottom — there were still old friends happy to come to my rescue. Johnny Speight was one of a trio of great writers who were to put me back on the road to the top. My white-knuckle ride on the roller-coaster had finally bottomed out. It was still a long way up, but at least I was facing in the right direction. I was back on the screen. The Big Screen.

—oOo—

As the fifth lead in a major movie, I was entitled to certain status symbols, like a canvas-backed chair on the set with my name stencilled on it. I could eat with the other major actors in the restaurant while the technicians and extras went to the canteen. And there was a space booked for me in the car park, among the Rolls-Royces and the Jaguars. Trouble was, apart from the chair which came free, I was in no position to take advantage of my reacquired loftier situation. For a start, lunch in the restaurant cost £3 10s 0d. It was very good, gourmet standard, but the prices were too much for me. After two or three visits, I took to the canteen where I discovered that exactly the same meal cost just six shillings. This obviously attracted the attention of the other top-liners and when they asked me why, I simply replied: "Can't afford it. I'm skint." They took it as a joke and wrote me off as an eccentric. But when I explained that you could get the same food at less than a tenth of the price, the others took to using the canteen too — I had created something of a trend which, no doubt, did not please the restaurant manager.

I needed my food because I was getting virtually no sleep. For while other leading members of the cast were staying either at their London homes or in expensive hotels nearby, I was commuting daily from Sapcote. Despite my prized space in the car park, I did not have a car so those three or four pounds I was saving on lunch were being put aside carefully by Muriel to spare me the nightmare of that daily trip. The millions who were to watch the film version of 'Till Death would scarcely have believed just how close to that fate came the Fifth Lead just to take the part.

Early starts are one of the great agonies of film making, for when producers have huge bills to meet for salaries and sets, when highly-trained technicians and hyper-expensive equipment are on hire, the idea is to get as much done in a day as is humanly (and sometimes, inhumanely) possible. In Hollywood, they sometimes start as early as 6am, which means that glamorous stars lead distinctly unglamorous social lives whilst working: it is more likely to be a book in bed at 8pm than champagne and starlets until dawn. At Shepperton, mercifully, our calls tended to come at about 7.30 or 8am, which was just about acceptable for most of the cast who lived just down the road. For me, more than 100 zig-zag miles away in the East Midlands, it meant the night shift.

When I was on an early call, it meant leaving our semi at 9pm the previous evening, starting a mind-numbing journey with a half-mile walk to the nearest main road to catch a Midland Red bus to Birmingham at a lonely country stop which very few people used. On some dark nights, the driver would not spot me at my lonely perch and would whiz past leaving me stranded until the next service came an hour later. When I did get aboard, I would travel to Coventry, get off and walk a mile across the city to the railway station. The train took me to Watford, where I would catch a few hours of cold and uncomfortable sleep in the waiting room before taking the connecting bus service to Heathrow Airport. Jumping off a few stops before, I would then struggle up the long drive at Shepperton just in time for make-up. Then it was straight before the cameras.

Such a glamorous life, being a film star!

Despite the rigours of this journey, memories of which still make me shudder, once before the cameras I seemed to light up. I became a total devotee of film making technique, revelling in take after take. Much of the television I had done, remember, had been live but even with that said, the differences between television and film making are stunning. Each scene tends to be shot from different angles, with one character saying his lines and then the director shouting. "Cut!" The cameras are moved, then the next character speaks his or her lines. Then "Cut!" again. A simple scene lasting a few seconds can take hours to get into the can. Even when the acting is judged satisfactory — and this regularly involves take after take — technical flaws can create a wasted day. Sitting to watch the rushes, the rough cuts of that day's filming, I was dismayed when one scene was chopped because the lighting was too grainy, then another because the sound technician had heard some intrusive noise. These scenes have to be re-shot and even then the process is far from complete. Editing is one of the crucial processes involved, and here the film editor, working with the director, can make or break even a great acting performance (David Lean, maker of *Dr Zhivago, Lawrence of Arabia* etc made his reputation as a film editor before becoming the world's most sought-after director). Then, of course, the director always has the final say. The great performances left on the cutting room floor are by no means an apocryphal legend, a series of stories invented by actors in a huff of wounded pride. It happens all the time.

However, I must not complain. Compared to what had gone before, film acting was both a joy and a doddle. Certainly, when you are working in supporting roles, the money is not bad. But how often you work is the key and that can sometimes be as little as two or three months a year. Spread out over a year, that adds up to not a great deal more than the earnings of a man with a steady job in a factory. Despite these drawbacks, I simply *loved* it. By the time *'Till Death* was over, we had scraped together enough money to buy a vehicle: not a car but a scruffy, rusty, second-hand van which looked decidedly ill at ease when it sat in my private space next to the limousines on the Shepperton parking lot. Once again, Bill Maynard's reputation as an amusing eccentric took another leap forwards.

I rang Richard Stone because I realised I was completely inexperienced at film making and asked him to get me any film role he could find, however rubbishy or minor. He was to take me at my word and in the next few years I was to appear in dozens of British pictures, including several of the *Carry On* movies which have become the strangest cult I have ever been involved with, although, quite frankly, I thought most of them were awful. Sadly, the *Carry On* films — and some even worse — keep cropping up on television so I am doomed never to forget.

At the time, however, such thoughts were far from my mind. I had discovered yet another new medium and it held me enthralled. My professional life, although not exactly booming, was finally paying the bills. And in my personal life, I was finally rebuilding the new Bill Maynard. I had discovered *The Power of Positive Thinking*.

—oOo—

One of the few advantages of being under-employed, perhaps the only advantage, was that it had given me time to think. For long years, I had been turning over in my mind why I had been such an arrogant idiot when I was making money that could, and should, have kept us in comparative comfort for the rest of our lives. I had begun to put it down to an inferiority complex born in my days in Rat Alley, a complex which had surrounded itself with a coat of armour plating to ward off anyone or anything which I judged to be patronising. I had to prove that I could out-act, out-spend, out-fuck and figuratively out-fight anyone who came my way. This was, I realised, part of an act, to ward off anyone who dared come close enough to look deeply into the real Bill Maynard. I might have been rich and famous but the urchin from Rat Alley was still there inside, hurting and hurtful by turn. I was determined that the rest of the world would not know this and created this shell of arrogance and brashness to keep the urchin hidden away. Normal people, with no such feelings to disguise, were repelled, but the armour worked in two directions: although it kept out intruders it also left me isolated from all but my closest family and a few friends. Then one day at a railway station bookstall, I picked up a copy of *The Power of Positive Thinking*, the best-seller written by Norman Vincent Peale, the American theologian. Now this book was once much discussed and much abused by the high-brow critics but it sold in its millions. It is a long and complex work but, thankfully, I had plenty of time to read and digest it. I will not pretend that I can break its message down to a meaningful precis in a few short sentences but to paraphrase, it summed up all the mysteries of Christianity in one simple sentence: "Do unto Others as You would have Them do unto You: the rest is propaganda."

In my darker days, I turned for solace to any potential source, including Christianity. I became a staunch supporter of the Salvation Army and would even have become one of its soldiers had I not realised that the press would have treated this as another publicity stunt. This would have damaged not only me but the Army, too, so I kept my views to myself. I experimented with Methodism, which with its rather severe forms of expressing faith appealed to me rather than the more flamboyant forms of Anglican worship. But it was the pure simplicity of *Positive Thinking* that struck home.

As I interpreted it — and there are no doubt many different interpretations — it meant treating other people as you would want them to treat you. There was no need to brag and bluster, unless you wanted brag and bluster in return. If you dealt with ordinary folk in an easy, pleasant manner, you would receive the same. This may well seem a little trite but it began to work for me in curious little ways. On my many train journeys, I had tended to ignore fellow passengers in case they remembered me and involved me in what I considered to be boring conversations. To them, I now realised, such conversations were not boring but deeply interesting, perhaps even intriguing, so why deprive them of such little pleasures? In the past on the train, I had read my newspaper and then left it on the seat beside me, not realising that fellow passengers might like to see it. I began to offer it around when I was finished with it and such a minor gesture brought the rewards of smiles and thanks.

I even took to carrying the bags of old ladies who could not find, or perhaps afford, a porter, where I had once upon a time rushed down the platform determined to be the first through the ticket barrier. How unbelievably simple all this sounds, for this is the way that most normal people behave. Suddenly, I was becoming *normal*, too, getting my rewards not in rounds of applause and big cheques but in smiles and genuine thanks. I felt that I had stumbled on one of the secrets of life and one of the follies of fame. It takes a single-minded determination to get to the top in any profession and in showbusiness more than most. In that blinkered scramble to the top, the ambitious cannot see the everyday things that are going on around them: the blinkers cut them off from that part of life. And once cut off, it can be extraordinarily difficult to come back, which is perhaps why so many big stars live in a pampered vacuum of isolation and, ultimately, self-delusion and despair.

The first to notice the change was, of course, Muriel, who made a point of meeting me at Leicester station whenever she could and had watched with growing fascination as I staggered down the platform time after time carrying some old lady's luggage. One day, there was no one needing a volunteer porter so I walked to her empty handed.

"What's up, Bill," she chortled, eyes full of delight, "Couldn't you find someone to help?"

I became so attached to *Positive Thinking* that I was later to buy dozens of copies to give to friends and colleagues. It took the sham out of my life and brought me back to earth. Once upon a time, when I was offered a drink in the pub, I would simply say no thanks, thus insulting the person kind enough to offer. After reading *Positive Thinking*, I would explain that I wouldn't take a drink because I was penniless and could not afford to buy one back. The answer was, almost invariably: "Who cares — get me one when you're flush again." I would get a smile, keep a friend and get a drink too, which is not a bad reward for a few simple words.

These were trivial little improvements, if taken singly, but they were to add up to a total of great significance, the final touches to the all new, improved Bill Maynard. By teaching against hypocrisy, it was also to give me the courage to stage one of the most satisfying moments of my life. For months I had been battling a growing loathing of my acts in the working men's clubs. Some of the dates I positively hated and now I realised that this hatred was in fact beginning to show in my act. I was actually projecting it at the audience, which is professional suicide for a comic. Bolstered by my newly-found film work, it was time for positive action.

One night, at a noisy WMC in the North-East, when I was dying on my feet unheard and ignored, I finally took that action. After a struggle, I quietened the noisome club. Then I said it: "Ladies and Gentlemen, I have finally realised that it was a mistake to come here. There are some good acts to follow and I wouldn't want to spoil your evening."

I walked out off the stage and out of the club, unpaid but ablaze with inner jubilation. It was something I had longed to do for months, if not years. And now I had finally done it. Even the concert secretary, who was standing by the stage when I passed, agreed. "You did the right thing there, son!"

That, to me, is *Positive Thinking*.

Chapter Nineteen

The Long Road Back

ALTHOUGH I did not realise it at the time, my roller coaster career had bottomed out some time before my ill-fated pantomime appearance at the London Palladium. The car that had carried me on this white-knuckle ride for so long was beginning to grind its way back upwards once again, but at a speed so slow that it was at first barely perceptible.

After the success of the *'Till Death* film, I was invited to appear as next-door neighbour Bert in several TV episodes, arguing with Alf Garnett on such subjects as pigeon racing. I got a few parts on other TV shows too, with the likes of Eric Sykes and Ronnie Barker. I even did a few episodes of *Coronation Street* as a pub singer in the Rover's Return, where, contrary to other stories which abound, the regular cast showed me great friendship and support (the show has a reputation for being hostile to guest artistes but I can say now that this is quite false). I also became a regular performer in a long series of 'B' movies which were so bad that I would dearly like to forget them — movies like the *Confessions of a Window Cleaner* and one called *A (W)hole lot of Trouble,* in which I played a recalcitrant labourer digging a hole in the road under the ever-pained eye of a local council official played by Arthur Lowe, later to become famous as Captain Mainwaring in *Dad's Army*. Arthur and I made several films together in atrocious conditions for something like £30 a day, which along with some stage work paid the mortgage and the Inland Revenue. Arthur and I had been around in the business for a long time but here we met some of the youngsters also on the way to the top. It was an intriguing time, but glamorous it most definitely was not. I remember one young starlet turning up to make her first movie and demanding: "Where's the make-up department?" We fell about laughing when Frank Searle, the producer-director, asked: "Who's got the tin, then?" This 'department' consisted of a single tobacco tin containing, if we were lucky, half a dozen well used sticks of make-up. I remember, too, one so-called 'wrap-party', the traditional celebration thrown when filming is finished. Frank Searle invited us all into the office — actors, technicians, the lot — and plonked a half-bottle of whisky on his desk. So much for the champagne lifestyle of making low-budget movies.

However, with some stage work coming in again and a regular diet of 'B' pictures, we were getting by in Sapcote (if you can call having beds to sleep in getting by!) but there was little cash to spare — the Inland Revenue were seeing to that. And along with my new positive mental attitude to life, I was changing physically too. My hair was beginning to recede, I had put on a lot of weight because I had given up smoking, and the hard knocks of life had put character into my face. I was never to achieve my aim of becoming a heart-throb leading man (in the traditional sense, anyway) but as I edged into my 40s, the time which all people dread but actors more than most, some of showbusiness's most astute eyes were beginning to see my potential as a 'character' actor.

This is a word that is often misunderstood. For generations, actors in the theatre, and later the cinema, had been divided into 'leading men' and 'character actors'. The former had, for most of the century, been the handsome hero type. In the 1960s, when 'kitchen-sink' drama swept the business, they had become young, working class lads. They were not handsome in the traditional sort of way but they were still young. Alongside these so-called leading men came the character actors and this is a genre in which Britain has long-excelled: in hundreds of films and plays, whether produced in Hollywood or Pinewood, on Broadway or in the West End, average performances by leading men and women have been made realistic and polished by taking place alongside brilliant performances from supporting character players.

Came the 1970s, however, and these distinctions were becoming blurred and particularly so in television. It was no longer *de rigeur* that leading actors should be young and prettily handsome; a new breed of writers were producing hard-hitting drama about *real* people facing *real* lifetime situations. As we all know, real people are not always handsome and desperate problems can arise for anyone at any stage of life. This new realism created a demand for actors who could play ordinary people facing extraordinary situations. It was time for so-called *character* actors to play *leading* roles. And at 40-something, the bloodied, battered but not yet bowed Bill Maynard had developed the looks, and the skills, to put some of these seminal works on the small screen.

The call came as a surprise for, as far as I can remember, I had never before met John Murphy, the casting director at Granada Television in Manchester. They had received a remarkable script called *Paper Roses* by the equally remarkable Dennis Potter, one of the leaders of this new vanguard in one-off television drama. Would I care to go to Manchester and discuss the part? Although Dennis Potter was by no means the great name he later became, he was already building himself a reputation in the business and his script positively sizzled. I went to Manchester like a shot, thinking that I had finally turned the corner. It was not to be that easy.

Although I do not know for certain, I suspect that the director, Barry Davies, and even more so, the producer Kenneth Trodd, had little faith in my ability to interpret the part of Clarence Hubbard, the lead character in *Paper Roses,* a one-time famous journalist who through age and drink was on the way down to Skid Row. It was a part that Dennis, apparently, had written based on his own experience of journalists he had known when he was a newspaperman, so it rang with conviction. It struck home with me, too, because I had come so close to living a similar part in real life; only the professions were different. Perhaps the producer and the director, men who remembered me from my stand-up comic days, thought that I was too lightweight for the part for they sent me away after the first interview with much h'mming and ha'ing but no concrete yes or no. I returned to Leicester in bleak disappointment. Then they asked me to go again. And again. And again. It took me three or four interviews before I eventually got the part — the part that was to launch the great climb back.

I based my portrayal of Clarence Hubbard on a well-known provincial theatre critic who had based his own image on that of Hannen Swaffer, at one time doyen of the Fleet Street columnists, all swish suits, silk pocket handkerchiefs, and flowers in the button hole — so my character had quite a pedigree. Dennis Potter, who came to the set regularly, his hands hidden in gloves to cover his rampaging psoriasis, always wore dark glass because his eyes were sensitive to the lights; some said that he had the eyes of an albino.

Dennis seemed to approve of the performance, although even he was not free to do exactly as he wished. In the first finale he had written, Clarence, taken off major stories and allowed to write only obituaries, had planned his own dramatic exit by writing up an exclusive story before it actually happened: he wrote the copy before going out to make the story. Having filed his story, he was supposed to walk into the middle of the road in Fleet Street carrying a can of paint. There, he was to sit down and paint the letters 'S ...H ...I...' in the middle of the road before being arrested and dragged off to who knows where, his career finished forever. In these days of non-stop expletives on certain television programmes, particularly American films, it is difficult to believe that this three-letter word was then considered to be far too risqué for the British viewing public and Dennis was asked to rewrite the ending. So I fell down a lift shaft to my death, drunk of course. This finale disappointed some of the critics but apart from that they were delighted: Bill Maynard received many congratulations as an act-oor in his first television starring role.

It took some time to find out that I owed it all to John Murphy, the Granada casting director, for I learned that he had fought tooth and nail for me to get the part in face of considerable opposition. Yet I barely knew the man and, I confess, until that point of time I had little respect for people in his job (I would have not got the 'Till Death role without the direct intervention of Johnny Speight). To me, they were just minor cogs in a very large machine, mere booking agents while the producers and directors made all the big decisions.

One night over a drink in The Stables, the Granada bar in Manchester, I asked John Murphy why he had gone to so much trouble to get me the role. "As far as I know, John," I said, "we had never met before this play, so why go to all that trouble for a stranger?"

He laughed. "That's my job, Bill," he said. "You may not have met me before, but I've watched you all over the country. I've been following you in rep for years and I always knew that you would do the job when the right part came along. I waited for years for that part to come up and this was it."

Here was a supreme professional who could see in actors facets that were hidden to others, a key player in making Granada one of the great centres of television drama. Poor drunken has-been Clarence Hubbard, a part so close to my heart, had brought me to the attention of the critics, the serious critics, and more too. After the broadcast, I received dozens of letters from journalists and fellow actors saying how much they had enjoyed my performance, some of them from journalists who had written highly unfavourable things about me in the past. So much for the adage, 'It's not what you know it's who you know…' John Murphy gave the lie to that.

—oOo—

If Dennis Potter and *Paper Roses* gave me a great push back up the ladder, another great writer and another great television play added rocket propulsion to the momentum: Colin Welland, one-time *Z-Cars* actor turned playwright, and *Kisses at Fifty*, the BBC TV play, took me hurtling back to top of the bill after more than a decade and a half at the bottom. *Kisses at Fifty* was a gem of observation on Northern working class life, a play without a hint of glamour yet a deeply moving account of how two people trapped in unhappy family and financial circumstances whip up the courage to take a gamble on happiness although it means losing almost everything they have: their friends, their families, their jobs and even their homes. Yet its hero and heroine were as ordinary as can be, he a stoker struggling to keep the boilers at his employer's mill firing, she a barmaid approaching middle age whose life has descended into the sadness of a vacuum empty of hope for the future. This was hardly James Bond material but the characters reached out to the viewers asking for sympathy and understanding — and won. Colin Welland was already well-known as an actor but it was this play that sent his career spinning towards the dizzy heights, too. He is now best known as the Oscar-winning scriptwriter for *Chariots of Fire*, whose acceptance speech at the Oscar ceremonies included the stirring cry, "The British Are Coming." This did not go down too well with American audiences as it is the famous quote from Paul Revere, one of the heroes of America's War of Independence from Britain.

The icing on the top of the wonderful *Kisses* script was the director, Michael Apted, who was also to make the transition to Hollywood as a major film director (but he still hasn't sent for me) and a marvellous actress in the bar-maid role, Marjorie Yates, who was to do me the most magnificent service: she allowed me to practise kissing. Screen kissing, it should be emphasised, because in my youth I had been quite adept at the real thing. Despite those in-depth private studies, I had only once before kissed a woman professionally and that was on stage in the theatre, where the audience are seated at a respectful distance. In this production, the kiss was to be in full close-up and it was absolutely integral to the plot. To explain, the title comes from an early scene in the play when it is my 50th birthday — the fact that I was in my early 40s at the time gives some indication of how the long hard years in the wilderness had aged me. Having washed and scrubbed up after my long, hard, dirty day's work, I call at the local pub for a lonely celebratory pint. There, some of the regulars wish me Happy Birthday and my eyes fall on the new barmaid, Marjorie. To my surprise, she asks for a birthday kiss so, urged on by my mates, I overcome my shyness and go behind the counter. There the magic kiss takes place and we fall immediately in love, two rather sad, rapidly aging people to whom a single embrace of real warmth sparks the desire for a new life together.

It was and still is a wonderful scene. But I was terrified.

In the early read-throughs, we sat in the rehearsal rooms at the BBC and went though our parts. Every time we came to the crucial scene, Michael Apted would simply say: "This is where you kiss," and pass on to the next dialogue. Everyone, including Marjorie, assumed that close-up kissing was part of every actor's working tool-kit, something you had learned rather like you learn to ride a bike: once you've done it, you never forget. I didn't have the nerve to mention my concerns to Michael for fear of sounding amateurish. But one evening, as rehearsals were breaking up, I approached Marjorie and said hesitantly: "I'm a bit worried about something. Would you mind coming in a bit early to tomorrow to ...eh ...practise?"

"Practise what?" she asked wide eyed.

I shrugged my shoulders apologetically: "Eh ...well ...the kiss..."

"The kiss?"

"Yeh, the kiss. You see I've never done it before in close up and I don't want to do it for the first time before lots of other actors. I was hoping we could practise ...well ...privately..."

"OK," she said happily and at that we both burst into laughter. Being the good sort and consummate professional she is, she turned up duly early the following day and she helped me lose my screen kiss virginity with tact and good humour. Fortunately, we both liked each other, so these secret kissing sessions were far from distasteful. Sadly this is not always the case: there are millions of television and film fans who watch with envy as their favourite actors and actresses go into deep clinches and murmur to themselves: "And they get paid for doing that!" What they don't realise is that these couples often have a deep loathing for each other and feigning passion under such circumstances is one of the most difficult demands of our strange job.

With the kiss suitably dealt with (and with some considerable success as later events were to prove) we began filming *Kisses*, partly in industrial West Yorkshire and partly in London, but there was another scene which was also giving me concern. Later in the play, having left home to be free of my bullying family, I am living rough, sleeping in a railway waiting room (shades of my 'Till Death film days!). I have lost my job and am looking for another one so that Marjorie and I can set up home together. This day I have an important interview and in order to look my best, I shave in the station loo — wetting my razor in a toilet bowl. This, I thought, was a little over the top so I mentioned my doubts to Colin Welland, saying I didn't think a man would do that in real life. "Oh yes he would," said Colin and went on to explain that the play was actually based on the real life experiences of a friend of his, a friend who had ended up shaving in a railway station toilet bowl one winter's morning because the taps to the hand basins were frozen up.

This information threw me back on to the horns of a familiar dilemma: Colin was absolutely right to insist on the scene, but had not written in any explanatory business to explain the washbasins being frozen. My problem was: dare I mention it? I was well aware that I was involved in a project of crucial importance to my future career. I was aware, too, that I had a reputation for falling out with some writers and this did me no favours when it came to casting decisions: don't use Maynard, he's a trouble maker. But throughout my working life I had insisted on the highest professional standards I could achieve, an insistence that had often cost me dear. What should come first now — professionalism or the possibility of personal progress?

Professionalism won, of course. "Perhaps you could write in something to explain about the taps," I suggested, somewhat hesitantly. "OK," said Colin and it was done. Once again, it had been proved to me that truly talented writers will accept a little query if they feel it actually improves the play; the work is the thing, not the ego. There are some leading actors and actresses who, of course, regularly demand rewrites to give themselves bigger and better parts, particularly if that means reducing the part of some rival professional. Writers, quite correctly, object to this very strongly. And I have said before, there are other writers who look upon any suggestion for changing their words as tantamount to rewriting the Ten Commandments. Colin Welland, an enormous talent, does not fall into this category as his later successes proved.

With Kisses in the can, I went back to any film work I could find, plus a few stage appearances, and by chance the play was broadcast while I was appearing in that humiliating pantomime at the London Palladium. And the star of the show, Edward Woodward — an established TV name from his spy series Callan — must have had a television set in his dressing room, a luxury denied to us peasants at the very bottom of the bill. My first indication of just how good things were to be, was when Edward came up to me on stage and whispered out of the side of his mouth: "You were doing sterling work on the box tonight, Young Maynard."

So I did not even see the first showing of *Kisses at Fifty*, the play which received rave reviews from the critics and put me once again back at the top of the TV pile. Its impact was so great that, after some 15 years in the wilderness, Bill Maynard once more became a household name. The phones at Richard Stone's offices never stopped ringing and the offers came flooding in thick and fast, for more television, more theatre, even more cabaret. Trouble was, I was contracted for some 16 weeks of this terrible time I was having in pantomime, so I was having to turn offers down. I dare not break my contract, of course, but I was furious to let such work pass me by. So I begged Richard Stone to find an actor who would agree to take over my spot at the bottom of the bill.

After a few days, another Richard Stone client, an old acquaintance of mine, turned up and said he might replace me but he would like to see the show first. That night, I retuned my normally exaggerated performance and played with quiet but professional decorum. Back home in Sapcote in the early hours of the following morning, I went down on my knees in front of Muriel — only half in jest, I might say — and said: "Let's pray that he agrees to take over." And he did, much to my delight, but even today I feel a little guilty at having conned him into such an unhappy show. I went to see him in the Palladium dressing rooms a few weeks later, offering to buy him a drink. All he did was to shake my hand and say, "You bastard ...you absolute bastard." I knew what he meant.

The long humiliation was finally over, even though I had still not paid off my debt to the Inland Revenue. Discussing this time, journalists have asked me if, once back at the top, I was tempted to return to the old life, to go back to the booze, the fast cars and the faster women. The answer, quite simply, is no. In a decade of relative stability, if not financial security, in my little semi in Sapcote I had realised just how empty and stupid my first years with the champagne set had been. It was a case of, I had been there and done that, and I was never once tempted to return. Muriel was now the rock of my existence and my children were growing into bright, ambitious young adults. All I wanted was to continue my work and that was now assured.

Kisses at Fifty was to win Colin Welland the BAFTA award for the best single television play of the year. It was an enormous boost to Michael Apted's career, an important stepping stone on his way to Hollywood, and it put me finally where I had so long wanted to be: accepted by critics and public alike as a serious actor. For a man in early middle age, this was a stupendous reward after so much travail. But I feel here that I should give a special vote of thanks to Marjorie Yates, who gave up her time to help me to overcome the embarrassment of my first screen kiss.

They showed that kiss in close up on a big screen at the BAFTA Awards when Colin won the top prize. I was not there to see it, as on the night of its first broadcast, I was working (thank goodness) and missed the show. I did see it again later, however, when Eamonn Andrews did my *This is Your Life* programme. As an erotic interlude, it probably does not rate in screen history alongside the famous beach clinch between Burt Lancaster and Deborah Kerr in *From Here to Eternity*. But if any single scene changed my life for the better, this was it. There is a certain piquancy, a wry sort of irony, in this, for while illicit kisses and more had once threatened to derail me forever, a totally platonic embrace with an admired fellow professional put me firmly back on the tracks. Thanks, Marjorie.

Chapter Twenty

Carry on Working

SO here I was, back at the top, and I suppose most people I knew thought that the money was rolling in. The fact of the matter was that, although the family finances had improved dramatically, I still had the Inland Revenue on my back and my income was still sporadic. Like footballers in those days, actors had still to enter the big-money league and one-off television plays, however successful critically, came along only rarely. When they did, they paid reasonably well but only for a few weeks' work. The only solution, to steal the well-known title of the film series, was to Carry on Working — at any part that came my way. Fortunately, they were many. To say they were varied is an understatement of some enormity.

In the mid-1970s, the press office of Yorkshire Television compiled a Bill Maynard biography to distribute among televisions critics as background material. It included a list of recent appearances and it was by no means complete, and I do not wish to present it as a series of triumphs. It was far from that: my credits ranged from *Kisses at Fifty* to *Confessions of a Window Cleaner*, which is truly the sublime to the ridiculous, but I use it here as an example of the sort of life a jobbing actor — even a newly reborn leading actor — must lead in order to make ends meet. Here we go:

Stage: *Babes in the Wood*, London Palladium (1972-73); *Crete and Sergeant Pepper* (Royal Court, London, May 1972).

Films: more than 50 in 12 years, include *'Till Death Do Us Part, One More Time*; six *Carry On* films; *Bless this House*; *Never Mind the Quality*; *(W)hole Lot of Trouble*; *It All Goes to Show*; *Adolf Hitler: My Part in His Downfall*; *Steptoe and Son Ride Again*; *You'd Better Come in Disguise*; *Confessions of a Window Cleaner*; *It Shouldn't Happen to a Vet*.

Television: *'Till Death Do Us Part*; *Dora*; *Love Thy Neighbour*; *Seven of One*; *Jokers Wild*; *The Orson Welles Mysteries*; *Coronation Street*; *Zodiac*; *Hunters Walk*; *Happy Days*; *The Way of the World*; *Journey to London*; *Love Affair*; *Father Brown*; *The Life of Riley*.

Radio: *Late Night Extra*; *The Bill Maynard Show*.

As I said, this was more like the tip of the iceberg rather than a complete list. As already recorded, I had done several of the great roles in contemporary theatre — Truscott in *Loot*, Archie Rice in *The Entertainer*, Oscar in *The Odd Couple*, Davies in *The Caretaker* — and many of the great Shakespeare characters. The incompleteness of the YTV list was probably my fault: throughout my life I have rarely kept any mementos of my career; press cuttings, photographs, reviews, theatre programmes and posters, all the things which many actors hoard, usually went into my dustbin after a few days. So to compile this recent biography for YTV was largely a matter of guesswork and, perhaps, voluntary amnesia — there were many performances I was happy to forget and others that I simply forgot anyway. But it is an interesting list because it shows just how much my career at this time ricocheted from one extreme to another and included the whole gamut of the media: stage, film, television, radio and (although they were not listed) a few cabaret appearances too. These, in particular, were at one stage to present me a completely new set of problems.

Even with the list before me, I can barely remember many of the parts involved. Anyone who has ever seen those American films from the era of swing music, starring big bands like Glenn Miller, Benny Goodman, or the Dorsey Brothers, will remember how the director showed the passage of time and progress by using shots of moving trains with headlines from local newspapers superimposed on the screen. This was how life became: a series of dates of varying importance and quality, in studios or theatres in towns and cities which passed in one continuous blur. Some, however, still stand out.

The Anglia Television play, *Love Affair*, where I played with the lovely Celia Johnson, was extremely well received by the critics, making a trio of important straight acting roles to go with *Paper Roses* and *Kisses*. It brought my first TV series, too, with *The Inheritors* from Harlech TV, a tough drama set in the world of wealth and big business. It was a time that introduced me to another great writer, Alan Plater, a Yorkshireman who had cut his writing teeth on hard-hitting episodes for *Z-Cars*, the classic BBC police series, but who had long wanted to try his hand at comedy. He did so with a BBC2 series called *Trinity Tales*, which was a 20th century send-up of the oldest classic in English literature, Chaucer's *Canterbury Tales*.

Instead of religious pilgrims making their way to Canterbury, however, this series depicted a group of Wakefield Trinity Rugby League fans on their way to the Challenge Cup Final at Wembley. Each episode told the story of one of the party, the literary device which Chaucer himself used. In my episode, I played the fryer — not a monk but a fish and chip fryer! It was experimental drama, well received by the critics, but perhaps went a little over the heads of many viewers, most of whom had never heard of Chaucer anyway. But it was intriguing, challenging stuff to play and Alan Plater and I built a relationship which was to serve us both well later.

The true significance of this plethora of roles good and bad, of constant travel and living out of suitcases, was that I was still *working*. This is a concept that might not at first seem overly significant to men and women in regular employment; going to the factory or office every day is such a regular phenomenon that it passes without comment (or, at least, it did until recent economic changes made jobs for life a thing of the past for millions of people). In showbusiness, however, work is not just a matter of earning cash, even when you are lucky enough to be doing it. Some 90 per cent of Equity members are 'resting' at any one time. Work is also a means of putting yourself out and about, to be seen by people who matter, who are planning projects about which you know nothing. In the previous chapter, I described how the Granada casting director John Murphy had watched me in rep for years before insisting that I was given the part that changed my life in *Paper Roses*. You never know who is out there in the audience, what plans they have afoot, or that you might unknowingly figure in those plans. This happened one night in the Palace Theatre, Manchester, when I was touring a play called *Cat in the Bag* by Joyce Raeburn.

It was a good play, one we eventually hoped to take to the West End, but those hopes never materialised. Although this was a disappointment at the time, that Palace performance was to be of great significance, for in the audience one night was a former insurance salesman turned scriptwriter called Harry Kershaw, another name to add to the growing list of talented writers whose careers became closely entangled with mine.

Harry, known as H.V. Kershaw, was a well-established star writer and producer at Granada Television, a Northerner of great wit and charm combined with a rare modesty. He had been one of the earliest scriptwriters on *Coronation Street*, one of the talents who laid the foundations for that show's stupendous success by moulding some of the greatest characters in television history. From there, over a period of some 15 years, he had progressed to become the *Street's* script editor, producer and finally executive producer. By the time he saw me in *Cat in the Bag*, however, he was coming to the end of his association with the programme. Like many creative people who had moved into management, he longed to go 'back on the road' as a writer. And, surprise, surprise, he wanted to try his accomplished hand at comedy.

Before breaking through into television, Harry had spent some 25 years selling insurance and had observed, with his then frustrated writer's eye, the goings on in that industry. Door-to-door insurance salesmen, who visited lonely housewives week by week to collect their dues, had, like milkmen, gained a reputation for supplying more than their professional services. For some time, Harry had been turning over in his mind the possibilities of basing a comedy series on such a character, a man who, although approaching middle age, still had the silver tongue and the scheming mind to sell himself as well as his insurance policies to lady customers. As I was to learn later, that character came alive in his mind when he saw me that night at the Palace Theatre. Just why I cannot imagine!

Working with the Welsh director Eric 'Taffy' Prytherch, who had been one of his collaborators on *Coronation Street*, he eventually approached me and asked if I would take the, as yet, un-named part. At this point, the series did not even have a title although a pilot show — a one-off programme designed to gauge public reaction — was being put together under the name *Happy Days*. Would I play the lead role, whoever he would eventually be? This, perhaps surprisingly, presented me with something of a quandary.

After all these long lean years, and at the cost of untold hardship for my family, I had finally made it back to the top as a serious actor. I was being offered lead roles in demanding drama although, I admit, I was also performing a lot of dross in between. Did I really want to go back into comedy? This was an extremely difficult decision, yet another turning point, and I hesitated for some time. I might have turned it down completely apart from two considerations, one obvious, the other more personal. The first and obvious point was that here I was being offered my first leading role in a *series* (I had absolutely no doubt that with Harry's track record, the pilot programme would be converted into such). That meant regular work and constant exposure to the public for the first time since the *Great Scott It's Maynard* days, and I remembered only too well the rewards that such exposure could attract away from television.

The second, more private, consideration can be put down to Harry Kershaw's unique charm. Not only was he one of the most respected writers in the business but he was also totally lacking in personal ego. He actually invited suggestions from the actors. More than that, he believed in creating a team, in which everyone could have his or her say on what they considered best for the show. In addition to all this, I was invited in on the ground floor, when the pilot was still in its birth pangs, and I was welcomed to help with the delivery. After long talks with Muriel and Richard Stone, I decided to go ahead: this, after all, was comedy acting, not stand-up comicry, and as I have said *ad nauseum*, all actors, however distinguished, long to play comedy at some point in their careers.

The pilot went out under the name *Happy Days* and, as I had expected, was well received. But we did not like the title for the series and tussled for some weeks to find a new one (my suggestion, in view of the insurance angle, was the *Policy of Being Frank*, but this was one of the few ideas that Harry and Taffy rejected). In fact, after several months, my character did not have a surname, just Frank. Then someone christened him Frank Riley and we had our title: *The Life of Riley*. And so we got down to the serious work of producing a seven-episode comedy series which, I can say categorically, is not that funny. In fact, at times, it can be positively infuriating. This is partly due to the way that such series are made and partly due to the curious demands made by having to be funny on schedule — and a very tight schedule at that.

—oOo—

A modern television studio is an enormously complex and crushingly expensive place. The cost of the equipment involved runs into tens of millions of pounds and the people who operate that equipment are extremely well paid. Even with a studio like Granada, one of the world's most successful independent television makers, that studio time must be shared out with great care between many competing productions. Because studio time is money, very big money indeed, producers quite rightly insist that programmes are nigh on perfect before they go before the cameras. That means rehearsal, lots and lots of rehearsal, but this can create its own problems, particularly for people trying to be funny.

Even before rehearsals proper start, there has been weeks of work: script meetings, read-throughs, costume and set design, script rewrites and more meetings. Then there is the set to be 'blocked-out' to see where various props must go. Only then do the actors begin to rehearse. After many more hours of this, any script can begin to sound distinctly unfunny. This is the stale period, the danger period for actors, because to be funny you have to *feel* funny and, before the deep probing lens of a television camera, a lack of conviction is communicated to the viewers in an instant. These stale moments came inevitably to *The Life of Riley,* even though it was one of the happiest shows I have ever worked on, and here I was able to make a positive contribution from lessons learned in my repertory days.

Back in the Playhouse days in Nottingham, Frank Dunlop had taught me some revered old theatre exercises for blowing away the staleness of long rehearsals. One of them involved the actors running through their parts at top speed, with no dramatic pauses and no break between various actor's speeches. This is a good method of ensuring that everyone knows their lines but can also bring some hilarious results. Another exercise demands that the actors speak each other's lines but within the character they are actually playing on stage, another excuse for clowning and cock-up. But best of all, Frank taught me *Whoops.* The idea is simple, the result can be side-splitting. One simply says *Whoops* and bangs the floor with one's foot before every line:

"Whoops. Who was that lady I saw you with last night?"

"Whoops. That was no lady…"

"Whoops. That was my wife…"

Played this way, even *Hamlet* becomes a comedy. When we used it on *The Life of Riley* it was uproarious. We could feel the tensions, the pressures, draining away. We were funny again. There are some writers and directors who would treat such larking about with a distinct po-face. Harry Kershaw and Taffy Prytherch encouraged it and the whole production benefited. They encouraged ideas on the scripts, too, which allowed me as usual to make the occasional suggestion. One night over a drink, Harry turned to me and said:

"I feel I should tell you, Bill, that I'm thinking of asking for an additional dialogue credit."

"That's a nice idea, Harry," I said, "but I don't really want one."

To which he replied with a twinkle: "It's not for you — it's for me."

The Life of Riley was a smash hit. It went to Number One in the ratings and actually took over from *Coronation Street* as the most popular show on the box. This was a result which, I think, shocked even Granada; under normal circumstances, their ultimate soap was knocked out of the Number One spot only by events like the Cup Final or Royal weddings. But it was not to last; things were changing in the Manchester hierarchy and for reasons which I still find difficult to understand, *Riley* was taken off after a single series. Harry and I were invited to do another one some time later, but it was pointed out by Granada's new head of comedy, Brian Armstrong, that, this time, I would not be allowed to change the script and would have no say in casting. I turned then down. Other things were afoot...

—oOo—

Being back on the box in leading roles had, as I expected, brought the offers pouring in, not just for television and theatre but for cabaret, too. People who had not picked up the phone for almost 20 years began to approach Richard Stone with bookings for cabaret spots. They were offering sums like a £1,000 a night for me to appear once again as a stand-up comic. This, financially, was the light at the end of a long dark tunnel, the opportunity to once again acquire security with, this time, the avowed intention of holding on to it. Trouble was, after years as an actor, I had forgotten how to do a stand-up act.

I discovered this to my cost at a major charity concert in Leeds where I had agreed to act as compere for a cast of top-liners that included Bill Dainty, Millicent Martin and Frankie Vaughan. All I had to do was introduce them. But a strange piece of dialogue between myself and Millie shook me to the core, for it brought home just how wide the gulf between variety and straight theatre had become for me. I was discussing how I should open the show and asked simply:

"Do you want me to go on from the side of the stage or should I come through the curtains?"

"Curtains?" admonished Millie. "The word is tabs."

And so it is: in variety, curtains are called tabs. In the theatre, they are called curtains. In a simple piece of trade talk, I had demonstrated just how far my professional life had changed. I knew fine well what tabs were. I had just forgotten the word. I was an actor now, not a comic, and for the first time in my life on stage my self-confidence crashed. I could not go on, I said. I did not

blicity still from the early 1960s.

In *You Too Can Have a Body*. The other male is Peter Byrne, who played Andy Crawford in *Dixon of Dock Green*.

Another scene from the same play – *You Too Can Have a Body* – this time on Australian TV.

Buttons in the pantomime *Cinderella* in 1961.

Playing Frank Harris in *The Bashful Genius* at Nottingham Playhouse in 1964. The other character is played by George Sewell.

As Justice Squeezum in
*Lock Up Your
Daughters.*

Back at
Nottingham
Playhouse, this
time as Bottom i
*A Midsummer
Night's Dream.*

...aying Big Daddy in *Cat On A Hot Tin Roof* at Derby Playhouse.

As Archie Rice in *The Entertainer* at the Royal Lyceum Theatre in the spring of 1969.

Sergeant Pepper in *Crete And Sergeant Pepper* at the Royal Court in 1972.

Breakthrough: as Clarence Hubbard in Dennis Potter's *Paper Roses*.

know what to do, I said. This caused some consternation backstage: Bill Maynard, frozen? Who had ever heard of such a thing? Finally, someone thrust a programme in my hand and, using it as a prop, I managed to stagger through the show. But I kept my eyes on the programme and barely looked at the audience all evening. I had fallen victim to the trait I had always scorned: I was using the audience as the Fourth Wall.

The following day, I made a panic phone call to Richard Stone. If I wanted to take more of these highly-lucrative cabaret dates, I explained, I would have to relearn my stand-up craft. And, living up to my long-time belief, I blurted out: "Could you get me some Butlins dates so that I can brush up my act?" Richard, I assume, must have thought I was having one of my funny turns again but he took me at my word. Almost. Instead of a 'few' he booked me 26 weekend dates at Butlins camps throughout the country. At £65 a time. I was to relearn old skills, of course, but it was to cost me a pretty penny…

Once again it was from the sublime to the ridiculous because, months before, I had contracted to do a major film called *Robin and Marian*, a Robin Hood-style adventure with some very big names indeed: Sean Connery as Robin, Audrey Hepburn as Marian, and Richard Harris as Richard the Lionheart. I was to play the king's bodyguard and it was very flattering to be in a company of such superstars. Only trouble was, the film was being shot on location in Spain and I was also contracted to do six months of weekend dates in the UK. Another fine mess…

Every Friday night when filming was done, I would be driven to Balboa Airport where I would catch a flight to London. Muriel would meet me at Heathrow and drive me to wherever I was due to appear — and the Butlins empire stretched as far as Ayr in Scotland. There, on Saturday and Sundays, I would do half a dozen spots, and then Muriel would drive me back to London. Then it was the early morning plane back to Bilbao and a long drive to the location. I had done it before, of course, by bus and train to make *'Till Death*, but at least in those days I was making a profit. This time, I was going all that way for £65 and, as far as I can remember, the air fares alone cost some £200.

One weekday evening over a drink, Richard Harris looked at me quizzically with those big blue eyes and asked in his broad Irish brogue: "Tell me this Bill, just where do you dash off to every weekend?"

He winked. He seemed to assume that I had a hot young woman stashed away somewhere. "You won't believe this, Richard," I blushed, "but I'm booked to do 26 shows at Butlins and I can't get out of it."

It was patently obvious that he did not believe me. But then, who would?

This was not what most people understand by living the Life of Riley and by the end of both film and Butlins tour I was virtually a physical wreck. But Frank Riley had done me one enormous favour. I sent off the cheque that, after years of near misery, paid off my debt to HM Inspector of Taxes. The millstone was gone. I vowed that it would never return.

Chapter Twenty-One

What a Life

ONE dark evening in 1973, I found myself on a train from Manchester to London with *Life of Riley* director Taffy Prytherch and Anne Wilkie-Millar, a top Granada production assistant who was — and still is — something of a legend in her own right, one of these people in television who do not get a lot of the glory but whose work is quite crucial: PAs are the people who mother-hen any production, making sure that everyone is where he or she should be at the right place at the right time when the cameras are ready to roll. Not an easy task when there tends to be an anarchic streak in many of the creative people involved. Anne was and still is, I believe, one of the cogs which has kept the *Coronation Street* machine turning smoothly over something like 30 years.

Yet despite this interesting company, I was not a happy man. The trip to London was, in itself, something of a bind and strange things had been happening in my life, both on the *Riley* set and at home back in Sapcote.

For a start, there had been rows back at home. My daughter Jane had now left school but had still to settle into the modelling career she had chosen. And night after night, she was leaving home by herself and going off to London, to do what I did not know. There is perhaps a good deal of hypocrisy involved in the relationship between any father and daughter and for pretty obvious reasons: fathers know how young men look upon young women and I perhaps knew better than most. I assumed that Jane had a boyfriend in London and I was far from pleased that she was spending so much time with him but never brought him home. Was something amiss? Apart from anything else, I kept asking Muriel, where was she getting the money for all this gadding about?

Muriel was, by this time, totally in control of the family finances: I had learned my lesson the hard way and realised that I was totally unfit to be in charge of the purse strings. Muriel kept the books, paid the bills, ensured that the taxman was paid and doled out living money for me whenever I needed it. Our financial worries were by now largely over but I still did not like the idea of a teenage girl shuttling back and forwards from London, for I knew only too well the cost involved. This had led to rows with Jane, who seemed to becoming increasingly irritated, but I put this down to typical teenage tantrums. Trouble was, this friction seemed to be getting to Muriel, too, and she was acting tense and withdrawn, something which I had rarely seen, even in our worse days in the showbusiness wilderness.

I would have been less worried had I known about the activities of my son, Martin, now launched on a promising career as a musician. Like me as a lad, he had shown a remarkable aptitude in learning to play a variety of musical instruments and he now had a regular spot as a singer with the Ken Macintosh band at the Hammersmith Palais, the famous London ballroom. As it happened, I had once worked with Ken in my brief fling as a band singer and was still close friends with both him and one of his former musicians, Denny Piercey, who was now working as a stand-up comic. One of his jobs was to do the warm-ups for the *This is Your Life* programme, telling a few jokes to get the audience in the mood for when the studio lights came on and the programme went out live. I spoke to Ken from time to time on the phone and, naturally enough, asked him how Martin was getting on. I suppose most parents glean information about their offsprings' activities this way, but in recent weeks, Ken had seemed curiously reticent on this subject.

Had he told me that, night after a night when the Palais closed, Martin was being picked up by a chauffeur-driven Daimler and whisked off to God knows where, the hypocrisy would no doubt have turned its other face: I would have assumed that Martin had found himself a young lady and good luck to him! This state of affairs had, inevitably, caused a good deal of gossip among the other musicians but Ken, in his wisdom, had decided to conceal the fact from me. So matters were somewhat strained on the family front and peculiar things were happening at work too.

I had a great friend on the *Riley* team, the actor John McElvey, who had appeared with me in the successful run of the play *Crete and Sergeant Pepper* at the Royal Court Theatre in London — in fact I had recommended him for *Riley*. Yet for some reason, John had taken a couple of episodes off and had gone off to Norway to make a film. It was this absence which brought about this evening trip to London for, as Taffy had explained to me, there was a *Riley* scene between John and I which needed to be re-shot and the only way that it could be done was for John to fly to London overnight, for us to shoot a street scene, and fly back to Oslo the following day.

This was something of a pain but Taffy had ensured my agreement by a subtle piece of blackmail: if, of course, it was too much trouble, we could write John out of the episode completely. He was convinced that I would not allow something that could possibly damage a friend's career and he was right. I agreed, rather grumpily, to do the overnight scene and here we were, sitting in a packed first-class carriage, me reading the script for the new scene. I was appalled.

Riley was, as I have said, written by Harry Kershaw, one of television's most talented and respected scriptwriters. Yet here in front of me were couple of pages of total bilge. "I'm not doing this — it's absolute rubbish," I roared. "I'll have to rewrite it myself." So I got out a pen and began to slash away furiously at the script. Anne Wilkie-Millar, who had witnessed many a scene like this in her years of shepherding temperamental actors, seemed particularly nervous. Perhaps we should have dinner in the dining car, she suggested, and talk it through over some food and a bottle of wine?

Somewhat ashamed of my outburst, I reluctantly agreed. The dining car was almost empty except for a group of four who followed us in and chose to take the table directly behind us. This also concerned me somewhat; with plenty of space available, I assumed they had recognised me and had chosen to sit there to earwig on our conversation. The meal began badly, with me still complaining about the script, and Taffy did all he could to indulge me, agreeing to any changes I suggested in a way which, had I been more alert, might have aroused my suspicions. As the food came and a bottle of wine went down, I began to calm down. I asked for a coffee and decided to enjoy a brandy, too.

Anne began to look even more unhappy: "I think we should get back to our seats."

"No," I said. "We're comfortable enough here. Let's finish our drinks."

Silence.

Anne: "We'll be arriving soon. We should go and get our bags."

Me: "They'll be all right where they are."

Silence.

Anne: "I"ve left my handbag back there. It could get stolen."

Me: "It'll be all right."

Anne: "Please, Bill. I'm worried."

Me: "Oh all right then..."

Back in a bad mood, we trudged back up the train. I plonked myself ill-temperedly into my seat. Then a blinding flash went off. I jerked upright, shielding my eyes against the glare, and suddenly men were climbing over the backs of seats towards me, pushing things which looked like weapons in my direction.

I was, to say the least, terrified. I thought we were being hi-jacked.

Campaigns by several different terrorist groups were at their height in the early 1970s. In those awful seconds, I thought I must have become caught up on one of their operations. Then a very large man pushed his way into the seat beside me and an Irish voice spoke to me among all the noise, the bustle, and the glare of the lights.

It said: "Bill Maynard, This is Your Life..."

Shielding my eyes and blinking more wildly than Claude Greengrass was ever to do, I looked up at the figure towering above me and into perhaps the most famous Irish face in the world at the time, Mr Eamonn Andrews, CBE. And in his hand was the famous red book. My first words on that programme were: "You bastards ...I'm going to kill my wife for this."

—oOo—

I have been asked a thousand times what it is like being the subject of *This Is Your Life*. No one word can describe it. It is is paralysing, moving, terrifying, joyous, sad, funny and tense, a mixture of emotions that, frankly, tend to register only later. For most of the programme you are simply numb, asking yourself: "Is this a dream, a nightmare, or is it really happening to me?" If I had to choose just one word to describe the making of the programme, I would give it the ultimate accolade, *professional.*

The most repeated question is: "Did you really not know it was going to happen?" and, in my case, the answer to that was a most definite no. But it was those very demands of secrecy that had, for some weeks, pushed both my private and professional lives to the very brink of turmoil. The *Life* producers have a strict rule that, should a subject — *victim* is perhaps a better word — gather even the slightest whiff of the fact that a programme is being made, it is instantly cancelled. They believe, and rightly so, that those few opening seconds, when the shocked subject is first shown the red book, are crucial to the rest of the programme; the surprise, the shock, set the scene and if viewers were to have the slightest suspicion that this is being feigned, then the show is flat on its back before it has even got onto its feet. There are virtually no lengths to which they will not go in order to preserve the secrecy and the resultant surprise. In my case, those included lies, subterfuge, conspiracy and even downright blackmail. Unusual ingredients, perhaps, for the creation of a family show, but they all went together to stir up a potent brew.

As I was to find out in detail later, as I ruefully put together all the little clues I had missed, I discovered that I myself had put the whole show at risk because of my own nosy personality. Those rows with my daughter, for instance, over those secretive trips to London. They had not been made to visit an illicit boyfriend but to meet with the *Life* researchers. She had filled them in with family background, giving names and addresses and family anecdotes, and taken them to meet people like my mother and father who were to appear on the show. Yet I had nagged her for weeks, to such a point that she finally had a blazing row with Muriel saying, "If he has just one more go at me, I'm going to tell him."

It took all her mother's great diplomatic skills to smooth out that particular turbulence but Muriel, anyway, was up to the neck in the conspiracy herself. Once again, I had added to her stress by unknowingly probing into opening wounds. I had, secretly, longed for Eamonn Andrews to walk into my life because I believed I did have quite a story to tell. But my friendship with Denny Piercey had exacerbated the situation because he would regale me with hilarious anecdotes about the shows where he had warmed-up the audience. This had led to a regular joke in my life when, in the middle of some domestic conversation at home, I would open, say, a cupboard door and say, "It's all right, Eamonn, you can come in now." In recent weeks, I had failed to notice Muriel going pale.

One day, however, I nearly wrecked the whole programme and, at the same time, caused a blazing row between my wife and my close friend, the said Denny Piercey. Muriel, as I have already mentioned, was an accomplished seamstress — she even made the costumes for an entire pop group which Martin had founded. One day, I walked in to find her working intently on a rather elaborate green evening dress.

"That's nice," I said. "You can wear that for my *This is Your Life*."

Once again, I must have missed the going pale bit because, as Muriel told me indignantly later, her heart had dropped like a stone. As soon as I had gone, she put in a furious phone call to Denny, asking him why he had let the cat out of the bag. For Denny, this was particularly distressing, for he was at risk on two counts: losing a close friend and probably his job, too, because anyone on the *Life* team who did break the code of silence was immediately asked to look for another occupation. To this day, I do not know if Denny or Ken Macintosh were aware of the reason behind those chauffeur-driven Daimler trips that Martin had been taking after finishing at the Palais. Far from having a rich lady lover, he was in fact being whisked off all over the country to introduce *Life* researchers to other potential guests on the programme. If Denny did know, he most certainly did not mention it to me. Muriel's angry phone call left him shell-shocked with the injustice of it all. My flip remark about the dress had been a total shot in the dark, a bit of banter which, by pure fluke, had hit the bull's eye. Muriel, of course, apologised profusely to Denny when she learned the truth.

This monster that had infiltrated my family did not stop there, however. My colleagues at Granada in Manchester were also drawn into the conspiracy and there, if anything, the subterfuges were even more elaborate than at home. Which is why I happened to be on that particular train that particular night, an innocent puppet whose strings were being pulled by dozens of invisible hands.

John McElvey was in the plot, of course, although he was never to fly back from Oslo to shoot that mythical retake. Taffy Prytherch, with his devious Celtic mind, had concocted the blackmail plot to ensure that I would not refuse to make the fateful journey; he knew fine well that by threatening to write John out of the show I would be left with no alternative but to go along. I doubt, however, that Taffy could have believed that his part in the drama would lead to grievous insults, for it was he, not Harry Kershaw, who had written the never-to-be scene which I had so-lambasted on the train. It was rubbish, of course, but Taffy had not put much effort into it; he knew it was never to be recorded. And Anne Wilkie-Millar, that ever present cool head, had been drawn in as a back-stop should anything go terribly wrong.

But it did not stop there. All those fellow passengers in the open first-class compartment were in fact trained technicians: cameramen, sound recordists, lighting experts, focus pullers, a complete studio on wheels, all with their equipment carefully stowed as innocent-looking luggage. When I had been lured down to the dining compartment for a long, leisurely meal, they had frantically begun to assemble their equipment, then hide it under the seats for my return, to spring into action the moment Eamonn, who had boarded the train at Watford, took out the red book.

To assemble this crew, in itself, must have been a major operation, for I did not know one of them. Should I have recognised someone, that might have given the game away. Considering the years I had spent in television studios throughout the UK, to assemble a complete crew of total strangers must have been a fearsome feat of planning. Even the four people who had so annoyed me by sitting at the next table in the dining car were plants. Their job, I learned later, was to stop me should I have decided to walk back to the compartment during the meal while the technicians were assembling their equipment. Just how they planned to do that I am not quite sure; there was some talk of engaging me in conversation and asking for autographs. In the mood I was in at the time, that was a ploy that would have met short shrift. Perhaps they had chloroform, handcuffs and a gag in their kit, too.

When it comes to covert operations, the SAS seem to be pretty good at their job. But next time the British Government needs to lift an embassy siege, they might consider sending in the *This Is Your Life* team. It would be cheaper and a lot less messy, for those guys could out-con any terrorist gang in the world.

—oOo—

But it did not stop, even there. Once that initial confrontation with Eamonn Andrews was on film, I was virtually under armed guard. The reason: they did not want to me to get a glimpse of any of the guests about to appear on the show in order to keep the surprise element going. When we arrived at Euston, I was escorted to a waiting limousine by uniformed security men, whisked around the corner to the Euston TV studios, and led into an underground labyrinth of dressing rooms. There were more security men at the junction of every corridor and I was finally thrust into a huge dressing room and the door clanked shut behind me. With another security man standing guard outside the door, I felt that I was back in the cells at Glasgow Central.

Here, there was more evidence of Muriel's work. Laid out were four or five neatly pressed suits so that I could choose what to wear for the following show. There were matching shirts and ties, socks and shoes, even cuff links, everything a man could need. With one exception: there was no loo! Since that first blinding flash on the train, I had not been alone for a single second and even I take exception about going to the lavatory accompanied. I hammered on the door and the burly security guard opened it.

"Sorry," I said, "but I must go to the loo."

The guard looked suspicious: was I trying to make a break for it?

"I've got to go," I begged.

He finally gave a critical little grunt, then summoned one of his mates from the end of the corridor. Together, they escorted me to the lavatory and stood guard outside. Then they marched me back. The door slammed behind me. All in all, an odd sort of start to one of the major experiences of a lifetime.

The strange thing is that I can remember very little about the show itself. I was, as I said, too numb to let much of it sink in. It started with the film of my encounter with Eamonn on the train. Then, the audience having been well warmed-up by my long-suffering mate Denny, the guests spoke a few words behind a curtain and then came on to the stage. It was, of course, live, something I had not done for many years, but the 30 minutes flashed by in what seemed like seconds. Mum and Dad were there, of course, and Muriel and the children, a little reward I hope for all they had suffered to get the show on screen.

Terry Scott was away filming but sent a funny tribute on film. Then came my old mentors: Jon Pertwee; Frank Dunlop, who talked about the Nottingham Playhouse days; friends like Johnny Greenaway, the jockey. John Neville, with whom I had extracted laughs from Shakespeare, was flown in from Canada as my surprise guest — he was running a highly-successful arts centre over there. What I remember most was the after-show party. They had laid on a sumptuous spread in the studio commissary, with champagne, smoked salmon and all the rest. To have all these people together in the same room was almost as important as the show itself. Then, after about an hour, the producer announced that they were to run the programme again. I sat down and watched it as if for the first time and, I admit, there were tears in my eyes.

This may seem on the sentimental side, but so what? Mine can be a highly sentimental trade, which can sometimes recompense for all the hard knocks it also hands out. This, after all, was a tribute to me made at considerable expense and with almost unbelievable cunning by some of best professionals in the business (although I received more of the cunning than the expense: my fee, I recall, was £50!). This was a tribute by fellow professionals and from friends and family, too, which is a pretty heady combination. It never crossed my mind all that long evening to say no and refuse to do the show as, I understand, have one or two potential subjects. Why they did that I shall never understand unless, perhaps, they had been better than I at picking up the clues and had decided against doing the show with the benefit of foresight.

To me, that verges on the churlish, for hopefully these shows give millions of viewers half an hour of pleasure, too, and that after all is the *raison d'etre* for all showbusiness. There are a lot of lonely people out there desperately in need of a little cheering up. I know that from the hundreds of letters I received after the show. To watch *This Is Your Life* makes them feel part of a family, too.

If any is needed, that seems to me to be justification enough for lies and subterfuge, conspiracy, blackmail and stress. Muriel, incidentally, never wore that green dress she was making. It went in the bin unfinished. Instead, she went out and bought herself an extremely expensive gown. Once again, opening my big mouth had cost be a great deal of money. This time, it was worth every penny.

Chapter Twenty-Two

Magic!

THERE IS a much-loved character in Sapcote called Peter Wright, who is as ordinary a working man as one could ever meet: he makes his living doing heavy labouring jobs like digging holes in the road and other such manual tasks. An unlikely candidate, one might think, to become the stereotype for one of the most popular characters ever to appear on British television, and even more unlikely as the progenitor of a couple of phrases which, for half a decade or so, were to become an everyday part of the English language.

Peter, despite his working man status, is like many of his type: he has a shrewd, rather wry, attitude to life and by the mid-1970s he had become one of my closest friends. Up until then, his one claim to fame was that he was a long-serving, hard-working member of the committee at the Sapcote Working Men's' Club. Peter attacks everything in life with great gusto. As a man of formidable strength, he throws darts so hard that only *he* can pull them out of the board. When he plays cheese skittles, that ancient Leicester pub game I described earlier, he hurls them so hard that they have been known to bounce off the table, over the safety net which is supposed to prevent such things happening, and knock holes in the walls and ceiling. On our cheese skittles forays around various pubs and clubs, he will point to a dent in the ceiling and say, "See that — I did that in 1966." His most famous exploit in this field was to clear the entire top shelf of a pub bar, sending bottles of whisky, gin, rum etc, showering across the bar in a scene straight from a film brawl in a Western saloon.

This vibrant enthusiasm goes into his work as a committee member, too, and he is a great force for organising special 'do's' and raising money for charity. His heart is always in the right place but sometimes his over-enthusiasm leads to confusion and much shaking of heads by other committee members who find Peter's pace of doing things hard to keep up with. It was this ferocious energy, coupled with an ever-present desire to help other people, that led me in my Nottingham Playhouse days to use him as a model for my playing of Bottom, the over-enthusiastic comic figure in Shakespeare's *A Midsummer Night's Dream*.

In the mid-1970s, Duncan Wood, my former producer of *Great Scott It's Maynard*, had become head of comedy at BBC Television and, after the success of *Riley*, he asked me if I had any ideas for a new comedy series. That concentrated my mind on a project I had been toying with for some years, to create a modern-day Bottom character in a contemporary setting. As a great believer in that adage, 'write about what you know about', I began to build in my mind a series set in a working men's club. With that idea in place, a character based loosely on Peter Wright became irresistible. Nothing happened.

Television is a curious medium in that it can create new heroes overnight, yet the ingestion period for the birth of those heroes can cover many months or even years. To get a series on the box usually means attracting the approval of one person, usually a producer or a top-rated writer, which when you have long-established contacts like mine is not overly difficult. But that is only Step One. The producer involved must then take the ball and run with it through a series of committees which he must convince of the likely success of the venture. These committees have to agree to invest very considerable amounts of time and money in a project that could turn out to be abject failure. So they tend to err on the side of caution.

After what must have been a couple of years or so, I telephoned Duncan Wood and asked him if there was any progress on my long-conceived baby. No, he said, but he was soon to move to a new job as head of comedy at Yorkshire Television. After such a length of time, would I be prepared to hold on for a few more months to see if YTV were prepared to do it? Although I did not know it, this was to be the start of a long and highly successful relationship with the Leeds-based company.

Yet more months passed and then I got the call I had been hoping for: YTV wanted to do a pilot of the WMC show and had been talking it over with yet another writer of great distinction, Roy Clarke, a Yorkshireman whose credits include *Open All Hours* and *Last of the Summer Wine*. Roy needed some background assistance with the WMC scene, with which he was not very familiar, and apart from anything else, they needed a title. Would I like to go up to Leeds and talk it over with Roy? I was on the train in a flash.

After those initial meetings, it was Roy Clarke who finally came up with the title: *Oh No, It's Selwyn Froggitt,* a name he dreamed up from God knows where. The character I had based on my mate Peter Wright had finally got a name and more, for two of Peter's pet sayings were about to become national catch-phrases: "Magic!" — with the accompanying double thumbs-up sign — and: "A pint of cooking and a bag of nuts," which was Selwyn's regular lunch at Scarsdale WMC (he had read in *The Times* that a bag of nuts contained more protein than a pound of beef steak and, as he said, "You don't have to do the washing up.").

To have Selwyn as a regular reader of *The Times* was another suggestion of mine and it is, I feel, a good example of what one does to build a convincing comic character. Peter Wright had been my original inspiration, of course, but one does not normally create a complete television character based on a single person, however endearing. Peter laid the foundations: on those we built what was in fact a very complex character. I wanted Selwyn to be more than just a lovable bear-like character whose wild over-enthusiasm regularly led him from disaster to disaster. Despite his lack of formal education, I wanted him to be intelligent, too, always anxious to improve himself. The easy route would have been to use the old clichés, like Malapropisms and Spoonerisms, but that would have made the character too one-dimensional. By getting him to read *The Times* and be an ardent student of dynamic word power, we gave him the breadth to spread the comedy over a wide range of subjects (although, alas, he did sometimes use some examples in quite the wrong context). We wanted people to laugh *with* him, not *at* him.

This is one of the golden rules of comedy that goes back through the centuries as far as the court jester. He was there to make people laugh, of course, but he was often the only person at court who could poke fun at the king. For other courtiers to do so would have put them at risk of, at best, exile from court circles or, at worst, an appointment with the axeman. The jester was allowed to get away with it as a figure of fun but that did not mean his jokes against the king were censored of pointed reference to policy matters, thin ice on which no other dared to tread.

In other words, all good comedy has a solid centre of truth. As entertainments secretary at Scarsdale WMC (a post Peter Wright never held in Sapcote, although he has been a committee member for years), Selwyn Froggitt, bumbler that he was, often made the other more worldly members of the committee face realities they would rather avoid. His reading *The Times* did, however, give us plenty of opportunity for good lines. After studying the advertisements for classical music concerts in London, Selwyn would one day suggest to the committee: "We've got to get the stage made wider and strengthened because we're going to have the London Symphony Orchestra, Sir Yehudi Menuhin ...and five houses of bingo." He was a wonderful character, Selwyn Froggitt, who because of his eternal willingness to take on any job and his relentless appetite for hard work, was always being cynically exploited by other members of the committee. Despite this, Roy Clarke's original script was somewhat at odds with the original concept and we met to discuss some rewriting. Now no one can doubt Roy's ability to create great characters — Compo, Norah Batty, Smiler, Auntie Wainwright and many others in *Summer Wine* alone testify to that — but at that meeting he admitted that he had difficulty in writing about situations he had not cultivated himself in his own fertile mind. Being the professional he is, he decided that he was not right for the job and asked me if I could find another writer. Now this was a serious crisis: we had high hopes for a long and successful series, but no one to write it. What to do?

As I mentioned in a previous chapter, I had worked on a rather different comedy series, the Chaucer spoof *Trinity Tales*, written by Alan Plater, another Yorkshireman, whose forte until then had been hard-hitting drama like *Z-Cars* and the adaptation of serious literary novels for television. *Trinity Tales*, about a group of Wakefield Trinity Rugby League fans making their way to the Wembley Cup Final, had been filmed in the most difficult circumstances. Most of the action had taken place inside a cramped mini-coach and that had caused almost unbelievable technical problems.

For a start, the soundman had been forced to lie on the floor of the van, out of view of the cameras, which made recording extraordinarily difficult: we, the actors, were cramped enough, so what this poor technician was suffering we could only guess. But at least we had a soundman; there was no space for the luxury of a lighting technician so we had to hold small spotlights ourselves, clutching them in our hands below seat level and lighting ourselves as we said the lines. In such circumstances, almost all the dialogue was in close-up and, as I explained earlier about my first screen kiss in *Kisses at Fifty*, a television camera virtually poked up one's nostrils is the most demanding, all-seeing, flaw-finding scrutiny any actor can face. This, I can assure readers, is not the ideal way to bring out the best in a performer but despite these problems, the making of *Trinity Tales* had been a deeply satisfying professional experience.

Much of this had been due to Alan Plater's wonderful scripts, which is a great compliment to the breadth of the man's talents. The leap from the grim reality of *Z-Cars* to *Trinity Tales* had been an enormous one because writers, like comics, need that very special deft touch to make people laugh. Alan had made that leap with great élan. Would he be prepared to put his reputation on the line once more and put words into the mouth of Selwyn Froggitt, a character he had never yet heard of? We made contact and, after reading the pilot, he agreed, a matter of considerable delight for me because Alan is another of the truly outstanding screen writers who welcome suggestions from the cast.

And so Selwyn Froggitt came to the small screen, the result of much close co-operation between Alan Plater and myself. Selwyn was immediately taken to heart by the British public and was yet another series to overtake *Coronation Street* as Number One in the ratings. This was, of course, a major feather in the cap for Yorkshire Television which, only a few years before, had been created by the Government licensing authorities by splitting the Granada franchise. This, in the early days of independent television, had covered the whole of the North of England across both sides of the Pennines. For the White Rose to knock the Red Rose off the top of the television pedestal was, of course, a matter for considerable glee.

Selwyn was first broadcast in January 1976, on all ITV channels, and the programme notes printed in the TV guides went to some length to explain the meaning behind Roy Clarke's inimitable title: "He sticks his thumbs up and says, 'Magic!' Everyone else sticks his head down and says, 'Oh no, it's Selwyn Froggitt.'" The show was to have long-term consequences for me because is established beyond doubt that I was a leading actor with the range to tackle many different roles from the sophisticated, gin-sodden cynic Clarence in *Paper Roses,* to clumsy, lovable Selwyn, the beer-drinking, nut-eating perpetual optimist who would never stop trying whatever went wrong. I remember many great episodes of the show but one in particular stands out, one which stood this adage of art imitating life on its head. This was a case of art imitating art (if television can aspire to that rather grand word *art)* because it was once again sparked off by my own personal experience. It was the day when Selwyn Froggitt thought he was to become the subject for *This is Your Life.* The idea came from my own traumatic experience on that show and Alan Plater wove a parallel conspiracy. This time, however, it was to end in pathos. The episode opened with a producer from a local radio station arriving at the Scarsdale WMC hoping to see Selwyn, the entertainments secretary, to organise a quiz show to be staged at the club. Selwyn was not there, so the producer spoke to the club steward, played by Ray Mort, who agreed to pass on a message. When our hero finally arrives, he is told that a man from radio — or was it television? — had been looking for him. Selwyn's eyes widen with delight. Was he a big fellow? Did he have an Irish accent? Was he carrying a big red book? The steward says well, he did have some sort of accent, Irish or perhaps Scottish, and he was carrying something under his arm (a clip board, as it happened).

"That's it," says Selwyn, agog. "That was Eamonn Andrews."

Then, in one of the most Selwynesque lines in the entire series, he adds: "They don't always do big stars, you know. Sometimes they do unsung heroes. *And no one is more unsung than me.*"

This conversation is duly reported to members of the committee and, always ready for a laugh at the expense of their over-the-top colleague, they begin to create an elaborate conspiracy to keep the joke going. This leads Selwyn into a world of subterfuge as he goes around his family and friends searching for clues to confirm his suspicions, constant questions which leave those involved totally mystified. Finally, Selwyn cracks and tells his long-suffering mother that he is to be on *This is Your Life* that evening. It does not happen, of course. Selwyn goes off to the club full of hope, only to help in the radio quiz show recording but waiting expectantly for the big Irishman who never arrives. When he returns home devastated later that evening, his mother comes out with another pearl of dialogue.

"I watched *This Is Your Life*, Selwyn," she says. "It was the Archbishop of Canterbury. It was very nice — but it was a bit religious." His brother, seeing just how disappointed Selwyn is, tries to console him by saying perhaps he'll be on next week.

"I'm not bothered," says Selwyn. "I was glad they haven't done me. 'Cos once they've done you, there's nothing left to look forward to..."

That was typical Selwyn Froggitt, always making the best out of a bad job. But that final line, only slightly rewritten, I had said myself to Muriel after my real-life encounter with Eamonn Andrews. "Trouble is," I had said, "now they've done it, there's nothing to look forward to."

This, I think, is a brief answer for the hundreds of people who have asked me how I go about creating a character. First you take a model, then you work closely with the writer, and, hopefully, a convincing, living person will emerge. You elaborate and expand, of course, but when you reduce it to its barest skeleton, real life is always the best basis for fiction.

—oOo—

After *Selwyn Froggitt,* I would never look back again, professionally. In my private life, I had been close to both Clarence in *Paper Roses* and Selwyn, so I could play them both not just with conviction but with real understanding; once again, I had been there and done that! In a curious sort of way all the disappointments and aggravation of my own life were giving me the depth to tackle widely divergent roles. And in establishing a close bond with Yorkshire Television, I had started on the road that would eventually lead to another great character based in no small measure on my real life experiences: Claude Jeremiah Greengrass. That, however, was a long way in the future.

In the meantime, Selwyn Froggitt changed my private life, too. For years, in the car at traffic lights, in the pub over a drink, in a restaurant over a meal, people would spot me, hold up two thumbs, and mouth: "Magic!" It is as good a catch phrase as you could want because it expresses pleasure and hope, and even today it always brings a smile to my face. I had one problem, however: how would my mates at Sapcote WMC react to their real world being exaggerated and exploited before millions via the make-believe of television. I need not have worried.

Almost every time I went into the club, some member of the committee would take me aside and say gravely: "I just want you to know that I am very happy with the way I am being portrayed." To a man, they associated with the television *personae* and never once complained that they were being misrepresented in any way, which they most certainly were. That, I think, is a tribute to the plain common sense of the ordinary working man. As for Peter Wright, my Bottom turned Selwyn Froggitt, he became a celebrity himself for a while. The press discovered that he had been the real life model for Selwyn and came to interview and photograph him. Now this made me even more worried because these down-to-earth Leicestershire folk are not given to flamboyance and in the tiny world of Sapcote, the presence of the national press is not always welcome. They put up with it for me because, away from the cameras, I have always been one of them. For ordinary working folk to be dragged into the spotlight could, I feared, make them resentful. And Peter, as I have said, is a very strong bloke indeed.

The first night I was in the club after Selwyn had gone on air, Peter came looming up to me and slapped me around the back with a force that, if I had not braced myself in readiness, would have floored me. Then he gave me a bear hug round the shoulders that took my wind away. He smiled.

"Thanks a bunch, Bill," he said. "You've made me a star."

Peter and I still have a pint together on a regular basis and he still orders 'a pint of cooking and a bag of nuts'. More rarely, he still says, "Magic!" and sticks up his thumbs. This, to me, is the most critical audience I ever face, my friends at Sapcote WMC. To remain firm friends, after perhaps appearing to send them up so mercilessly, is one of the most gratifying experiences of my life. Good people, these Sapcote folk. I was proud, despite the fact that I was back in the money again, that they never changed their attitude towards me. And that means they have continued, to this day, with their merciless ribaldry at my expense.

—oOo—

Selwyn Froggitt brought stability and peace of mind at home, too. Once again we were financially secure and this time Muriel was keeping her sensible fingers tight on the purse strings. The children, now young adults, were building their own careers and Muriel and I were able to spend more and more time together. This was to be the happiest period of our lives together and this remarkable closeness, hewn out of so many troubles, became a talking point in showbusiness where, as anyone who reads the tabloid press knows, long and happy marriages are as rare as rebates from the tax man. The relationship was picked up by YTV PR department and during the Selwyn run, they issued the following press release:

Bill Maynard

There are two people in particular of whom one-time top comedian turned successful actor Bill Maynard took notice whilst Yorkshire Television's new situation comedy series, *Oh No, It's Selwyn Froggitt,* was in production.

One, naturally enough, was the producer and director, Ronnie Baxter. The other was ...his wife, Muriel.

For Muriel, married to Bill for 27 years, attended every dress rehearsal and frequently, after completing a scene, Bill went over her and asked quietly, "Was that all right?"

Bill explains: "Muriel goes to my dress rehearsals but never becomes involved in anything I do before that stage. Consequently, she is seeing the show afresh and can sometimes pick up faults and other things which could stand improvement better than those who have been working on it all the way through.

"It is not a case of Muriel being my sternest critic — but she is completely honest with me and is the one person I can really trust.

She isn't particularly experienced in the business but she can assess a production entirely independently as an average viewer would see it. And that, after all, is what it's all about."

These were the bare bones of the situation. What had happened, personally, is that Muriel and I had fallen back in love again, a mature, mutually-supportive love that transcended anything we had known before. It has been long held by many writers that true love can only grow through shared sufferings and, particularly in showbusiness, there are many examples to support the opposite reaction: rich, successful couples, whose main problem in life is knowing what to do with their immense wealth, often seem to become bored with each other and end up in the divorce court. As far as I can tell, the killer for those marriages seems to be boredom. And whatever can be said about our marriage, Muriel and I had never had time to be *bored*.

It is true that Muriel did catch a train Leeds every Friday to watch the *Selwyn* dress rehearsals but she did it, not out of some sense of duty, nor to act as some sort of overseer of my work. She did it because she loved it. She would have a day looking round the shops in Leeds, meet me for afternoon tea in the YTV canteen, and then we would go to the rehearsal together. During the performance, she never said a word nor would she ever have dreamt of doing so. Afterwards, I would go to her and ask what she thought. Most of the time she would say, "Great." But, on occasion, she would say, "I didn't understand that bit about so-and-so..."

Now here was the voice of the outsider, the representative of the average viewer. Many of the tiny faults she picked out had been caused by a script rewrite that had not been carried all the way through, so that a line of dialogue later in the episode was following an earlier line that had been cut and was therefore unexplained. Muriel picked on these with unerring accuracy, to the benefit of the show as a whole. A few changes would be made before recording, the audience would be welcomed on to the set, and off we would go.

These were the good times, the best of times. We did not know that they were soon to end...

Chapter Twenty-Three

All Good Things…

UNLIKE the sound working class folk of Sapcote, there are some people in television who can face in two directions at the same time. Whether actors, writers or producers, they fight like devils to get on to the box for the fame and fortune it brings. Once they are there, they adopt airs and graces and look down their noses at their fellow artistes and even at the medium itself: "Just passing the time here, Darling Luvvie. I should really be back in the theatre — the real theatre." There are not many of them, and most of those do not survive too long, but their presence can be poisonous to colleagues striving to do professional work.

I had met this syndrome before, when the Nottingham Playhouse was moving from its cozy old converted cinema to its multi-million-pound purpose built theatre, the types who thought that the public should be made to watch Shakespeare and the other classics, like it or lump it. Most modern drama, and comedy in particular, is strictly for the peasants. They take their pay with alacrity, of course, and conveniently close their minds to the fact that the money came in the first place from the audience's wallets. But having banked the cash, they deliver their part of the bargain with condescension, treating the audience — whether in the theatre or watching on television — with contempt. Many of them, it almost goes without saying, have come up the 'proper' way in the theatre, via the drama schools. To an old pro like me, who had risked all to get the training that had been handed to them on a plate, these people are anathema, the kiss of death to any company or show, however happy.

The 1970s had been a great decade for me, the time when I drew back from the abyss and re-established myself — and, more importantly, my family — both professionally and financially. As the decade began to draw to a close, I was thoroughly enjoying my work and *Selwyn Froggitt* was about to go into yet another series. Then one day I walked into the bar at the YTV studios in Leeds and stood behind a couple of the cast who were unaware of my arrival. As I waited to be served, I heard one of them, a woman, say to her partner: "I'll be glad when this dreadful series is over. I can't wait to get back to some decent drama..."

I walked round her to confront her and saw her face go ashen.

"You won't have to wait long, love," I said, "because you won't be in the next series."

It was time for a change. Many people wonder why actors willingly leave successful shows when the public, the studios and, in the case of ITV, the advertisers are demanding more. There is rarely any one single reason, rather a series of reactions which begin to set in more or less at the same time. The most important of these is that the writer begins to run out of ideas and in Selwyn's case, Alan Plater was in such demand that he was able to turn his hand to many other pet projects. Actors suffer similar pangs because, to keep a character alive, you must change him slowly but surely over many performances to retain elements of surprise and freshness. Otherwise, the character himself becomes stale and that could cause the public to lose interest. Then you get the disaffection among the company, as the overheard conversation in the bar had proved. It was time to lay Selwyn Froggitt to rest.

Having contracted to do one more series, Alan and I agreed that we needed a change of scene, that the Scarsdale WMC had become just a little hackneyed. So Selwyn got himself a job as the entertainments officer at a run-down holiday camp and off he went to the seaside. Needless to say, my Butlins experiences gave me a rich seam to dig in search of new humour and it also gave us the chance to create a new cast of supporting actors. My two friends at the bar were duly written out and I hope they enjoyed themselves back on the boards.

As with all Selwyn's adventures, it started badly and got worse. On the way to the camp, he manages to upset an irate Welshman on the bus by dropping his luggage on his head. It had become a running joke in the series that Selwyn had an unexplained but pathological dislike of the Welsh. But when he finally arrives to take up his exciting new post he finds, alas, that the man he had brained on the bus is in fact his new boss, the camp manager. After their first meeting, Selwyn storms out of the office, slams the door, and a great crack appears in its glass panel. On their next confrontation, the crack has been given a botched repair job with sticky paper. He slams the door again, and another crack appears. This was one of the best running gags of that last series because, by the end, the panel was no longer glass but a mass of sticky paper.

That much-abused door had become virtually a metaphor for the show. By now, both Alan and I were tiring of papering over the cracks, both figuratively and professionally. We decided that Selwyn Froggitt had nowhere else to go. It was a decision taken with regret, because it had been a joyful show to work on for the vast majority of its run. But, like sportsmen, we decided it was better to retire at the top rather than risk the slippery slope to oblivion. So where to go next?

Re-established now as a major player, I could possibly have been forgiven for taking a break at this point, to sit back and put my feet up and live off my newly-accumulated savings for a year or so while taking the odd plum role on the stage or cabaret to keep the coffers topped up. But the lad from Rat Alley was still there inside, starting immediately upon a new scheme once I had tired of the old one. A new scheme was afoot that was to intrigue and challenge me and, later, to prove an absolute Godsend. I was about to become a film maker in my own right — thanks to a famous potato crisp manufacturer in Leicestershire.

This was not, I should point out, a television commercial for potato crisps (although I have done such commercials, including playing the baker in one of those famous Hovis ads, which is still being repeated from time to time after a period of some 30 years). The crisp project was in fact a new venture in my life, a move into commercial video films which were then in their infancy. Major companies were beginning to realise that in-house videos, for training purposes or as part of a sales pitch, were a highly effective method of getting a message across. As a well-known television face, I was being to asked to star in such videos and the pay was very good. But my real interest in this new branch of the media lay not in front of the cameras...

For years now I had been working in front of camera and, I suppose, I had become pretty proficient at it. But in all that time, I had been taking a keen interest in what was going on behind the cameras, a fascination which had sparked on my very first day on the *'Till Death* set. I had watched directors, cameraman, lighting and sound technicians going about their business and, like many an actor before me, had begun to toy with the idea of becoming a director myself. As in everything else I had ever done, I realised that to put these years of observation into hands-on practice, I would have to learn many of the mysteries of the director's craft, skills like camera angles, film editing and all the other tricks in the magic box which turn light and sound into convincing images on screen. This new field of commercial videos, I decided, was where I could learn these skills, adding yet a another string to the Maynard bow. Soon, I was to set up my own video production company, Charterhouse Films, which was to serve a crucially important purpose in the most desperate years of my life. It could have made me rich. Instead, as I will reveal later, it was to keep me sane. Once again, the roller coaster of my life was poised for yet another sickening downwards swoop. This time, I was not to blame.

—oOo—

As it happened, my sojourn away from the small screen was to last only a matter of a few months. A script which, as is the way of these things, had been bouncing round the broadcasting world for a couple of years finally landed on a desk at Yorkshire Television, whose occupant's ears pricked up with interest. On quitting *Selwyn*, I had let it be known that, in future, I would like to do drama rather than comedy but would consider comedy if I thought it to be very good. The script of *The Gaffer* seemed to encompass both worlds.

This show had had a curious ingestion period even before its birth. It had been written by a then unknown, Graham White, whose family owned a small engineering firm in Derby. Quite rightly, Graham had written a short comedy about life in a fictitious engineering company but he had written it as a *radio* script for the BBC. There it had lain in some filing cabinet for a couple of years until Graham, finally losing patience, had asked for its return. Then, as a long shot, he had mailed it to the drama department at YTV with a question: would it have any potential as a TV play? The answer, the powers that be decided, was yes — but it needed a great deal of work.

This, remember, was the late 1970s before Margaret Thatcher had begun her war of attrition on the trades unions. Labour relations in Britain were an international bad joke. Many of our great industries were crumbling under a combination of militant trade unionism and bad management. The country had earned the nickname, 'The Sick Man of Europe', and at one stage striking grave-diggers even refused to bury the dead. This was fertile ground for a black sort of comedy, virtually a satire taking a small engineering company as a microcosm of the seething whole. *The Gaffer* seemed an opportunity to poke a finger of fun at this chaos, using humour like the court jesters of olden days as a weapon to point out the sheer folly of it all.

Trouble was, the script was not all that funny. It was brilliant in many other ways, hitting the nail directly on the head when it came to the absurd gulf between employer and employee, particularly when the employer concerned was a crooked, cunning old so-and-so with pressing financial problems that forced him to go to almost any lengths to keep his company afloat. That was the drama side of the show which appealed to me, the basis of truth which all good comedy must possess. But comedy, even black comedy, is wasted unless it actually makes people laugh: make them laugh first and then they might stay around long enough for the more serious message to sink in; fail to make them laugh and they switch to another channel.

YTV sent me the script and, like them, I could see the potential. I might do it, I said, but only if I could meet the writer and discuss first the transformation required to turn a radio play into a television series and, from then on, have the right to contribute ideas which would beef up the comedy. That meeting was duly arranged and Mr White, anxious to have his baby screened, agreed to my proposals. Believing that everyone was happy, I signed the contract.

The Gaffer was never to acquire the great success of *Riley* or *Selwyn Froggitt* but it did run to three series over a couple of years. One of the reasons for this was its transmission slot. Yorkshire had, at that time, made a lavish production of J.B. Priestley's *The Good Companions*, the glorious tale of a travelling theatre group, but other ITV companies were bickering about taking it. There was a lot of politicking and, as a compromise, it was decided that *The Gaffer* would go out in a pretty awful slot: mid-evening on Friday nights when, as everyone in TV knows, most of Britain is in the pub. The reason, I understand, was that the network hoped *The Gaffer* would encourage viewers to stay tuned to ITV for the rest of the evening programmes. Despite this, *The Gaffer* reached Number Three in the ratings, the first time, I believe, that a Friday night comedy had ever got into the Top Ten.

In this story of success against the odds, I hope my contribution was important. Apart from playing the part, I had gone to considerable lengths to develop Fred Moffatt, the Gaffer himself, into a believable character, using both my old skills as an actor and some newly acquired from my technical interest in my commercial video business.

One of our major problems had been to establish Fred as a chancer from the very opening scene. In this, my son Martin had unwittingly sown the seed. Martin by now had a busy career as a session musician and singer, darting around the London recording studios for an hour here, half an hour there, recording a few bars and then rushing off to the next session. To help him meet this hectic schedule, he had borrowed one of my cars and, one day when I got into it, I saw that the back seat was awash with parking tickets, 20 or 30 of them still pristine in their un-opened plastic covers.

"Don't worry about those, Dad," said Martin chirpily. "It's a hazard of the trade. I pay them off in job lots whenever I get the time."

This, I thought, was an ideal scene-setter for *The Gaffer*. So the show started with a shot of Fred Moffatt climbing into his battered old Rover outside the Queen's Hotel in Leeds city centre and throwing yet another unopened parking ticket onto the back seat.

A simple shot, perhaps, but it immediately established Fred as something of a rogue with little respect for authority. And I did not just contribute the idea but set some new production standards, too. That scene went out *before* the opening title credits, a novelty then but now much used, and what's more, the scene ended in a freeze-frame shot, the process by which the moving image freezes into a still photograph, giving it considerable impact. This was a technique I had been experimenting with in my commercial video work and had found to be particularly effective. I only agreed to do *The Gaffer* if YTV gave us freeze frame facilities, another production first for a British comedy series.

There had been problems, too, in selecting the type of car that Fred Moffatt should drive. Graham White's script had asked for a Rolls-Royce which, considering the fact that the man was fighting a non-stop battle against bankruptcy, I considered over the top. Eventually, we gave him a battered old Rover, the boot of which was always full of various engineering spare parts. This car became famous for its unreliability which is not, after all, what one would expect from a successful engineer, another twist to the Fred Moffatt character exhibiting his extreme reluctance to spend money he hadn't got!

The car also gave me an opportunity to create a new opening gag for the show each week. One day, for instance, as I am driving into the factory yard, Ginger, one of my workers, says: "Gaffer, your engine's making a funny noise."

"Yes," I reply. "The only thing on this car that doesn't make a noise is the hooter."

Freeze frame.

That car became a character in its own right. It was a running joke that its brakes did not work so that, every time I pulled into the factory yard, I would stop by running it gently into a line of old oil drums. One day in rehearsals, after a period of heavy rain, I did not realise the drums had filled up with an evil mixture of water, old oil and rust. That was the day I chose to hit the drums a little too hard and drenched Ginger and half the crew from head to foot with this watery black slime. They had to go off to change, which did not please the director, but unfortunately the cameras were not running at the time: that would have been a wonderful piece of footage for the archives.

In the meantime, I was also making other important contributions to the show. The script had called for all the cast to speak with Yorkshire accents but, after Selwyn Froggitt, I was not eager to play in another all-Yorkshire situation. There was no reason for this, I explained, because any engineering company will have employees from all parts of the UK. The cast, my secretary Pat Ashton, the shop steward Russell Hunter, and one of the workers, Don Crann, a fellow former stand-up comic who I had recommended for the role, came from an area which ranged from Scotland to the East End of London. They reacted with delight when they were allowed to act their roles in their native accents (although I myself had to use a Yorkshire accent because the series was set in Leeds). This made the cast happier and, in my opinion, contributed to the authenticity of the show.

Finally, there came the scripts. Reassured that I was acting with the writer's blessing, I had a regular date with *Gaffer* producer-director Alan Tarrant at his flat in Leeds. After the first read-through of a new script on a Sunday afternoon, Alan would invite me home where, as a gourmet chef of some distinction, he would cook me a good meal and, over a bottle of wine, we would do the rewrites. When we actually filmed the show before an invited studio audience, I would always introduce Graham White as the writer. He would stand up and take a bow to their applause which, I thought, must have given him a great deal of pleasure; a few months previously, he had been working away at the family business near the railway station in Derby. Now he was in showbusiness and reaping the plaudits.

Now there may well be people who will cast a critical eye over this passage. I had, indeed, taken a very strong lead in the making of *The Gaffer*, contributing in every sphere from props via casting to technical advice and script rewrites. I had done so for the benefit of the show as a whole, throwing years of hard-earned experience and observation into the mix. Perhaps some would say that, as an actor, I had interfered too much. To them I can only say that I thought that these arrangements had been ironed out before I agreed to do the show. In the writer's case, in particular, I was working with an unknown quantity and genuinely believed that his work was benefiting from my input. I had built up a close working friendship with the director and, after all, *The Gaffer* had become the first Friday night comedy show to get into the Top Ten ratings.

I was pretty happy with life. I did not know that my world was about to fall apart...

—oOo—

Towards the end of the third series of *The Gaffer*, I noticed that things were beginning to change. A certain tension had begun to cloud the atmosphere on the set. I should have been perhaps more worried about this than I was, but I had other, more serious, concerns on my mind. Back home in Sapcote, Muriel had begun to feel unwell and had been to see the doctor. One day, Graham White took me aside and explained that he was beginning to run out of *Gaffer* ideas but had been thinking of another project. Would I mind if he took a break after the present run and perhaps come back with another series in a year or so? I didn't mind at all. I had plenty of other things to do, with stage bookings, the burgeoning video business and, above all, my growing worries about Muriel's health. Then the remaining scripts began to arrive later and later, so that in the end they were being handed around as we were finishing the filming of the previous episode, giving us a ridiculously short time to prepare for the new one.

The situation worsened when, one evening, as I was beginning to rewrite one of the scripts, Alan Tarrant intervened: "Why are you rewriting that, Bill? I don't think you should rewrite the scripts any more."

The cracks were beginning to show. Hadn't I been rewriting the scripts for all the three series and why had he never objected before? He shook his head and I let it go; I was not in the mood for a row. A couple of days later, during a break on the set, I popped into Alan's office to phone home. There, on the desk, lay a letter with my name on the top of it. It was addressed to Alan with copies to various heads of department at YTV and it was signed by Graham White. I did what everyone would do in the circumstances: I read it. And to my mounting anger, I found that it was a vitriolic attack on me for allegedly ruining White's scripts with constant rewrites.

I was livid. I rushed out to Alan and blazed away at him. His reaction was that I should never have read the letter — it was private. Mine was that, both as a friend and as director, he should have told me about it. This did little to assuage my fury so I insisted that Graham White must henceforth be banned from the set. I never wanted to meet him again and, if I did, I was very likely to chastise him.

I did meet him once more, however, at the wrap party that was to ring the death knell for *The Gaffer*. I was angry that he had had the temerity to turn up, so I strode up to him and growled: "I'm going to give you the chance to take one swing at me. Then I'm going to tear you limb from limb…"

He did not take me up on the challenge. Instead, he pushed past me and went to complain to Alan Tarrant. It was a bitterly unhappy end to a series that, at its best, had been very good indeed. But this wasn't the end of my world. That came later when I went back home to Sapcote and found Muriel crying.

"I'm sorry, Bill," she said simply. "I've got cancer."

Chapter Twenty-Four

Roses for Muriel

URING those long years in the wilderness, I had explored many avenues of Christianity in search of a personal sort of faith. As I wrote earlier, I was less attracted to the more elaborate forms of worship but had found comfort in simpler beliefs, like the Salvation Army and the practical, down-to-earth philosophy of the *Power of Positive Thinking*. That faith was to be tested to near destruction in the next three years as I watched the woman who had taught me the meaning of true love battle with wit, courage, and doggedness against the evil which was destroying her from within.

Love, like beauty, is, I suppose, in the eye of the beholder. People lucky enough to find it, and hold on to it, must enjoy and suffer its pangs in their own different ways. Muriel, with her steadfastness in the bad times, with her refusal to lay blame when blame was due, with her determination to give an extraordinary family as ordinary life as possible despite huge odds, taught me the difference between love and lust. She reformed me without acrimony and without obvious effort. She taught me that making love is a stroke of the hair, a squeeze of the hand when you are hurting, a smile of encouragement when things are going badly, as she had done so many times when I was battling with the noise and the smoke and the barracking of the drunks when I was forced back on to the club circuit. She had sat silently for hours in late night television studios, a constant back-up, a shoulder to lean on, a source of advice which, though sparing, was always direct and honest. My most trusted critic. Not only did she forgive but, outwardly at least, she also forgot, creating a stable home for me and the children, a haven of peace and reality in my largely make-believe world of work.

If there is a God, why would He allow the destruction of such a creature? And if that destruction were preordained, why decree it at such a time? Surely, after all she had suffered and fought her way through, she was entitled to a few years of quiet happiness at the heart of the family she had so gallantly held together, unfettered by financial concerns and gossip about her husband's indiscretions?

It was not to be.

Her first operation, at the best private hospital I could find, led to complications. The cancer seemed to have been removed but she developed an embolism, a life-threatening blood clot, and was rushed to a National Health Service hospital in Leicester for a second, even more complex, operation to remove the clot. Then came a long, tense period of treatment with drugs like warfarin, to prevent further clotting. She was treated with great skills and kindness by the staff and, night after night, I slept at her bedside in an old garden chair. Then it was time to come home. Once again, it seemed, the Family Maynard had survived the crisis. Once again, the reason for that survival was Muriel's determination to win through.

For the first time in my life, I was glad *not* to be working — or at least working at my acting craft. *The Gaffer* had come to its somewhat sorry end and even though much in demand, I began to turn down new roles. I was needed elsewhere and, for the first time since I was a child, that place was home. Muriel, although cheerful, was still weak and was suffering untold indignities as the after-effects of her operations. These she handled with a perky disdain, refusing to have her daily routine displaced. She would potter in the garden which she loved so much, do as much cooking and sewing as her strength would allow. It was almost back to normal but a normality we had in fact never known: I was at home, for the first time, taking my share of the family responsibilities.

It was now that Charterhouse Films Ltd, my corporate video company, came into its own. Like many things in my life, Charterhouse had come about almost by accident. In my last run as Selwyn Froggitt, I had signed up to do a series of TV commercials for Holt's, the motor car spares group, for a pretty arcane product which repaired leaks in radiators. Not a subject for a lot of comedy, one would imagine, but Selwyn managed to inject a feeling of fun into the ads. These were quite successful and began to earn me substantial sums of money. Along with my acting earnings, the cash was gushing in once more and that, I knew from lessons hard won, would eventually mean another large tax bill. At long last, financially sane as well as secure, I consulted my accountants and they suggested two alternatives: either pay out large lumps of cash in tax or invest some of the money in capital equipment, more tools of my new hi-tech trade.

The result was Charterhouse, a company created when I invested heavily in the very latest video recording equipment. I bought not just cameras and sound recording equipment and all the necessary studio gadgetry but, the jewel in the crown, equipment for a complete tape editing suite. Now, at last, I was able to get behind the cameras and, by overseeing the final editing, was in total control of the final product. I could be writer, performer, director, editor, producer and chief accountant, which gave me absolute scope to back my own judgment for both business and artistic merit. Charterhouse Films came into being as a tax loss. This little company was to become, for three long years at least, my saviour.

The reason was I was now totally independent financially. I did not have to travel to distant theatres or television studios to earn my daily bread. I ran Charterhouse from our semi in Sapcote, promoting our services among companies based mainly in the Midlands, doing the deals, signing the contracts, writing the scripts in co-operation with the clients' advertising and PR companies, and editing the finished product with the help of a trained film editor. Much to my surprise, this tax loss operation turned into a flourishing business, winning orders from travel agencies, hosiery and double-glazing manufacturers and many more. But there was much more to it than money. It meant that I could be at home with Muriel.

This was one of our better times. For a year or so, I worked happily at home for most of the time. When I did go off to do some film work, there was always someone with Muriel. This was usually our daughter Jane, who was growing more like her mother every day, resourceful, cheerful, tactful, but knowing what needed to be done and making sure that it was done. If Jane were not there, it would be one of our many helpful neighbours, for which I once again give praise. When it comes to crisis, the working folk of Sapcote came out in their real colours, ever helpful, fetching and carrying, tidying up the house, running errands, always on hand but never intrusive. When they were needed, they came with neither question nor complaint. Their little kindnesses complete, they would fade away again until the next time. Riches cannot, and had not, bought these mercies. Curious though our lifestyle might have been, the long hard years had made us one of them. We were part of the community and, when need arose, that community rallied around.

It was about as close as we ever got to normality. If I did go off to work for the day, I would be back home in time for supper. In the summer, I would join Muriel on a tour of the garden, now approaching full maturity, bursting with flowers and shrubs and trees. She would point out any new developments — a plant in flower here, a shrub in bud there — and together we would do those little jobs that all gardens require: a bit of weeding, a new plant to put in here, seeds to sow there, a length of hedge to be trimmed, blooms to be cut for the house. Then we would have a quiet meal which Muriel had prepared herself, perhaps a glass of wine on the good days, watch a bit of television and then an early night.

This is true love.

Then the pains began again, pains in different parts of Muriel's body. More doctors, more tests. It went on for weeks, for months, and I could see that this darling creature of mine was in ever-growing agony. This is the worst of it, suffering with a loved one but helpless to do much to relieve that suffering. These were the times when, if anything, it was Muriel who strived to keep up my spirits, rather than vice versa.

When the news came, it could not have been worse. The cancer had spread to her lymph glands. After every other source of treatment had been tried, and failed, they was only one choice: a third operation, this time even more traumatic, involving the removal of large tracts of cancerous material leaving horrendous wounds. As usual, Muriel took it all like a Trojan, but one night when the pain was very bad, she asked me to cuddle her and whispered in my ear:

"I knew it couldn't last, Bill," she said. "I knew we were not allowed to be this happy."

—oOo—

After that operation, Muriel was never the same again, physically. Mentally, she maintained her old resoluteness, her determination never to give in. She was no longer able to walk and we bought her a wheelchair and I would push her around the back garden so that she could see her beloved plants, or into the village for a breath of fresh air and a little shopping. There, in the street, neighbours would stop and chat and Muriel would swap local gossip with them, bright as a button.

Back home, she was mainly bed-bound but this did not stop her activity. She had always enjoyed drawing and painting, and in her bed she became an accomplished amateur artist, painting at first in watercolours then, as her grip on the brushes weakened, turning to coloured pens and crayon. She chose subjects she had always adored, like still-lifes of flowers and birds, and we hung the paintings on her wall so that she could have her own indoor garden. One of them was a drawing of a pair of lovebirds on a branch, a creation that was her particular favourite. The house was never empty. She had round-the-clock nursing care but when it came to dressing those horrendous wounds, Jane would do it most of the time: a bonding of mother and daughter that must have been repeated over the ages since men and women lived in caves. There were friends by the score, neighbours and some of my showbusiness colleagues, dropping in to see her for a few minutes' chat that would leave her, although exhausted, with a smile on her face. There were doctors, of course, all the time, and anyone else we could think of who might possibly be of use: faith healers, herbalists, practitioners of many forms of alternative medicine. We even tried hypnotherapy which, at least, seemed to dull the pain. For a while.

Most of all, there was me. Desperate to do some work to keep my mind off the impending tragedy, I had bought a large van for all the Charterhouse equipment. This, along with my film editor, I installed on a parking space outside the house so that I could pop out of the house and into the van, do a few minutes work before going back to Muriel's bedside. That, I think, is how I kept my sanity.

We knew the end was near when Muriel began to give away the paintings that now festooned her bedroom walls. Whenever particular friends or neighbours dropped in, Muriel would invite them to take their pick. One by one, the paintings disappeared. In the end, only the two lovebirds were left. When that last visitor had gone, Muriel reached out and took my hand.

"I'm glad they left the lovebirds, Bill," she whispered. "I wanted you to have that."

—oOo—

I tried to sleep in the next bedroom but tossed and turned all night. I heard a final slight moan and rushed to her. She was unconscious and I telephoned the doctor in a cold sweat of terror. He arrived within minutes and asked to be left alone with her. Then he came to the bedroom door.

"I'm sorry, Bill," he said. "She's gone."
My sheet anchor. She was gone.

—oOo—

We buried Mrs Muriel Williams, known to the world as Mrs Muriel Maynard, at the little parish church of Sapcote, Leicestershire, on a summer's day in June 1983, aged 57. She had been approaching the time in life when, by richly deserved right, she should have been looking forward to a peaceful, prosperous and serene old age, things she had experienced only too briefly in a lifetime of hard work, dedication and too many disappointments. But we had agreed, Martin, Jane and me, that it should not be a *funereal* occasion: Muriel would have hated that.

So we stocked our little semi just round the corner with crates of champagne and I ordered 300 red roses to be laid on her coffin. Those roses, I asked the vicar, should afterwards be handed singly to each of the mourners as they left the church. All her life, Muriel had loved flowers and the sight of the little old church would have thrilled her: it was piled to the rafters with sprays and bouquets and wreaths, a panoply of colour in the grey cool light of the church, their scent drifting up to the high-arched ceiling. Many of those single roses, distributed by the vicar, still exist today. Some mourners took them home and pressed them in books. Others dried them, pressed them, and mounted them in frames, where they hang of the walls of their homes alongside the paintings and drawings that my wife gave them.

Most poignant of all, perhaps, is that a bush of the very same rose now thrives in my daughter Jane's garden not far away in Leicestershire. One of Jane's friends had a father who was a keen horticulturist, who took the rose from Muriel's coffin and persuaded it by some green-fingered magic to strike root. Then, unknown to Jane, he grew it on until it became a healthy bush in its own right. A few years later, the friend dug it up, carefully wrapped its roots, and presented it to Jane who had married and was setting up her first home. It went into the new garden in pride of place and, as Jane and her family moved on to bigger and better things, it was dug up and transplanted twice more.

Such a vagrant life might not be the ideal existence for the average plant but perhaps, in some mystical way in that little Leicestershire church, this rose had absorbed some of Muriel's determination. Now installed in its fourth home, in the garden at Jane's converted farmhouse, it has finally come to full glory. In

1997, after 14 years on the move, it finally had its say: it bloomed magnificently, throwing out 40 or 50 flowers, each as perfect as the ones that had once lain on a wife and mother's coffin.

Muriel would have loved that. And she would have loved the fact that there is another rose in the Muriel story, too. After her death, I had divided the best pieces of her personal jewellery between Martin and Jane, but there was a substantial amount remaining, jewellery which we had bought as a hedge against inflation. Its presence in my now quiet and lonely home brought back too many painful memories. I decided to sell it and donate the proceeds to charity. But which charity?

To my surprise, that jewellery raised £10,000 and, although this substantial sum was burning a hole in my pocket, I had not yet decided how to distribute it. One day, listening rather disinterestedly to a programme on BBC Radio 2, I heard that Harkness, the famous rose-growers, were offering the right to name their latest creation to the highest bidder. The money would go to the Save the Children fund and the naming ceremony would take place at the Royal Chelsea Flower Show, spiritual home to every gardener in Britain and a large chunk of the rest of the world too.

And, as fate would have it, the £10,000 exactly covered the winning bid.

I didn't go myself. Instead, Jane went to the grandeur of the Royal Chelsea Flower Show to name the new Harkness rose, surrounded by a crowd of people ranging from aristocratic stately home owners to old ladies with a few square yards of suburban soil (which they tend with just as much affection). The rose is a small, pink patio specimen which gives off an abundance of blooms, and it now grows in tens of thousands of small gardens throughout Britain — gardens not unlike a certain one surrounding a small semi in Sapcote, Leicestershire. It is grown by many of our friends, too, because Harkness asked for a long list of names and addresses to which they supplied free specimens.

It is called, of course, *Muriel*.

I can't think of a more fitting memorial. She would have loved to have her own rose. She would have appreciated the fact, too, that some of her jewellery had gone to feed starving children in the Third World: all her life, she had fought tenaciously for her own children's' futures.

—oOo—

The roses must have been coming into bud in Sapcote on that June day in 1983, when we laid her to rest. I don't think I noticed, for most of the time I was simply numb. Then, while the wake was under way and the champagne was being drunk to an accompaniment of home-cooked refreshments prepared by Jane, friends and neighbours, I slipped quietly out of the back door and got into a chauffeur-driven car and was whisked away to Heathrow Airport.

The roller coaster was under way again, on an eight-year journey that was to take me, quite literally, to the ends of the earth and back, a journey of escape from loneliness, a quest for oblivion, a desperate search for peace. These were the blackest moments of them all. Alone in hotel bedrooms overlooking the Pacific Ocean, or in theatrical guest houses overlooking Margate beach, I would think of Muriel with a heart-rending mix of longing and guilt, of happiness and regret. In those darkest of nights, I would sometimes try to comfort myself by remembering the old theatrical exercise that Frank Dunlop had taught me at Nottingham Playhouse, the one when you put *Whoops* at the beginning of every line of dialogue to brighten up a sad and stale rehearsal.

I even started a poem but I was never able to finish it. The one stanza I did finish reads thus:

Whoops! Whoops! Whoops!
They said if I said, *Whoops!*
Everything would seem all right.
Whoops! Whoops! Whoops!
Why isn't it working?

Chapter Twenty-Five

Wanderings

I SUPPOSE few men slip out of their loved one's wake and jump on a plane to New Zealand. It was the beginning of a series of wanderings that was to last for some eight years when I was almost continually on tour. My life was once again dividing into alternative decades of dizzy success and sickening disaster: the 1950s had been the way to the top; the 1960s the way back to the bottom; the 1970s hauling myself back again; and, the bitterest blow of all, the 1980s started with Muriel's illness. This was the decade when I plunged myself into work as a touring actor in the theatre, once again turning my back on television. It was, perhaps, my equivalent of joining the Foreign Legion, except that I did not sign on to forget — that I shall never be able to do. But the only way way I could push aside the pain, to get some relief however temporary, was to immerse myself in a non-stop schedule of work in the company of friends.

The New Zealand trip had been broached some months earlier, while Muriel's illness was getting increasingly desperate. *The Gaffer* had been a big success Down Under and I was invited to host a telethon to raise money for various New Zealand charities. I had turned it down, of course, but a couple of days after Muriel died, I picked up the phone and asked my agent to see if the offer was still open. It was — but I would have to leave in the next couple of days. Cruel fate decreed that my last possible departure date would be the day when we laid Muriel to rest.

This was an agonising decision but, deep inside, I knew I must go. To have remained alone in the Sapcote house, with the memories of Muriel all around me, was unthinkable; I had real doubts about my ability to keep my sanity.

And there were now few ties to hold me: Martin and Jane were now adults with their own lives to lead and the little family home was in good hands. For years, Muriel had been immersed in her work as my secretary-manager, handing all my business affairs, and that had given her little time for housework. My friends and neighbours two doors away, Brenda Seal and her husband Tony, had been helping out with this and they agreed to keep an eye on the house as, indeed, they still do to this day. Brenda does any housework necessary and Tony, a skilled carpenter and boat fitter, can tackle maintenance jobs much better than I could ever dream of.

With the domestic side of my life in good hands, there remained only my professional career to consider and here I suddenly realised that I was totally free. Much of my striving to get back to the top had been driven by a desire to prove to Muriel that I would make up for all our earlier turmoil. Muriel, herself, never asked for this but I was driven to it to restore my own pride in her eyes.I wanted to repay her in my own small way for the suffering I had caused.

Well, I'd done that, done it better than even I, in my arrogance, ever thought likely, and now she was gone. With her went much of my motivation. With no one to please but myself, I realised that I did not care very much what happened to me personally. I had money in the bank and I could pick and choose — and what I chose was the touring theatre, where I would be surrounded by friends old and new, where the evenings would not be lonely because I would be at work, where the days would be spent in different towns or cities in many different parts of the world where I could explore and keep my mind active. The alternative, to have sat alone in our empty house in Sapcote, would have destroyed me.

So off I went to New Zealand on a nightmare 26-hour flight. Once there, my feet barely touched the ground for three hectic weeks. Not only did I appear on television for hours upon end, but I also toured large areas of the country, meeting local people and making public appearances in places like shopping malls. It had been well reported in the New Zealand press that I had come straight from my wife's funeral and this brought out in the New Zealanders extra warmth and sympathy from a wonderful people who already possess those characteristics in large measure, even under normal circumstances.

One group in particular went out of their way to comfort me: the local Maoris. Coming as they do from a one-time warlike tribe with ancient traditions of the spirits of the departed living on forever, they have a very different attitude to death to the average European. They see it with regret, of course, but also as a transition to better things, a cause almost for celebration, subdued but celebratory none the less.

I was invited as guest of honour to a nearby Maori settlement for a special *hungi*, a traditional feast centred round the carcass of a whole lamb which has been buried surrounded by hot stones and left to cook underground for two or three days. There I sat as honoured guest while, for me and Muriel, they performed their traditional death dance to say goodbye to the departed but at the same time to wish her well in the spirit world. Muriel would have been overwhelmed because this was no morbid dance, there was no morbid 'death march' music, but a vibrant, noisy, joyful affair not unlike the *hakka,* the fearsome dance that the All Blacks Rugby Union teams perform before the kick-off at international matches. Except this was a gesture of support and friendship rather than one of intimidation.

This ritual and the feast that followed moved me deeply (the lamb, incidentally, was the most delicious I have ever tasted). Afterwards, I thanked the chief and asked if there was any gift that I could contribute to the settlement: a set of swings and slides for the children's playground, or perhaps some sports equipment for the school? The chief smiled and pointed out, a little ruefully I thought, that although the *hungi* was a traditional feast, the modern world had encroached even here and the meal was now served on stainless steel dishes. The settlement's set of such utensils was reaching the end of its useful life, so would I consider donating a new set? I was delighted, even though the gift involved two or three hundred dishes.

Another stroke for Muriel. From time to time, when this memory comes back to me, I find a little smile on my lips. Every now and then in the South Pacific, an entire settlement of happy, friendly, supportive Maori have a ritual feast and they do so from dishes presented at a memorial to a wonderful woman. If she is there in the spirit world, I hope it gives her a smile too.

That New Zealand tour lasted only a few brief weeks but helped me, partially at least, to adjust to life on my own. But the long flight back was a nightmare, for I dreaded going back to Sapcote. Once back in my empty little house, the despair came back with a vengeance. For several days, I pondered my future. I would give it all up, I decided. What I wanted was total anonymity, a total impossibility in the UK or in many other countries where my television series had been shown. I would go to France, I decided, and take a job as a barman or a manual labourer, learn the language and build a new life away from the spotlight.

Then, on cue as ever, the phone rang…

—oOo—

The musical *Annie*, the story of an orphan girl helped on in the world by a lonely old philanthropist, has a huge cast and most of them are very young. To take such a show on tour, complete with elaborate sets, costumes, and demanding musical scores presents the sort of logistical problems that a small army must face when going into battle. But transport and accommodation, long rehearsals with theatre orchestras essential to the success of a major musical, are not the only problems. There is the law, too.

Since the days of the music hall, British law has insisted that youngsters appearing on stage can do so only above a certain age and only for a given number of hours in a given period. The rest of the time, they must be provided with a proper education and rest periods. These are sensible precautions to stop the wholesale exploitation of youngsters — a regular feature of Victorian times for touring theatre companies, variety artistes and circus people. Sensible and proper as they are, they create a nightmare for anyone contemplating such a tour with a show like *Annie*. It meant, for instance, that at any one time we must have two Annies, one working and the other back at school. It would be impossible to take a whole chorus line of youngsters on tour, so at each venue local amateurs with ambitions for a professional career are recruited from dancing schools and theatre groups, a practice that has been common in pantomime for many years but one which Equity, the actors' trade union, watches with eagle eyes to ensure that amateurs are not being used as sweated labour to the detriment of professionals whose roles they could take.

All this having been said, the part of Daddy Warbucks, the millionaire who helps Annie to a better life, is a cracker, a big, expansive character role ideally suited to big, expansive actors. This was the role I was offered by my agent, Richard Stone, a few days after my return from New Zealand as I sat alone in Sapcote pondering a future role as a *garçon* in some remote French cafe. Richard, of course, was well aware of my state of mind and thought that what I needed was work, work and more work in a show as big and complex as he could find. He had put out feelers and, out of the hat, had come up with the ideal elixir for my new life alone.

I agreed to tour with *Annie* and this helped me through the next 18 months with barely a minute to pick at my psychological wounds. Playing Daddy Warbucks was a non-stop whirl of activity, a week here, a fortnight there, at major venues throughout the United Kingdom, from the South Coast to Scotland, from East Anglia to Wales. There was, of course, the core of a professional cast that went the whole way from start to end, but in each town there were new youngsters in the chorus and a series of Annies, all of whom needed to be treated with support and understanding. Working with young people, and particularly with girls of not much older than 11, became totally absorbing. To them, of course, I was a figure of some awe. Nervous young performers, however, are not at their best so I went to great lengths to break through this barrier of awe and help coax the best performances out of them. I was Daddy Warbucks both on and off the stage and helping these youngsters along gave me enormous satisfaction. It also, of course, kept me very busy indeed.

The *Annie* tour lasted some 53 weeks, with breaks in between and, in particular, at Christmas where I played pantomime, another chance to be with a handful of trusted professional friends and young people in the chorus, to be surrounded with laughter and activity at this critical time of the year when lonely people feel their loneliest. It was just the beginning of a decade of escape.

I played in J.B. Priestley's, *When We Were Married* at the famous Whitehall Theatre in London, and in a play called *Strippers* by Peter Terson, set in the North-East night club scene I had known so well, at the Phoenix Theatre in Charing Cross Road. This was another part close to my heart because I played a down-market comic who also managed a troupe of striptease artists touring the clubs.

He did a 15-minute stand-up act in between the strip acts and I took the part only on condition that I could rewrite the stand-up act. Here I was very much on home ground. I took over the role from Alan Haughy, a Geordie actor who had played opposite me in *The Gaffer*

"I know what you've come for," said Alan in the theatre bar after I had gone to watch the show for the first time. "There is no chance of me going to the West End."

Any guilty feelings I had about taking his place were tempered by the fact that I had got him the part in *The Gaffer*, which was a big boost to his career.

This is the time when I did everything I could to be in the company of old friends. When I was offered the part to tour as Henry Hobson in *Hobson's Choice*, I asked if the part of young Willie Mossop, who marries Henry's daughter Maggie and ends up as the hero of the piece, could go to Don Crann, the former stand-up comic who had joined me on *The Gaffer*. When he was accepted, I took him aside and gave him a serious ear-wigging.

"Listen here, mate," I said. "This is the best part in the play so when we go on tour, you will get all the best reviews. I'm telling you this now, so that you won't get carried away when it happens."

I was right and he did. But it was great fun. We even got a part for Don's wife, Lisa David, who graduated from one of the minor roles as Maggie's sister to play Maggie herself, the female lead. This she did with considerable flair and, with both Mr and Mrs Crann getting rave notices, this was a very happy tour indeed.

When it came to putting time and space between me and Sapcote, my old adversary-turned-friend from the London Palladium pantomime turned up trumps. He had started his career in showbusiness in management anyway — as I have said, he used to bring me my pay packet when I was working for the Lew Grade organisation — and had now turned back to management and had become a very successful producer. He has a great flair for getting long tours to run smoothly, which is something of a rarity in this business.

This time, he had put together a tour which, even by his standards, was complex indeed. The play was pretty straight forward, the light comedy *There's a Girl in my Soup*, but the itinerary was mind-bending: half a dozen shows in the Gulf States in the Middle East, then on to South-East Asia to Bangkok, Singapore and Jakarta, and half a dozen far-flung destinations which I can no longer remember. The tour was sponsored by British Airways, a connection that was to prove very useful later, and it was intended for the dinner theatre circuit — a sophisticated concept in which important local guests, and most of the British expatriate community, were invited along to an expensive meal to be followed, not by after-dinner speeches, but by our play.

Many of the countries we visited were, of course, ruled by strict Muslim principles and *Girl in my Soup* was presumably chosen because, although a little risque, contained no hard-core sex. Nevertheless, it had to be vetted before public performance by an Eastern equivalent of the old English Watch Committee. As most of these guys did not speak English anyway, we showed them the play, gave them a slap-up lunch, and off they went happy. Whatever the locals thought, the ex-pats loved it.

As I said with a sweet smile to my old sparring partner from our panto days: "I'll never work *with* you ever again . . . but I'll work *for* you any time you like."

—oOo—

The years passed quickly in a haze of travel and work. From time to time, when I was working in Britain, I would find myself passing Sapcote on the M1 motorway and, on the occasional weekend, I would spend a night or two there. I would visit my daughter nearby, and have a pint or two at the Sapcote WMC with my old mates — and then rush off to the next date. Slowly, painfully, the wounds were beginning to heal.

I have made no secret of the fact that I adore women. I love their company, their loyalty, their softness, their often contrary views on life. And, of course, I've always liked to stay awake with them (as opposed to sleeping with them). As the end of the 1980s loomed, I had been celibate for five or six years but, most of all, I missed the focal point that Muriel had been in my life. To the travelling actor, away from home for months on end, the fact that there *is* a home, however rarely seen, is an immense comfort.

I don't think I ever made a conscious decision about this but I found myself thinking that I should try and find another Muriel. Not a replacement, because that would have been impossible and I realised such, but someone who could give me back that focal point, somewhere to turn my mind as I lay alone in some hotel bedroom far from home. There was a passing fling with a young actress which even I realised was doomed. And every night when I got home after saying goodnight to her, I would hear Muriel's voice saying to me: "Don't be a silly old sod..."

Then I made a few hesitant dates with women from outside showbusiness, something I had never done before. These, too, ended disastrously and made me realise just how wide is the gulf between an entertainer's lifestyle and that of people in more normal walks of life. On these dates, over a nice dinner, strangers would approach me as though I were an old friend, engaging me in conversation, asking for autographs, or taking photographs. These women, nice though they were, could not cope with such attention although, to me, it was both welcome and normal — even though I had not been on television for several years, people still remembered me and treated me as one of the family.

One night after such a failed date, I lay in bed wondering if it would ever be possible to find another partner who could cope with the fame, with the travel, with the constant separations. It occurred to me that the only person likely to cope was a woman who had experienced celebrity herself, or who had been partner to a celebrity, someone who understood the rules and the vagaries of a showbusiness life.

For a widower pushing 60, bald, fat and no longer a sex symbol, this seemed to be an impossibly tall order. But life is like a jigsaw puzzle. There are pieces scattered all over the board and, one feels in exasperation, they will never fit together. I did not know that, by the most remarkable series of coincidences, by the longest of long shots, another major piece in the jigsaw of my life was about to pop into place.

Chapter Twenty-Six

Voices From The Past

A S YET another decade came to end, I was still moving about Britain like a pin ball in an amusement arcade machine, making the lights go up in theatres from one end of the country to the next. For me, the 1980s had not been the Greedy Eighties but the Endless Eighties. I was working non-stop, and earning good money on the stage, and a lot of the time I was reasonably happy. But even six years after Muriel's passing, there was an emptiness, a lack of focus. I did not know that yet another part of my jigsaw of a life was about to drop in place as a result of a series of coincidences that spanned some 30 years and, quite literally, three of the four corners of the Earth.

One day the phone rang and up spoke a voice from the past: Paul Desmond, the American comic who I'd last seen in Australia during that wild tour when I had gone on my last extra-marital fling with the wild Aussie redhead. Paul was having a hard time Down Under at that time and eventually found himself out of work and broke. As a man who understood these things, I had given him a bed in my apartment and we had become firm friends. It was, I thought, just one of the many friendships that grow on tour, two of many ships that pass every night for the working actor, and when Paul had gone back to the States I thought we would never meet again. This is quite normal in the ephemeral world of entertainment.

Back home, Paul had built himself a good career and, when he telephoned that fateful day, he had arrived in the UK on the QE2 where he had been entertaining cruise passengers. He was due to fly back to the States but had a couple of free days in England. Could we arrange a meet? Great, I said. I, too, had a rare couple of weeks off in my touring schedule so I invited him to come and stay in Sapcote. We could have a few beers and talk about old times, which for me was as good a way as any of passing my non-working evenings. I did not know this was to be the first link in a very long and, even viewed from today, staggering chain of events.

I showed Paul around my home county and one night as we reminisced he mentioned a name which caused the hairs on the back of my neck to stand up as though someone had run an electric shock through me: Tonia Bern-Campbell, the widow of Donald Campbell, the speed ace who had been killed when his speedboat cartwheeled out of the water while he was trying to beat the world water speed record on Lake Coniston in Cumbria.

The reason for this electrifying effect was not that I merely knew Tonia but that, during the wild days in Soho, she and I had enjoyed a short but passionate affair, an affair so dangerous that I had ended it because I feared it would break up my marriage. Tonia, a talented singer and cabaret artiste, and I went our separate ways and, some time later, I had read in the newspapers that she had married Donald Campbell. After his tragic death, she had resumed her professional career and for years in my travels round the globe, I had almost dogged her footsteps. In Australia and South Africa, she had become a major star.

Even in a professional world jam-packed with characters of every hue, Tonia stands out as a one-off. Born before World War Two, she was the daughter of wealthy Belgian hoteliers, so wealthy that as a child she had been driven to school in a chauffeur-driven Rolls-Royce. Then, when she was a young girl, the Germans had invaded and had commandeered the family hotel as the local military headquarters. The war years caused her untold suffering, and both her elder brothers died in harrowing circumstances, one of them in a Nazi death camp. With the war over, she was a teenage girl with nothing to her name but an outstanding musical talent. At the age of 17, with only the clothes she stood up in and a few sheets of music, she moved alone to London determined to put the past behind her and build a career as an entertainer.

We had met in the 1950s, when she appeared as a guest on *Mostly Maynard*, having demonstrated the necessary combination of real talent and a gritty ambition to succeed under her own steam. Our working worlds were very different: while I was entertaining the male thrill-seekers at The Windmill, she had become a cabaret star on the caviar and champagne circuit, performing with sophistication and wit before dinner-jacketed audiences at the Savoy or the Café de Paris. If there ever needs to be proof of the law of physics which says that opposite poles attract, this was it. We were both a long way from home and we threw ourselves into an affair of almost uncontrollable passion. Almost. The intense heat of the affair frightened me and I backed off. We had never met since...

Now it so happens that Paul Desmond lives in Palm Springs which, by American standards, is just down the road from Los Angeles. As an entertainer, he spends much time in LA and its suburb, Hollywood, and one night as we sat remembering mutual old friends, the name Tonia Bern-Campbell cropped up. I was electrified as I listened: Tonia, Paul revealed, had built a big success in America. As a singer, she had performed at the Carnegie Hall in New York and at the even more famous Hollywood Bowl. From music, she he had gone into making TV commercials, moved from there to roles in popular TV soaps, and had eventually ended up presenting her own morning TV show. In a town where celebrity is all, she had combined this with building a reputation as a society hostess, whose dinner invitations were much sought after by the powerful people who make Hollywood tick.

This story did not surprise me at all. I had always known she had great talent as an artist. It did not take much imagination to guess that her sophisticated European ways, her ability to speak seven languages, the faint but alluring accent of a natural French speaker, her knowledge of fine wines and food from her childhood in a luxury hotel, all these things would make her a winner on the brash Hollywood scene. Here, as I was soon to learn, money and *class* are rarely synonymous and one spends a great deal of time trying to acquire the other. No, I was not at all surprised to learn that Tonia Bern-Campbell had become a Hollywood success. I was, however, surprised that she had never remarried.

What Paul said next, however, came as a bombshell.

"The funny thing," he went on with a mischievous twinkle in his eyes, "is that I met her at a party a while back and when your name came up, she opened her purse and showed me some photographs. They were snapshots of her and you together, taken back in the 1950s. Strange that a woman carries around pictures like that after 30 years or more. You must have had quite a thing going, the two of you..."

I was stunned. I know, of course, that all women carry photographs in their handbags but, in most cases, only of their closest intimates: a husband or a boyfriend, their children or parents. That this woman, with a glittering new life built Phoenix-like from the ashes of a dreadful tragedy, should have my picture among her most treasured possessions left me speechless — not one of my normal states of mind.

Paul watched me impishly as this nugget of information sank in. I could not begin to grasp the implications. As I struggled to find something to say, Paul grinned: "Why don't we give her a call?"

"What? Do you have her number?"

"Of course."

"But what would I say…?"

"How about, 'Hello Tonia, it's Maynard. How are you?'"

After much cajoling, I lifted the phone and the miracle of modern communications joined my little semi in Sapcote to, as I was to discover, a luxurious bungalow set high in the Hollywood hills, one of the most prestigious addresses in one of the most prestigious cities in the world. I felt like a tongue-tied schoolboy struggling to whip up the courage to ask for his first date.

I recognised the unmistakable voice immediately.

"Tonia," I said hesitantly, "a voice from the past…"

"Hello, Bill," she purred. "How are you?"

"I'm fine."

"Where are you?"

"At home. In England."

"That's a shame. When are you coming to see me?"

—oOo—

I don't recall much more of that call. Paul went on the line and exchanged a few pleasantries and the receiver went down. I sat staring at the phone, aware that something important had happened, but not quite sure what it was. For the first time in years, powerful emotions were being unleashed and this I found not a little frightening. What to do?

"I'm flying home for a week or so until the next cruise," said Paul. "Why not join me?"

I thought he was joking. But he piled on the pressure. Eventually, the thought of a little adventure began to appeal — I had not had a holiday as such for some ten years. I might go, I said, but not just to see Tonia. It would be nice to see Palm Springs and get some desert air and while in California, we could take in San Francisco, the city where Paul was born and which I had always wanted to visit. As for Los Angeles, I did have a contact there — an American casting director who had married an English musician I knew — and had a standing invitation to drop in. As for Tonia, if we had the time, we might just say hello.

British Airways nearly strangled this budding romance at birth. We tried the booking office to get another seat on Paul's flight but no, there was not a chance — the flight was already heavily oversubscribed. That's that, then, I said, almost with a sense of relief. Then I remembered contacts made with BA when they had sponsored that long Far Eastern tour. With Paul still egging me on, I pulled a few strings. Thirty minutes later, the airline rang back and said that, somehow, they had found me a seat. As it happened, it next was to Paul's reservation. *Go West, young man*, they used to say in the days of the American pioneers, *and build a new life*. I was no longer young and had long given up hopes for a new life. This, I vowed as we got on to that plane, was just a fortnight's holiday.

I insisted that we stuck to the agreed schedule. Although we landed at Los Angeles, we avoided the city and drove straight to Paul's home in Palm Springs. After two nights there, we planned to set off for a tour of San Francisco, with Paul proud at the thought of showing me around his home town. On the way, of course, we would have to pass Los Angeles so I might as well call in and see my casting director contact. There is always a demand for English actors in Hollywood and who knows...?

Back in LA after three days of non-stop travel, it became necessary to stay overnight in order to see the casting director. Well, I said, it would be churlish to stay in the city and not say hello. I picked up the phone.

"Hello Tonia, it's Bill again."

"That's nice. Where are you now?"

"In LA. Just round the corner, in fact."

"Wonderful. You'd better come round..."

So off we went into the Hollywood Hills, to a house that came straight out of a movie made in that place. Tonia was, as usual, in the middle of a dinner party for important business contacts, her agent and accountant among others, and I felt distinctly like an intruder: a balding, sartorially inelegant Englishman arriving unexpectedly out of the night in the company of glistening, groomed, successful Californians, all sleek and sun-tanned and Gucci from head to toe.

I was aware of the puzzled glances in my direction, glances that moved with disguised but distinctly raised eyebrows from my dishevelled hulk to

Tonia, all blonde and long-legged and exquisitely groomed, and then back to me. Despite this, the electricity was already crackling across this elegant table, darting between us and the silverware and the crystal wine glasses. These guests may have been puzzled but they were by no means unreceptive to these rippling currents. One by one, they stood up, made their excuses and left (One of them told me later: "I don't know how you do it, Bill, but I thought the air itself would catch fire that night.").

When they had gone, Paul Desmond, who had driven me hundreds of miles in the past 48 hours on top of the long flight from Heathrow, lay on a settee and fell into a deep sleep. We were alone for the first time in more than 30 years.

"Let me show you the house," she said, and gave me the conducted tour, stopping in every room to gaze out of the picture windows over the pine and palm covered Hollywood Hills, aflame with the gleaming floodlights that stay on throughout the night around the homes and swimming pools of the great film stars, the producers, the directors, the writers and all the other top-of-the pile people who make this place the glitz capital of the world. Then she stood before me, looked up, and said:

"Aren't you going to kiss me?"

We embraced and three decades fell away in three seconds. For a while, we stood in silence. Then she said: "When are we going to get married?" Of all the emotions that were running through me after that kiss — and there were many — the one I remember most was sheer terror. I had absolutely no doubt that I was back in love. I had absolutely no doubt that if there was ever to be another woman in my life for ever, this was she. I was in absolutely no doubt that finding her again had been one of the luckiest acts of Fate in a fateful life. But could I go through all that emotional turmoil again? That was the terror.

I took the coward's way out. I hastened to Paul, shook him awake, and said we must leave immediately. We swept out of the driveway in a hail of dust with Paul, still half asleep, shaking his head in bewilderment and asking what had gone wrong. That night, back at our hotel, I rang a bemused British Airways and asked if they could get me on a flight to London. But hadn't I booked a return flight in ten days' time and hadn't the trip been organised with some difficulty in the first place? It's an emergency, I said. And it was.

The following day, from the airport, I plucked up the courage to ring Tonia again and, thankfully, she was not at home. With relief, I lied to her answerphone, saying that I had been called back to England to make a TV commercial. Sorry to let her down, I said, but there was a lot of money at stake. I would be in touch.

When I finally dragged myself through the front door at Sapcote, totally exhausted from four of the strangest days and nights of my life, Tonia's voice spoke to me from my answerphone.

"You swine," she said. "You've run out on me again."

—oOo—

On that horrendous flight home, across North America and then across the Atlantic, I had plenty of time to think. It was some six years since Muriel's death and, as I said earlier, I longed for someone to share my life with, someone special to give me a point of focus. I knew, too, after my fumbling attempts to romance ladies from outside the world of showbusiness, that such a woman would be a rare find indeed. Now I had found her...

Tonia was not only fully aware of the pains as well as the pleasures of celebrity. She had also suffered, if anything, more than me. Her childhood had been full of genuine horror, whilst mine had merely been the grind of poverty. She, too, had fallen from great wealth, although from no fault of her own, and she understood the insecurity that can bring. She, too, had lost a dearly-loved partner, because in her marriage to Donald Campbell, she had become a full-time member of his team, helping out in the workshop with his cars and boats, cooking and even doing the laundry for the mechanics. She dressed in oily overalls and joshed with the press who were in constant attendance whenever a record bid was under way.

Donald's horrific death had haunted her professionally, too, because when she gamely tried to put her life back together by taking up again her cabaret act, she found that audiences in Britain no longer laughed at the sophisticated patter she interspersed between songs. She was the most famous widow in the country and, the British being what they are, they found it difficult to laugh with a figure of high tragedy. Facing up to this lack of response she, like me, had travelled the world, hoping to bury painful memories under a mountain or work. Like me, those travels had eventually led to more success, to a secure, settled and safe way of life.

The similarities in our lives, the instincts those similarities gave us to provide mutual support and understanding, were quite outstanding. And if all these musings seem a cynical weighing of pros and cons, let us make no mistake about the most important issue of all: we were deeply in love. There was little doubt about that when we gazed at each other for the first time in 30 years, across that littered dinner table; even total strangers to me had felt the vibrations. What little doubt there could be was instantly destroyed by that solitary kiss — and that is as far as it went that first night in LA.

Yet, in many other ways, we were chalk and cheese.

First, we had to contend with the spirits of the dead. I was still in love with my memories of Muriel and knew that no one could ever displace that love. And Tonia had been faithful for years to the memory of a brave, gallant and ultimately doomed man, a great Englishman from the heroic mould that has produced so many of the breed.

Could we create a relationship which allowed for the presence of such memories of the past in a way that would not cloud the present?

Then there were our lifestyles, poles as far apart as it is possible to be in the Western world — and in this I am not speaking of simple geography. She lived in a gleaming bungalow on one of the world's most glamorous suburbs. I lived in a semi in Sapcote. For lunch, she would go to the Beverly Wilshire Hotel and sip chardonnay in the Californian sunshine, nodding to some of the most famous faces in the world as they passed by. I would have a pint of bitter and a bag of nuts at the Sapcote WMC and talk about greyhounds with the men who had been my models for Selwyn Froggitt and his cronies. She dressed in designer clothes from Rodeo Drive, the most expensive shopping street in the world. I padded about in tracksuit bottoms, T-shirts, and scruffy old trainers.

Could these two worlds possibly mix? These are the questions I had pondered on that long, lonely flight back from LA. I had decided, more or less, that the whole situation was an impossible dream. Then I switched on my answerphone and there she was, calling me a swine.

Timorously, I picked up the phone...

—oOo—

Amazingly, Tonia took my abject apologies with fine good humour. For several days, I wooed her long distance. Then the banter turned more serious. We couldn't go on like this. We decided that we would have to meet to see if the magic could survive after a few days in each other's company. We chose New York, a halfway house for both of us, and agreed to rendezvous in a fortnight's time. The following day, the phone rang again.

"I can't stand it any longer," she said. "I can't work. I can't eat. I can't sleep. I'm coming today..."

I was waiting for her at Heathrow where, as many a celebrity has discovered to his or her cost when on clandestine liaisons, press photographers stake out virtually every flight, hoping for a shot of a famous face coming or going. Here were two famous faces, two highly unlikely faces together: the widow of a great hero and a stand-up comic turned actor. Here was the smell of a good story and the press pack were due to descend like an avalanche. Before they got on to our trail, however, we had 48 precious hours to see if our lives could fit together. In those two days, I wanted to show Tonia England, the real England, *my* England. The question was: could she share it too?

Chapter Twenty-Seven

Transatlantic Marriage

W E had a few precious days of privacy before the press avalanche rolled over us and, while Tonia was in the air over America and the Atlantic, I had carefully planned every move. This was, I knew, a situation which called for some subtlety — not one of my stronger points — but also had to be something of a trial run. Here were two adult, experienced people with wildly differing lifestyles and yet in some ways we were acting like star-crossed teenagers. If this were to more than just another wild fling, certain cards had to be laid on the table, certain barriers had to be faced and broken down. After our meeting at Heathrow, I drove Tonia north in a state of considerable trepidation.

She had, of course, spent many years in England, first as a young entertainer, then as the wife and widow of a very famous man. But most of those years had been passed either in the more well-heeled parts of London or, when helping Donald with his record bids, in expensive hotels or luxurious rented properties. She had seen very little of ordinary England, Little England, and — let's face it — there are fewer more ordinary places than Sapcote and, in that ordinary village, fewer more ordinary homes than my little semi.

She watched the passing landscape with interest as we sped up the M1. When we turned off through the rolling fields of Leicestershire, she murmured appreciatively at the greenness of the countryside with its thousands of trees and lush hedgerows: this is just about as different as you can get from the Hollywood Hills, with its arid pines and occasional palms, country so tinder-dry that forest fires from time to time destroy hundreds of multi-million dollar properties (if it's not the fires, it can be the mud slides in winter plus, of course, the ever-present threat of a catastrophic earthquake which Californians live with all their waking moments).

Then the red brick cottages of Sapcote came into sight, winding down the little main street, and the spire of the parish church where we had laid Muriel to rest. This, of course, was my biggest fear: could the living come to terms with our memories?

This was the first hurdle and Tonia took it as though it weren't there. In fact, for her at least, it *wasn't* there. She began to talk about Muriel and our lives together as though she were still alive, a welcome member of the family, almost as an old friend. This openness, this immediate acceptance of the fact that there was and always would be a part of my life into which she could never intrude, was the first great reassurance. When we finally drew up outside the little house, *Muriel's* little house, her first remark was to compliment me on the state of the gardens, with their carefully chosen and well-nurtured trees, plants and shrubs. My wire-taut nerves relaxed a notch under this soothing balm.

We had a quiet meal and then, inevitably, it was time for bed. Here, once more, I was acting like a fumbling schoolboy. I did not know until later that Tonia was just as nervous as me.

I had, of course, given Tonia a room of her own and had left her to unpack her things in peace and quiet. On our way to our separate rooms, we embraced on the tiny landing and it seemed as though a lightning bolt had struck. Reluctantly, but breathlessly, we parted and went into our own rooms. In mine, I changed into the somewhat singular night attire that I have worn for years: the Arabian djallaba, a cotton shift which buttons from the neck and covers the whole body down to the feet. Modest in my djallaba, I knocked nervously on her door and said I would like to wish her goodnight. The rest is strictly private, although I will say that I did not sleep with Tonia that night and have never done so since; when we are together, we still have separate rooms. However, to use a phrase I have coined, I did and do stay awake with her rather a lot...

It took some time before Tonia confessed that she, too, had been schoolgirl nervous about that first night together after 30 odd years. So nervous, in fact, that she had sought advice from a women friend in LA, saying that she knew she would have to go to bed with me if the relationship were to continue but she was terrified of doing so after a long period of celibate living.

The friend, I believe, advised her to let nature take its course. It did.

—oOo—

The following day, I awoke bright and chirpy as a lark. Two of my worst anxieties had been allayed. First, I knew now that the memories of Muriel and Donald Campbell would not cripple this new relationship. What's more, I even had the feeling that Muriel would have encouraged it: she certainly did not speak to me that night with her familiar "Silly old sod…" remark which had come so often before as I sought to find a new love in my life. And as to the sex thing, that had been absolutely no problem at all. But there still remained the great obstacle of lifestyle. Could a woman like Tonia really build a lasting relationship with a man who lived the way I did?

I had plotted this bit with great care. I was determined that Tonia should be under no delusions about my *modus vivendi* so that second day I took her for another long drive across the England she had never really seen. We could have gone to somewhere elegant and expensive, like Stratford-upon-Avon, York or Bath, the sort of places that attract the average American tourist like a magnet. Instead, we went to Cromer in Norfolk, an archetypal English seaside town, with cockle and whelk stalls on the front, amusement arcades and shops selling funny hats and rock with the word 'Cromer' running all the way through.

As much as I like these picture postcard clichés of the seaside, I had chosen Cromer from a dozen other similar resorts for one very good reason: it was the last place I knew that still had genuine *pierrots* working a variety show on the end of the pier, a cozy mixture of song, dance and stand-up comicry which, although I had gone on to bigger things, was still very much part of my conception of my working world.

I was intrigued to see how Tonia would take such a show, accustomed as she was to the elegant supper-theatres in Los Angeles or the private showings of yet-to-be-released blockbuster movies in the mansions of the Hollywood moguls. Then, as we walked along Cromer sea front, eating fish and chips out of newspapers, people began to stop me and ask for autographs (no easy request with a handful of chips) or pat me on the back and wish me well. Then, I distinctly remember, two old ladies approached, thanked me for the pleasure my shows had given them in the past, and turned on Tonia.

"You'd better look after him, lass," said one of them. "He's a national treasure."

Tonia shrilled with laughter and they shook her hand too. When they had gone toddling off, I turned to Tonia and saw that her eyes were agleam with pleasure.

The Bill Maynard Crash Course on the Real England did not stop there. On Day Three, I took her a few steps further down the class system ladder by literally going to the dogs: a greyhound track where, once upon a time, I had spent many happy hours. It was not even a licensed track, strictly regulated by the Greyhound Association, but a so-called 'flapping' track where private greyhound owners, the types who keep the dog at home as a pet rather than send it to expensive training kennels, test their animal's speed against long-time friends and rivals.

These tracks attract a huge range of people, from genuine dog lovers to petty villains of every hue: unlicensed bookies, tipsters, pick-pockets, plainclothes CID men keeping track on the whereabouts and spending habits of petty criminals, the whole gamut of working class (or non-working class) English life. Here, too, I was mobbed by old mates and fans, who offered me tips on the races or pints of beer at the bar. There was one character there who had always interested me, a dog-track regular who dressed habitually in an Army surplus greatcoat, a red neckscarf over a collarless shirt, and a pair of tattered mittens. He was to come in very useful in a few months time when I went back to work but, in the meantime, I was enjoying my night at the races.

In America, no doubt, such tracks — if they exist at all — would not be the sort of place where a couple of famous entertainers would want to be seen in public. But, as I explained to Tonia back home that night, this was part of my world, my *real* world. Did she think she could share it?

"I love it, Bill," she said. "And I love you too." Thus our troth was well and truly pledged.

—oOo—

They have probably never before seen a day like September 4, 1989, at Hinckley Register Office, an unpretentious local government building where Births, Marriages and Deaths are registered in this one-time mining and hosiery town in Leicestershire. Another decade was drawing to a close in a blaze of headlines.

It had taken the press only a few days to track us down after that first sighting at Heathrow and by now they were camped outside my door in Sapcote. Their columns were full of speculation about the romance between Tonia and me — the *Daily Mail* even carried a full-page article about an impending marriage, the page trimmed with bows and bells — and, this time, they were dead right. The day after our trip to the dog track, I applied for a special marriage licence and, three days later, we arrived at the register office to be met by a barrage of flashbulbs, TV cameras and hordes of reporters. Even Tonia, accustomed as she was to Hollywood razamataz, was stunned.

It did not stop there. Some bright executive in the Jersey Tourist Board had read about the forthcoming wedding and had made contact, offering us a lavish, all-expenses-paid honeymoon in the Channel Islands. We had made no other arrangements and, a precursor of things to come, we did not have much time available: we both had professional commitments, this time in different hemispheres. We accepted — here was another part of Britain that Tonia had never seen — but had not anticipated the treatment that we were about to receive.

We were met at the airport by a red convertible and driven through the streets to waving throngs of holidaymakers and locals alike, all blowing kisses and shouting best wishes. Every time we went out, we were besieged: in theatres, restaurants and night clubs, people stood up to cheer and clap as we entered. Hollywood itself could not have done it better — Royal honeymoons have received less coverage. All this, I think, rather bemused poor Tonia, accustomed though she was to the spotlight.

Then, it was time to say goodbye and begin a marriage routine which, I have to admit, is far from normal. Tonia was due to finish a TV play in Hollywood and I was contracted to make a film in, of all places, South Africa, with two actors from, would you believe, Hollywood: Burgess Meredith and Don Ameche. It was, as it happened, a total disaster. The film, called *Odd Ball Hall,* was perhaps the worst I have ever made and, even worse still, it was the first Hollywood movie in which my name appeared above the title, the ultimate accolade from Tinsel Town. It was never even released on the British cinema circuit although years later, it did appear on video. I watched it and wished I hadn't.

That first separation, the first of many, set the standard for a marriage which, unorthodox though it is, has given me back the prize for which I had searched so long: a point of focus, a sense of permanence. This must, at first sight, seem a great paradox because the vast majority of our time is spent 6,000 miles apart. For over seven years now, we have pursued our separate careers on separate continents. And the reason for that, quite frankly, is that I no longer find Hollywood a pleasant place to be.

In the beginning, I would fly out to LA every couple of months or so when Tonia was working and she would make the return trip when I was booked up. But for me, the tinsel soon developed a tarnish. For a start, there is an artificiality among many of the people there which I find repugnant. The ambitious kowtow to the powerful and they in turn kowtow to the more powerful. It is always difficult to know, outside our own small circle, if people are speaking the truth or merely what they think you want to hear. As a plain-speaking Englishman, I find this extremely distasteful.

Then there is the town itself, a town where no one in their right mind would wander the streets, as Tonia and I had done eating fish and chips on the front at Cromer. And, of course, in Hollywood, no one comes up to you in the street to slap you on the back and thank you for pleasures past — the hand that slaps you on the back in certain parts of LA is likely to be holding a knife. The boy from Rat Alley, the boy who once gazed in awe at the silver screen in the flea pits of Leicestershire, the boy who once dreamed of being up there with the best of them, had grown too accustomed to life in a real community and genuine friendships with genuine people. Whatever the reason, that boy turned his back on the film capital of the world.

Strangely enough, Tonia, the ultimate LA sophisticate, had reacted in absolutely the opposite way. She comes to Britain — or to my son's place in France — as often as she can. Most of the time, we stay in Sapcote and do all the things I have always done: visit the WMC or the local pubs to hear country bands, have couple of drinks and play cheese skittles, even go to the greyhound track from time to time. Most curious of all, she has become an absolute *aficionado* of that most British of entertainments, the humble pantomime.

She was entranced when she first came to see me in panto, so much so that she wanted to become involved professionally. So every Christmas now, you will see Tonia Bern billed as playing The Fairy or some similar role in theatres ranging from Manchester to the South Coast. By doing panto, with its mix of old pros and amateurs from the local drama and dancing schools, Tonia, like me, gets a sense of family, something which is perhaps lacking on the Hollywood scene. It also gives her the chance to get in front of a live audience once more, which may be challenging but also gives a performer the greatest satisfaction available in this strange business of ours.

I must emphasise, however, that Tonia and I never play in pantomime together. I know only too well the frictions that can arise when married people work together in the theatre and I am determined that they should never be part of our lives. This means, however, that even when we are both in England for Christmas, we are rarely together. The exception is Christmas Day, the one day off (apart from Sundays) in the pantomime season. Even this calls for a major logistical effort.

If we are appearing reasonably close together (ie, within a hundred miles or so) I jump into my car after my Christmas Eve performance and drive to Tonia's theatre. If the distance is too great, I send a car for her. Then, while the world lies asleep waiting for Santa, we drive to Sapcote for a few hour's sleep. We go to my daughter Jane's house for Christmas lunch, back to Sapcote for Christmas night and then, on Boxing Day, it is back to our individual theatres.

I assume that, to most people, this is a very strange way to spend Christmas. Most people would also assume, I expect, that Tonia, 6,000 miles away from her own luxurious home in the relative warmth of California, would strongly object to spending most of Christmas Eve on some lonely motorway in uncertain weather conditions that can range through rain and snow to fog and frost. This, she assures me, is not the case: our Christmases have become a much-anticipated ritual and all that really matters is that *we* are together.

Sailors, who spend lonely months away at sea, have a phrase for it. They call it a *Honeymoon Marriage,* where the brief periods spent together are just that. I have three or four honeymoons every year and for a man of my age, that can't be bad. Once again, the pendulum had swung. A new decade was upon me, I had a new and beautiful wife and the memories of the past were no longer nightmares. Time, perhaps, to put my feet up and ease myself into gentle retirement. Bang on cue, as ever, the phone rang...

Chapter Twenty-Eight

"It's Not The Lead, But..."

MY long-serving (and some might say long-suffering) agent Richard Stone had by now gone into well-earned retirement and the Richard Stone organisation had been left in the very capable hands of several wonderful ladies. The phone call came from the head of the drama department, Meg Poole, who explained, perhaps a little warily, that my old friends at Yorkshire Television were planning a new series. It was based on the comings and goings surrounding a police station in a small country town set among the rolling, heather-covered hills of the North York Moors in the early 1960s. It was not to be a crime series in the traditional sense of the word — the place would not be littered with bodies and the hills would not be alive with the sounds of the wailing sirens and screeching tyres of non-stop car chases. Instead, it would be more of a study of rural life with a strong family bias.

"What they are looking for is a local rogue, a poacher and petty villain, who can inject a little humour into the piece," Meg went on. "It is not the lead, but YTV feel that there is the potential here to create an outstanding character who, one day, might spin off for a series of his own."

And so Claude Jeremiah Greengrass came into my life, a character who may have been tailor-made for me. Here is the boy from Rat Alley aged 60, still on his perpetual search for a new scheme, a dodgy ploy, which would put some tax-free cash into his back pocket to maintain his expensive tastes for Scotch and slow racehorses. That's how he is now. At the time of the first phone call, he was little more than a sketchy outline on paper, an outline with little shape or substance, a minor character with a peripheral part in what, after all, was a story about life in a rural nick.

At this time, as I said in the last chapter, I was financially secure and old enough to take things easy. After playing the leading roles in three highly successful television series, I had become accustomed to having considerable input in any new project I cared to contemplate, more input than, in some cases, a certain type of producer or director would care to accept. Yet here was a part which would entail my playing down the bill to Nick Berry, a young actor who a few years before had made his name in *EastEnders*, the BBC soap, as the London bobby gone north, and his doctor wife, Niamh Cusack. It was their close, and eventually doomed, relationship which was to give the series its name: *Heartbeat,* a pun which combined the couple's very different working interests.

Now I must emphasise that playing the lead in any production, whether in film, television or the theatre, is not to me a matter of ego-tripping. Of course it is flattering to have your name on the top of the bill, the position I had striven for over half a century when my work as a child entertainer is taken into account. If it were merely a matter of billing, I am actually in favour of having the cast credited in alphabetical order which, although it would leave me well down the list, is a fairer method than the sometimes hit-and-miss process by which actors are judged on their so-called 'star rating'. The billing is almost an irrelevance as far as I am concerned, but what does matter immensely is that matter of having some form of *control* (although that, in itself, is not a word I particularly care for). This means that your ideas and suggestions are listened to with greater respect the higher up the bill you are. As I have made clear time and time again, I like to make contributions to any production I am involved with and feel that, after all my hard-earned exper-ience, any suggestions I make are worthy of serious consideration.

This had led to my being accused of arrogance at many points in my career. I accept that, to people who have not worked with me before, that could well be the image I project, but I prefer to call it confidence bred of experience. I feel I know as well as most how to create a convincing character and, when it comes to comedy, I have had so many years' experience in the difficult art of making people laugh that I have a right to be heard: after all, I have to speak the lines and if people don't laugh, it is me who gets the blame as far as the public is concerned, not the writer or the director. In this I make a rod for my own back and it has been said of me that I am more interested in pleasing the audience than the TV companies that pay my wages. Well, so be it...

So here I was, being asked to play a supporting role in a programme which no one thought — including me — would last for more than one or two series. I could have turned it down. But, on the plus side, there were just too many good things in its favour.

For a start was the executive producer Keith Richardson, who is also Head of Drama at YTV, a department which I had never worked for before and one which I felt would benefit my career. Another plus factor was the fact that I knew the original writer, Johnny Byrne, who had produced the first scripts by adapting the novels written by Peter Walker. Peter had actually been a beat bobby in the Whitby area of North Yorkshire and had based his books on real-life experience. Johnny Byrne and I had worked together on the film *Adolf Hitler: My Part in his Downfall*, taken from Spike Milligan's tragicomedy war memoirs of the fighting in North Africa and Italy. Then came the worry about turning down any part. For the vast part of my working life, and particularly after the big crash in the 1960s, I had grabbed at any role I could find, partly out of a sense of insecurity, partly from the need to earn a living. Now I had the luxury of putting such considerations behind me, but I had another bad decision on my conscience: I had already turned down the lead in Dennis Potter's *Pennies from Heaven,* the controversial and sexy quasi-musical which I had rejected because of the bad language in the original script. When that had eventually appeared on the screen, most of the expletives had been cut, which made a nonsense of my objections. To rub salt in the wounds, the role I declined was taken by Bob Hoskins and, let's face it, it didn't do him any harm.

Of all these plus points, however, the one which attracted me most came from Meg Poole's words: "There is the potential here to create an outstanding character who, one day, might spin off for a series of his own."

Now if there was ego involved in my decision, here is where it lay. Meg and the creative people at YTV knew only too well that here was the offer I could not refuse. To build Claude Jeremiah Greengrass from a shadowy outline to a major figure in his own right was a challenge that I could not resist.

And on top of all this, the money on offer was good — much more than I thought the part was worth.

So I said yes. I did not realise that I was about to become one of the best-

As Sergeant Ellis in *Adolf Hitler, My Part In His Downfall*, the film based on Spike Milligan's book of the same title.

In Colin Welland's Play for Today, *Kisses At Fifty*, which was broadcast on BBC TV in October 1972.

As Dad in the comedy sex romp film *Confessions Of A Window Cleaner*. Also pictured are Anthony Booth, Doris Hare, Robin Askwith and Sheila White. The baby is Lyn Harris.

complete change of tone: as the padre in Thames TV's two-hander *Paradise Island*, which
so featured William Franklin.

Playing the King's bodyguard in *Robin and Marian*, which starred Sean Connery, Richard Harris and Audrey Hepburn.

Playing millionaire Sefton
Garrett in TV's *The
Inheritors*.

he film
houldn't
pen To
Vet.

With Celia
Johnson in the Anglia
TV play *Love Affair*.

Magic! Playing the title role in *Selwyn Froggitt*.

A handy all-rounder. Playing for the Lord's Taverners in Guernse

Another title role, this time *The Gaffer*.

ﾕde Jeremiah Greengrass from *Heartbeat*.

**Newly-weds –
Tonia and me.**

**An idyllic retreat in
Charentes, Maison de
Maitre**

**La Vie
Française!
Enjoying a
glass of re
at Maison
de Maitre.**

loved characters in the history of British television (and in dozens of other countries, too, for that matter). Nor did I have an inkling that Greengrass was to grow and grow throughout the 1990s, not only providing constant work but also keeping me right at the top of my chosen profession as I approached my 70th birthday. It had taken a very long time but now I was making all the right decisions...

—oOo—

Just who is Claude Jeremiah Greengrass? A difficult question because he is a man of many parts. There are men like him in most country villages — indeed, in any community — and in some ways they are products of their environment. Farm work, particularly on the desolate high moors of North Yorkshire, is hard graft and not overly well paid — even if you can get it which, in these days of ingenious farm machinery, is not easy. There will always be men who think they can find better ways of earning a crust than actually taking up hard graft even though, in the end, they end up working harder at not working than if they had taken a proper job.

In the small Leicestershire towns where I spent my childhood, such men would turn to activities on the borderlines of legality, like become bookies' runners before off-course betting was legalised, or selling around the pubs trinkets or gadgets that had 'fallen off the back of a lorry'. In more remote rural areas like North Yorkshire, a bit of poaching would come naturally, or perhaps dealing in horses or farm livestock of dubious origins. To an extent, these activities are tolerated, if not actually condoned, by most of the community — unless, of course, the local 'rogue' happens to be caught red-handed with a couple of the squire's pheasants stuffed in his pockets. So Greengrass may well be a rogue but he is not a hardened criminal — a tight-knit community would not tolerate such a man in their midst and he would soon end up either in exile or in jail.

This, then, was the lovable rogue I was asked to develop: a man who is a constant thorn in the side of the local bobbies but never a serious threat. This allowed the writers to develop the characters of the policemen, too. Part of Nick Berry's role, as a one-time London bobby transformed to the country-side, was to create an arms-length relationship with Greengrass by taking the more sophisticated view that, although not actually harmless, Claude could be a useful source of information on what passes for the rural underworld. In contrast, Sergeant Blaketon, a country-bred bigot of the worst type, takes the view that Greengrass must be stamped on at every conceivable opportunity. So in many ways, Greengrass is a catalyst for the various reactions between the men at the nick.

This, then, was the character that I was asked to build. He was an interesting man, a key player in the everyday lives of Aidensfield folk, but at the beginning he lacked a great deal of humour. This was the ingredient I was asked to supply and, as the series progressed, it became, in my opinion, more and more essential as a counter-weight to some of the sadness: the death of Nick's wife, when Niamh Cusack asked to be written out, being an obvious example.

To provide such humour in what is, after all, a drama series is far from easy. I did not want Greengrass to become a simple figure of fun, the village idiot that everyone laughs at. He also needed to create a sympathy from the audience when some of his schemes go wrong after all his plotting and scheming. Although he lives in considerable squalor, he could not be a dirty old man either: reprehensible, yes, but repulsive definitely not. And although his schemes are regularly thwarted, he must not appear stupid: if those schemes did not at first appear to have a reasonable chance of success, the final denouement would have no impact. So I was asked to build a wily, intelligent, schemer with, despite all his drawbacks, an underlying heart of gold. The entire history of English drama and literature is alive with such characters, from Chaucer via Shakespeare to, dare I say it, *Selwyn Froggit* and *The Gaffer*.

When the first read-throughs were called at the YTV studios in Leeds in 1990, I already had the skeleton of Greengrass, courtesy of the first scripts. My job, as I saw it, was to put flesh on those bones. I started, as always, with the feet: get those right and the rest of the physical character follows. And old pair of army boots helped me create that bent forward shuffle that has become so much a part of Greengrass.

With the walk in place, he needed some personal gestures which would be forever his. In search of these, I turned as ever to the people back in Leicestershire who I had been observing with an actor's eye for decades as they went about their everyday business. Peter Wright had been my model for both Bottom and later Selwyn Froggitt, so was there anyone else in my personal circle from whom I could draw inspiration?

Now it so happens that I have one acquaintance whose operations as a wheeler-dealer are regularly the subject of considerable conjecture. He is a businessman ready to turn his hands to many things and, like many such an operator, he chooses to play his cards very close to his chest. From time to time, his mates lose patience at the secretiveness and ask him, outright, just what he is up to at this particular moment. Faced with such alarming directness, he begins to blink. Further pressed, the blinking gathers pace and is accompanied by much stuttering and prevarication. By this time, the questioner has usually lost interest so the question rarely receives a straight answer.

This, I chuckled to myself, was an absolute natural for Greengrass and so was born the most famous blink on British television — a gesture (perhaps *affliction* is a better description) taken straight from real life. At the risk of being repetitive, there is no better basis for creating art. So far so good. Greengrass was growing fast, the joint product of several writers, my invented walk, and a blink stolen from an old acquaintance. The next step was his costume and here I was to encounter one of the rare problems on the *Heartbeat* set.

I had been involved in run-ins with some of the backstage departments at Yorkshire Television in the past, most notably when I insisted that *The Gaffer's* car be changed from a Rolls-Royce to a battered old Rover in the interests of authenticity. This time, it was not props but wardrobe that caused the conflict. In the first rehearsals, they wanted me to wear a black Crombie overcoat, battered but still formal, far too formal in my opinion. It was the sort of coat some small-time crook might wear in the inner city but, in my opinion, was totally out of place in the countryside and even further out of character for Claude. In that case, said a rather huffed member of the wardrobe department, did I have anything else in mind? And I had. Exactly. For in the many hours I had spent mulling over Claude's character, my mind had done back to that man at the greyhound track, the man wearing an army surplus greatcoat, a red neckscarf tied over a collarless shirt, and, to top it all, the mittens.

It is perhaps strange that such a humble and rarely-worn item of clothing as a pair of mittens can say so much about their owner's character. They are, of course, cheap but can only be bought at places like army surplus stores. They are worn by people who, patently, want to keep their hands warm but at the same time their fingers active and ready, just in case there is a passing pie to thrust them into.

Market traders wear them on frosty mornings, for it makes it easier for them to pick up their goods and pass them to the customer. It also makes it easier to count the cash and give out the change. My man at the race track probably wears them for the same reason, when he is handing money to or picking up his winnings from the bookie. Fagin wore mittens in *Oliver Twist*, all the better for picking a pocket or two. And although Claude Jeremiah Greengrass never actually picks a pocket, one suspects that he might be sorely tempted if the prize were right. There was some consultation between wardrobe, director and producer and eventually, Claude got his mittens, his khaki greatcoat, and his red neckscarf. Once again, I had interfered with another department, sticking my nose into someone else's business, done a job I was not paid to do. Perhaps it was arrogance and, if I put my case too bluntly, I apologise. But I have to wear the bloody things and in the world of television trademarks, there can now be few better known than my costume. And it was cheap, too.

Greengrass was now almost complete. But, being a countryman, there was one final touch lacking: his dog, which, I believe, was included at the instigation of Johnny Byrne. All countrymen may not actually own dogs but, in the eyes of television viewers, they are expected to have one. And this brought me up against that much-quoted theatrical adage, *never act with children or animals.* The reason behind this bit of stage wisdom is not so much that children and animals are difficult to teach — in fact, they can learn quicker than many an old pro. No, the real reason is much more self-centred: animals and children can be so good that they steal the show and few actors willingly give up the spotlight for a rival. I had reason to be wary.

Many years before, I had toured the country playing Launce in the Shakespeare comedy *The Two Gentlemen of Verona.* One of the stars of that play was to be my dog, Crab, played by an oversexed Jack Russell supplied by a training kennel. I had been taught to control the dog by saying, "Sit!" very emphatically and looking him straight in the eyes. Sure enough, Crab would sit and stay sat, peering out into the audience as I spoke my lines. Trouble was, from the very first night, we drew howls of laughter from parts which The Bard himself had never intended to be funny. I came off mystified.

"What the hell were they laughing at?" I asked the smirking stage manager.

"The dog," he chuckled. "As soon as he sat down, he developed a huge erection and it stayed up through your whole performance."

Now The Bard at his best can be very bawdy indeed and Shakespeare audiences tend to be pretty broad-minded. But one can only image the reaction of the Mary Whitehouse brigade if a well-hung mongrel began to display his wares in the middle of a family television show. Such a shot would, of course, never be broadcast (although it would no doubt make a prized out-take for private showings among TV staff) but such a situation would involve retake after retake. And as much of the *Heartbeat* filming takes place in pretty bleak weather on those windswept Yorkshire moors, I did not relish hanging around for hour after hour whilst canine passions cooled.

I need not have worried. Enter Sue Beale, one of the unsung heroines of *Heartbeat*. Sue is a professional animal trainer who runs a company called Whoofers. She supplies and trains all the animals used in the show and this being a rural production, that means lot of animals of almost every shape and size: horses, cows, sheep, pigs, foxes, rats, even moles. And it was Sue who introduced me to Alfred, *aka* Tramp.

Once upon a time, when I was Selwyn Froggitt, strangers in the street would give me the double thumbs-up sign and shout "Magic!" For almost a decade now, since I became Greengrass, the first thing anyone I meet asks is: "Where's the dog?" For Tramp, to use his real name, has become a star in his own right and, like all stars, he has quite a story to tell. In its canine way, his story is not dissimilar to mine.

Tramp is a lurcher but not a true lurcher — I know this because I looked it up when, in their hundreds, people began asking what sort of dog he is and I thought they deserved a proper answer. By definition, a true lurcher is a cross between a greyhound and a collie, which is what makes them such good hunters: the speed of one combined with the herding skills of the other. Other lurchers are a mix of any other breed cross-bred with either a greyhound or a whippet. And this is Tramp, half-greyhound, half-Bedlington terrier. Like me, he started life at the bottom.

He actually hails from a broken home and was rescued from an RSPCA dog's home by a lady teacher who, I understand, lives near Huddersfield. It was there he was discovered by Sue Beale, animal talent scout *extraordinaire*. *Heartbeat* needed a trainable lurcher and Sue, as ever, came up with the answer. We got on like a house on fire from our very first meeting because, with Sue's training, he had become an old *pro*. Whilst we are filming, Sue is on set with him all the time and takes him home at night. Sometimes, when she has other dogs in training, she brings them along too. She says this is to get them accustomed to the atmosphere of a television set, with the lights and the noise and the bustle, but personally I think it is so that they can watch Tramp act. Because, make no mistake, he is an actor. Like most dogs, he will spend most of the day half asleep in some cozy corner. But as soon as he hears the word, "Action!" he is up on his feet, eyes bright and shiny, ears pricked alert.

I am quite convinced that he knows when he is on camera and, over the years, our relationship has become a close bond. I do, of course, take biscuits on set with me and reward him for a good performance, praise which, like all actors, he seems to appreciate. But all actors will turn on good performances if the biscuit is big enough. With Tramp and I good friends, the final piece of the Greengrass jigsaw dropped into place. Even before we went on camera for the first time, I felt we had got him right. He would grow, I knew, because all characters must grow if they are to stay alive. But even I did not anticipate what a giant of a character he would become through, at the present count, seven series covering virtually the whole of the 1990s. I owe a lot to my blinking friend from Leicestershire and the greyhound track character in the khaki greatcoat. And Alfred, too, of course.

Chapter Twenty-Nine

Heartbeat Places

GOATHLAND until 1991 was a quiet village of grey stone houses nestling in a folding valley which dissects the rolling North York Moors. Lying as it does in a national park just off the main road to Whitby, the picturesque fishing port-cum-seaside resort where Bram Stoker wrote the first *Dracula* book, it has always attracted its fair share of summer visitors. This means that, for a village of its size, it is well endowed with accommodation: a rather expensive hotel and several friendlier ones, part hotel, part pub.

Until then, it had two claims to fame. It is part of a steam railway system, abandoned by British Rail but reopened by enthusiasts determined to keep alive the great days of steam. And the valley is also dominated by the top-secret Fylingdales Early Warning Station where, for years, RAF technicians trained their huge radars to the east on a 24-hour lookout for Russian bombers or, worse still, Russian intercontinental ballistic missiles. It was this station, with its now-demolished golf ball structures the size of cathedrals, which would have given the people of Britain the infamous four-minute warning that they were facing nuclear annihilation.

The tourists who made their way along the winding roads over the moors from York or Scarborough or the North-East came for different reasons. There were the train spotters and the young families who wanted to show the kids what a steam engine looked like and perhaps take a ride in the railway's vintage coaches. There were the defence buffs (and probably some spies, too) who would spend hours gazing at the sinister golf balls on Fylingdales Moor, and the country lovers who came to walk the hills through the bracken and the heather. And there were the motorists on the way to Whitby, with its ancient cliff top abbey and bustling fishing port, who would stop off in Goathland for a pub lunch and a look around the picture postcard village with its huge area of open common (much of which, incidentally, is owned by the Duchy of Lancaster and is therefore, technically, the property of HM The Queen).

The locals were a mixed bunch, too. The majority were dyed-in-the-wool Tykes, proud of their county and proud of their community, many of them hill farmers forever fighting the elements to raise their sheep in some of the toughest terrain in Britain. Among them lived a sprinkling of wealthy in-comers, well-to-do couples who had made their money in the towns and the cities and who had bought their bijou country cottages and retired to enjoy the country life. Another section of this group were the weekenders, the subur-banites wealthy enough to afford a second home, who had snapped up cot-tages once occupied by local farm workers and tradesmen, and used them for a few weekends a year and perhaps a week or so during the school holidays. In doing so, they had pushed property prices beyond the reach of local couples who, as often as not, could not afford to set up house and home in the village where their families had lived for generations.

This is a scenario which is familiar in pretty rural areas throughout Britain. And although the incomers make serious efforts to blend into the local com-munity, there are often underlying divisions and resentments. In Goathland, those divisions came bubbling to the surface when news leaked out that York-shire Television were planning to film a major television series in the village. The community split into two halves: the ones who welcomed any development which would bring additional income and a few jobs into the village; and the others who did not want the peace and quiet of their rural idyll shattered.

A small but vociferous protest group developed and, eventually, a village meeting was called. These events were watched with some misgivings by senior YTV executives who were worried about something much more serious than the potential for adverse publicity. They knew that the making of a long, complex and extremely expensive TV series in such a small village would depend to a great extent on the goodwill and cooperation of the local com-munity. They therefore breathed a sigh of relief when the majority of the villagers voted to welcome us in with open arms.

Goathland was about to be put on the map. As Aidensfield, fictitious home to PC Nick Rowan (Nick Berry), his doctor wife, Kate, (Niamh Cusack), the bigoted Sergeant Blaketon (Derek Fowlds), and the local poacher and rogue, one Claude Jeremiah Greengrass Esq. And, for better or for worse, Goathland will never be quite the same again, for this century at least and, the way things are going, well into the Third Millennium.

In the first three or four series, *Heartbeat* was shot almost entirely on location and that, as the YTV bosses had so correctly envisaged, demanded the closest co-operation, and sometimes considerable patience, from the good folk of Goathland. On screen, as one scene slickly moves into the next, few of our millions of viewers have the slightest conception of what has happened in between those scenes, of the travelling, of the reorganisation, of the moving of tons of equipment and dozens of extras, of the trucks moving along narrow country roads jammed with all the paraphernalia demanded by a modern location unit: the props wagon; the catering wagons that can produce anything from mugs of steaming coffee to a four-course *haute cuisine* lunch in half an hour; the mobile make-up and costume departments; the caravans in which we actors can put up our feet in the hours that sometimes pass before we are next needed before the cameras. We even take our own portable loos.

Within hours, real-life Goathland, going about its normal business, can be transformed into dream-world Aidensfield. Goathland Post Office, a real-life going concern, becomes Aidensfield Stores when our sign goes up to obliterate the real thing. The Goathland Hotel becomes the Aidensfield Arms in the same way. All modern cars must be moved from the High Street, for *Heartbeat* is, of course, set in the 1960s and we have our own fleet of period Morris Minors and Ford Anglias. This, of course, can be a pain in the neck for the real-life Goathlanders who want to pop down to the Post Office and collect their pensions.

The modern glass-and-steel BT phone kiosk outside the Post Office has to be removed because it is out of period. And in our trucks are hundreds of yards of rubber matting which cover the offensive double yellow lines which now ban parking in real-life Goathland (largely thanks to us, as I shall explain later). Double-yellows may have been introduced in the big cities in the 1960s but it took years for them to invade rural villages (and many people, including me, think they should never have been put down in such places in the first place).

So Goathland became a quick-change village, changing hats as quickly as the late Tommy Cooper did in some of his most famous sketches. But that was just for *exterior* shots. For many of the interiors, the changes demanded were even more exacting, in both time and skill, and for that there is no better example than the junkyard Greengrass calls home. When these shots were filmed in Goathland I, in fact, had two homes and they were some three miles apart. If anything demanded the support of the local people, this was it.

The back door of the Greengrass tip is, in fact, a farm owned by Mick Atkinson and his wife, who suffered long and hard for several years to make *Heartbeat* a success. In real life, they have a wonderful kitchen which is a delight to live in, brimming with that rustic charm much loved by glossy life-style magazines (and slavishly copied by thousands of city dwellers pretending they live somewhere else). In other words, far too good for the slovenly Greengrass.

So every time we were filming in Goathland, and a scene demanded shots of Greengrass in what passes for his home, a YTV crew would move into the neat Atkinson home and — a lovely phrase this — *break it down*. That meant carefully removing every stick of furniture, every cooking utensil, every picture and carefully storing them away. Then they would set about junking those pristine walls to give them the required dingy look. With walls and curtains suitably filthy, they would move in 'my' junk furniture, which had also been stored with equal care. That in place, they would make the elaborate mess with which Greengrass surrounds his domestic life: unwashed plates and cutlery, piles of old newspapers, bits of sacking and, of course, a corner for Alfred.

After filming — and that could sometimes last for only a few hours — the crew would move in again and repeat the entire process in reverse including, after every session, completely repainting the Atkinson kitchen. I suppose there are many people who would love to have their kitchen redecorated regularly by professionals, for free at that, but to have it done every couple of weeks or so seems to me to be a little over the top. The Atkinsons took it in their stride, however, and soon became firm friends with many of the actors and the crew. Unfortunately, the Atkinson front door was not suitable for exterior shots so if you ever saw me emerge from the front of the house, I was in fact coming through a door at another farm three miles away owned by John Jackson and his family. They, too, suffered with great forbearance as our trucks packed their working farmyard to get a few minutes, perhaps only a few seconds, of Greengrass on film.

Scenes like this would be under way throughout the Goathland area when we were on location. Businesses changed their names and signs, locals would play extras dressed in 1960s-style clothes and, in the winter months at least, they even lost the use of one of their local pubs for days on end, something which would tend to upset the regulars at many of my watering holes back home in Leicestershire. In the early days, we took over the Goathland Hotel bar completely, recompensing the landlord for his loss of genuine trade. The *Heartbeat* crew were not, however, restricted just to Goathland. The police station and Nick's police house were some 60 miles away in Otley, a thriving market town in the beautiful Wharfe Valley north of Leeds. These were chosen for their authenticity. They had the advantage of being much closer to the YTV studios in Leeds but still a long and difficult journey from Goathland. Moving from one to the other with all our equipment was like moving a small army and it presented another major problem: the nightmare of continuity.

Stepping out of a door which is three miles away from where it appears to be can present minor problems. Stepping out of a police station on to a high street which is 60 miles away, when several days have passed between the internal and the external shots, is tempting the devil. And in this case, the devil manifests his evil ways with, from a television production point of view, his most relentless weapon: the English weather. Although in the same county — admittedly England's biggest county — Goathland and Otley are immensely different places, geographically, geologically and, in particular, meteorologically.

On the high North York Moors, only a few miles from the sea, easterly winds can sweep in a whole gamut of weather conditions within the passing of a few hours: mist, rain, gales and, in mid-winter, heavy falls of snow. In Otley, sheltered as it is in the Wharfe Valley, weather conditions are much milder but, like everywhere else, it can rain and rain and rain. This presents the continuity people with massive headaches for, should Nick Rowan walk along the high street towards the nick (an exterior shot in Goathland) when there is heavy snow on the ground, and allegedly a few minutes later, come out of the nick (in Otley), into bright sunshine with not a snowflake in sight, the viewer has the right to raise an eyebrow. This can cause havoc with the continuity of any episode so, where possible, any day's shooting schedule should have an alternative interior schedule so that we actors are not kept hanging about doing nothing if the weather turns foul.

That's the theory. There is one regular set of circumstances when we can only keep our fingers crossed and hope for the best: the location night shoot. *Heartbeat*, quite rightly, prides itself on the amount of outdoor location shooting it does. That, after all, is why it is based on that beautiful stretch of moorland. But, outdoors, you cannot fake night-time scenes; you cannot turn down the lights and pretend it is dark because the viewer could see that you are faking. So in the interests of realism, night shoots are a pretty regular part of the *Heartbeat* schedule and because Greengrass is a character of nocturnal habits, I tend to be in many of them.

So off we go to the woods (most of my poaching activities take place in woodland, of course) and the mobile army turns up: cameramen, lighting men, soundmen, the line producer, the director, the prop men, the caterers and the mobile loos. Once this army is in place, the show must go on and to hell with the weather. We shoot in rain and in gales and sometimes in the snow and, surprisingly enough, the results are often sensational, some of the best footage ever seen in a British drama series. But for those who think the life of a TV actor is one of pampered luxury, try working when you are drenched to the skin, your fingers almost paralysed with cold, your feet slithering in the mud or tripping over invisible branches, with the rain stinging your eyes as you face the glare of the lights. This, however, is nothing compared to what the crew have to endure. Unlike us cosseted actors, they have to be there for every scene on every day.

Those are the nights when you wish you were comfortably retired, tucked up in bed with a drink on the bedside table and a good book on your chest. Then you see the rushes and your professional pride swells: it was worth it after all. For these episodes, I should like to thank the *Heartbeat* mobile army. I never fail to wonder at the technical expertise, the detailed planning, the huge logistical effort needed to gather all those skilled people and their mountains of equipment in the same place at the same time, particularly when the place is some rainswept wood on the North York Moors and the time is after midnight. The SAS could not do better.

—oOo—

In some ways, *Heartbeat* became the victim of its own success. Even though the first series went out in a killer slot — that time on a Friday night when most people in Britain are in the pub — it immediately went to Number Seven in the ratings and it has rarely been out of the top five ever since. This, for a drama series as opposed to a soap, is a phenomenal success and it is now part of life for tens of millions of viewers in this country and for many more millions abroad: it gets prime time slots in Australia, New Zealand, Canada and more than 30 other countries. But that success brought its problems, particularly in Goathland.

Sometimes the power of television sits up and bites you, even an old pro like me who has worked in the medium virtually since its birth as the country's most popular form of entertainment (there were some broadcasts before World War Two, of course, but they were restricted mainly to the London area and to the few upper echelon homes which could afford the then extremely expensive sets). It is so easy, *too* easy, to become blasé about the way you can be infiltrated into millions of households, to become a friend, even a member of the family, of tens of millions of people you have never met. Then something happens that sets you a-thinking about the benign monster you have helped to create.

Popular television series have taken such a grip on the nation that they are no longer looked upon as fiction. They develop a life of their own. People want to meet the characters, as opposed to the actors, as though they were living human beings. Most of all, they want to see where and how these characters/people live. And this has given rise to a completely new form of holidaymaker, the television tourist.

Any town, village or district which becomes associated with a major TV show becomes a tourist honeypot. Yorkshire is blessed with many of them. The filming of the James Herriot novels in *All Creatures Great and Small* changed the area of North Yorkshire west of Goathland from the Yorkshire Dales to 'Herriot Country'. *The Last of the Summer Wine* did the same for Holmfirth, a small Pennine mill town in West Yorkshire, on first sight a highly unlikely spot to become a major tourist venue. Over the Pennines, *Coronation Street* has always been a studio set but Granada have been forced to build a tourist village next to their Salford studios to cater for hundreds of thousands of fans who demand to see the real/imaginary thing. Now they can buy a pint in The Rover's Return.

Heartbeat was to do the same thing for Goathland. We began to notice it towards the end of the first series and, as the years passed, this remote village was to become as busy as Piccadilly Circus at rush hour. There is a certain irony to this because we, as the people who had created the interest in the first place, began to suffer from the effects.

As I have explained, the arrival of our transport in the village nearly swamped the place. Our mobile army of something like 50 people already took up most of the available beds when we were on location, filling the hotels and B & Bs. Most of the locals accepted the disruption of their High Street with good humour and, indeed, many of them became such close friends that they offered some of our technicians accommodation in their own homes.

Then the tourist cars began to arrive, first in their dozens, then in their hundreds, which made clearing the street to make way for our 1960s vintage motors even more difficult. Then the coaches began to arrive, first from local venues like York, then great gleaming monsters from all parts of the country, tipping hundreds of people on to the already crowded streets. 'The Heartbeat Tour' had become a must for the television tourists. Then we lost one of the key sets, the Goathland Hotel, which was our pub in *Heartbeat*. We had, as I have already recorded, hired the bar for days on end during the quiet winter months. Now there were no quiet months in Goathland: the coaches and cars came summer and winter alike and it was no longer economical for the hotelier to turn away such trade. We were, as the saying goes, hoist with our own petard.

As this is being written, we are well into the seventh series of *Heartbeat,* a run which itself will involve 24 episodes, and now most of the interior shots are filmed on sets in an old mill at Farsley, an industrial town between Leeds and Bradford, where much of *Emmerdale* was shot. Under its great arched ceilings, many of our sets have been faithfully recreated: the Greengrass house and the pub from Goathland, the police station and Nick Rowan's police house from Otley. With all these facilities in the same building, we have cut hours of travelling and the average time for the filming a one-hour episode has been cut from 11 days to nine.

This does not mean, however, that we have abandoned Goathland to the tourists. All exterior shots are still done in that little village among the heather on the North York Moors. I go there and stay at my favourite pub, the Inn on the Moor, among people who have become some of the closest friends of my life. It is not quite Sapcote — indeed it is a very different place from Sapcote — but it is the next best thing. We may have brought the place some problems but we have also brought it a considerable prosperity and international fame. The fact that, after some eight years of disruption, the majority of the villagers still welcome us with big smiles and open arms speaks for itself.

Chapter Thirty

Heartbeat People

TELEVISION is, of course, a world of big egos. This is unavoidable when dozens of highly-talented, highly-paid people work together and all have highly-developed individual skills. These, however, must go into a joint pool: making a successful series is, above all, a team effort and a lot of those skills tend to overlap. This can create tensions which, if handled properly, can make an important contribution to the success of the show. If handled badly, they create the potential for disaster.

So although *Heartbeat* has given me seven of the happiest years of my professional life, to pretend that it has always gone smoothly would be to lie. There have been rows and virtually every one of them has been instigated by my own good self. Almost inevitably, most of them have arisen because of my refusal to speak what I consider to be unreal lines or lines which are supposed to be funny and aren't. This lifelong habit of changing scripts does not go down well in some quarters and has given me a reputation for being difficult to work with, an allegation I refute but which lingers nevertheless. In a seven-year run and still counting, with producers and directors changing every couple of years or so, it was inevitable that some producers would arrive on the *Heartbeat* scene with, it appeared to me, a determination to take Bill Maynard down a peg or two. Some of these problems arose because of the way the programme is made. First, there is the studio hierarchy. In overall charge is the executive producer, a key Yorkshire Television staff appointment. Next in line is a freelance producer, the producer who makes many of the important decisions, like appointing the director. The director controls the filming, the writers and, in the case of new parts or guest parts, has a large say in the choice of the actors. Unlike a one-off play, when the writer tends to be on set for much of the filming and readily available for consultation, *Heartbeat* scripts can be written six months or more in advance by commissioned writers who we, the actors, rarely meet. Their scripts then go through a long process of rewrites, with many of the aforementioned having their say alongside three script editors. By the time the cast see the words they are paid to speak, they may have been changed many times. They are, of course, always highly professional but, perhaps because of this long rewriting process, they can sometimes lose their sense of spontaneity. This applies, in particular, to the humorous content and as Greengrass supplies most of the humour in the show, this directly effects my performance. This is when I tend to get my pen out, usually at the request of, or with the connivance of, the producer or the director.

This can be anathema in some circles — a mere *actor* rewriting scripts. Presumably, the people who object believe that actors are merely puppets, robots to be pushed in front of the cameras to mime a few words while someone else pulls their strings. This, I insist, is most definitely *not* how it happens. As a pro I know and respect all the efforts other members of the team put into the making of *Heartbeat*. But to the viewing public it is we, the actors, who make or break the show: if it fails, we carry the can. And after 60 years in the business, I am damned sure that I will not let it fail if I think I can make things better.

I do not, however, go in for wholesale rewrites. I do not, for instance, rewrite other people's lines (although, I admit, some actors do approach me on set and ask if I can come up with a better line for them than the one in the script). But I do read every syllable of Greengrass dialogue, rehearse it to myself, turn it around on my tongue and, if I think it can be made better, I try to do so. Spoken dialogue often sounds very different than it reads when down on paper, and in my days as a stand-up comic, I had come to understand the rhythm of delivering funny lines, a skill which is atrociously difficult to acquire — if, as a comic, you do not get a laugh every 15 seconds you are dead. I could quote many examples but I will content myself with just one.

In the series we are filming as this is being written, Stratford Johns, another old pro who made his name as the irascible Inspector Barlow in *Z-Cars*, appears as a guest artist as my brother, a man with roguish tendencies similar to those of Greengrass but ones he had used to more success: he has, for instance, found himself a wife rich enough to own a Rolls-Royce. Stratford has come to visit me and, needing to make an urgent phone call, has been forced to go to the kiosk in the village. When he returns, he asks irritably:

"Why don't you get a phone put in?"

In reply, I was supposed to say: "What? On what I've got coming in?"

That is, shall we say, an adequate line. It keeps the dialogue going but it is, let's face it, hardly side-splitting. So I rewrote it:

"Why should I? No one ever rings me anyway?"

I will give to 10-1 that this gets a smile when the show is broadcast (it certainly did on set, and television technicians are a supremely critical audience). A simple line of a mere eight words it can barely count as wholesale butchery of the script, but in my professional opinion it is a line which will give the viewers some pleasure. These days, working under our latest and, in my opinion, best producer, I am allowed to make such changes by simply discussing it with our associate producer, a wonderful Scottish lady called Pat Brown, who is always on set to smooth away minor problems. But it was not always thus...

We have had, now, five producers and three of them were quite splendid. My relationships with the other two were, shall we say, somewhat fraught. One goes back to the time when Greengrass's part was growing show by show and there were people, I believe, who thought he was growing too big for his boots. The producer finally let it be known that I would no longer be allowed to change dialogue. Furious, I asked for a meeting and was invited to have a drink in the YTV bar. No, I said, this was something I did not want to discuss in public. In my room we had a face-to-face that lasted for three hours. I was so angry that I even considered quitting the show. This producer left after that series.

My second confrontation came with a producer whose views, to me, verged too far towards the politically correct — not an attitude of mind with which you would associate Claude Jeremiah Greengrass. New to *Heartbeat*, this producer gave the impression of having been warned about me and seemed determined to prove who was the boss. And although no attempt was made to take away my right of making script changes, I was told this had to be done at least two weeks before shooting and must be approved at producer level.

Now this was patently absurd. For a start, a lot of the best ideas for new lines actually come on set when filming is under way, often as a result of talks with fellow actors or because some prop does not work in practice as it is supposed to in the script. It was the former that brought about about the telephone gag with Stratford Johns. Then came the fact that the producer was rarely on set anyway, which meant we had faxes going backwards all the time with my suggested changes being answered by the producer's suggested changes to my suggested changes. It is quite impossible to be spontaneous under such circumstances and, as I said, spontaneity is one of the key sources of good comedy. Anyone who has been to watch a good stand-up act in a night club knows that some of the best gags come *ad lib* in the verbal duels between the comic and customers. This time, I felt I must appeal directly to Keith Richardson and, as a result, he fortunately approved the system by which I could clear any changes with Pat Brown, a system which has worked happily to this day. The producer, incidentally, departed after that particular run.

This attitude, as I have said, has given me a reputation for being difficult in some quarters and, believe me, that is a reputation which I could well do without. It does not help to make enemies of producers and directors and writers and there are many actors who happily go with the flow. That is the way to an easy life. Trouble is, an easy life has never been one of the luxuries I have enjoyed because, without wishing to sound pompous, I have this unshakeable belief in artistic *integrity*. An actor who knowingly speaks bad lines without protest lets everyone down: himself, his fellow artists and, most seriously of all, the audience.

We are not puppets. We are professionals and as such should approach what we do professionally. I have been doing it for 60 years now and, should I need to defend myself against charges of arrogance, I would like to remind certain people in the business that I have worked happily, and very successfully, with a long list of writers who names represent a roll of honour in British television and film: Johnny Speight, Dennis Potter, Colin Welland, Harry Kershaw, Alan Plater, Andrew Davies and many, many more, not to mention a list of directors far too numerous to mention — so I won't.

I rest my case.

—oOo—

With these minor skirmishes sorted out, I settled down to the longest, happiest and most satisfying period of my working life. I had a beautiful wife who, although 6,000 miles away most of the year, was a constant source of support, solace and fun (as my phone bills prove) and there were our three or four honeymoons a year. My children were married and providing me with grandchildren and I had suddenly developed a new family: the *Heartbeat* family.

In this, I am not being sentimental or dewy-eyed but factual. When you work with people over seven years or more, when you share their leisure time in beautiful surroundings on the Yorkshire Moors, when you see them getting married and having their own children, you realise that you are part of a family. Location shooting makes great demands while it is under way but, unless there is a night shoot, the evenings and days off are spent together and shoptalk gives way to the gossip of the day as in any ordinary family.

In the early years, Nick Berry and I became very close. This was, of course, his first lead role although he had already become famous via *EastEnders*, and this is no easy part to play for a young actor. I watched him learn to deal with the pressures, both on and off the set, and remembered all the mistakes I had made in my young days. I became, I would like to think, an avuncular figure to Nick, someone he could turn to for advice in this new bewildering world of public acclaim, that thrilling but daunting time when you realise that wherever you go, you are recognised, and that a normal existence is no longer possible.

When we were not filming, I would take Nick to see the seaside shows in Whitby and Scarborough, a world I had lived through and still regard with great affection, but which were entirely new to Nick. As an old-timer, I was able to point out some of the tricks of the trade and give him advice on money matters. After all, few people know better than I how young men unaccustomed to wealth can squander it with absolute abandon. Nick, I believe, will never make those mistakes. In fact, I know he won't, for he certainly has shown no signs of doing so up to now.

Then he married his girlfriend, Rachel, and they had a son, Louis, and now I see less of him. When in Goathland, they have a private apartment in another hotel and, very wisely, try to live as normal a married life as possible. Nick has now announced that he will be leaving *Heartbeat* and I shall watch his future career with great interest.

I greatly missed Niamh Cusack, who played Nick's doctor wife in the earlier series, when she asked to be written out. She was, I thought, very important to the success of the show and I even went to her caravan and spent several hours trying to talk her out of her decision to quit. Niamh comes from a legendary Irish theatrical dynasty — her father was the late and great Cyril Cusack, one of the finest actors of his generation — but she was having a baby and wanted to spend more time at home, another sensible decision. I have absolutely no doubt whatsoever that she will go later on to rival her father's achievements. I thought her departure would adversely affect the ratings but in this I proved to be wrong. After her television death, Nick was left as a single dad with all the problems that entailed. This story line, created out of necessity because of Niamh's departure, actually added a strong dash of social realism to the plot and, as a result, our viewing figures jumped by a couple of million.

Derek Fowlds has become not just a friend but more of a sparring partner. Derek had made one of the most dramatic changes of roles in recent television history, from the wide-eyed innocent under-secretary in *Yes Minister* to Sergeant Blaketon in *Heartbeat,* the man the viewers love to hate. Few people remember that he started his showbusiness career as straight man to a fox: he was Mr Derek to Basil Brush, the manic puppet who got a great many of his laughs by humiliating poor Derek. This, I think, is a part of his career that Derek would prefer to forget, even though Basil Brush was one of those rare children's acts which attracted a huge adult following. This, sadly perhaps, was not to be because I have had a long association with Basil's creator and operator, Ivan Owen. He was one of the lead actors when I got my first ever full-time professional date at Butlins all those years ago.

Derek, unlike me, is a drama school product, and we have formed what is virtually an off-stage double act. Using the snooty tones beloved by old West End act-oors, he addresses me always as 'the vaudevillian' and asks questions like: "Who allowed that music hall clown on the set?" I reply with rather unkind references to his early relationship with the rear end of a fox. This knockabout teasing helps fill in the long hours on stand-by but, so far at least, I believe I have had the last word ...for the moment.

In one episode of *Heartbeat,* there was a story line about a cattle disease being spread round Aidensfield by foxes. It was a case of all hands to the guns and everyone, including Greengrass, was asked to take part in a fox cull. My part was a night scene where I had to shoot a fox (a stuffed fox, I must assure animal loving readers) as it emerged from its den. It was a particularly filthy night for filming, even by Goathland standards, and everyone was anxious to get it done and get to bed.

Then, as the fox emerged from its hole in the ground, I shouted: "I'll lay six to four that when that fox comes out, it will have Derek Fowlds' arm stuck up its backside."

Collapse of film crew. Derek has been plotting his revenge for that one for some years now. I'm bracing myself, Derek.

—oOo—

Many of my closest friends in the *Heartbeat* family are not, however, my fellow actors. Whilst in Goathland, they tend to stay at a rather expensive hotel but I, the lad from Sapcote, prefer the more intimate atmosphere of the Inn on the Moor, a rambling pub-cum-hotel run by a former London policeman, Malcolm Simpson and his wife, Judy. I am not impressed by bowing and scraping and they treat me as one of them. I even help out in the place: from time to time, I will go to the cash and carry with Malcolm and help him load the car. As a man with an eye for a bargain, I sometimes pick up the odd item for myself. The Inn on the Moor is where most of the directors, the PAs and some of the technicians stay, including my stand-in, Joe Gallagher. Joe is a musician I met whilst making *Maynard's Bill*, a programme about pub bands and entertainers that YTV filmed in the Leeds area. Another regular guest is Dinny Powell, my stunt double. I am getting a little long in the tooth for running across the moors or through the woods being chased by Blaketon or the squire's men, so when you see Greengrass disappearing in haste over the horizon in some scenes, it is Dinny, not me, wearing the famous khaki greatcoat. Other regular guests at the inn include two of my closest friends among the *Heartbeat* family, Christine and Tony Edmondson. When I started on the show, Tony was a third director — a lowly figure known as the 'runner' — and Christine Sharmon was the production assistant. Since then, they have married and now have two sons, aged four and two, and Tony is post-production co-ordinator. So I have watched their careers and their private lives grow like a proud uncle.

Joe Gallagher stands in for me when they are setting up the cameras and the lighting for a new scene. This, I admit, is a bit of a luxury, as is the driver who now picks me up in Sapcote and takes me up to Yorkshire for filming. That's about as far as my star treatment goes and I suspect that the fact that I am an old-age pensioner has a great deal to do with it.

The Inn on the Moor is also where I meet many members of the public, for this is where many of the trippers stay on their *Heartbeat* tour. They seem to be surprised to see me sitting alone in the lounge, having a cup of coffee and reading the paper.

Much of the time in Goathland, however, I am on my own. This does not mean that I am lonely, just alone. When I am not filming, I go off to pursue some of my interests, like seeing the seaside shows or, more and more, combing junk shops or auction sales for minor antiques. I use the word minor because I am no big spender and, apart from anything else, should I buy a major item of furniture there is so little room left at Sapcote that I would have to sell something else to make space. My main interests are antique porcelain and crystal ware, items which take up little room and which I use all the time. It gives me great pleasure to drink a cup of tea from fine bone china or a glass of good wine from sparkling crystal. This pursuit has created a funny but friendly rivalry with John Simmons, who runs an auction house in Saltburn, just a few miles up the East Coast. That rivalry even gave me a few lines for one of my favourite *Heartbeat* episodes.

I can't even remember what I was bidding for, but it was certainly an item of no great value. Here is the script which, from real life, went straight into Greengrass's mouth when he attended an auction in the show:

AUCTIONEER: "I am bid £18. Do I hear £20?"

ME: "£19."

AUCTIONEER (PEERING OVER HIS SPECS): "Would you like to me to lend you a pound, sir?"

RIVAL BIDDER: "£20."

AUCTIONEER: "I have £20. Do I hear £22?"

ME: "£21."

And I got it. It was a game, of course, but only partly so. I saved the pound and got a laugh from the assembled bidders. The schemer from Rat Alley is still at it, still looking for the bargain, and still getting a laugh. Muriel would be proud of me.

Finale

SO WHERE do I go from here? The answer to that is that I don't really know but, as I look my 70th birthday in the eye, there are still many things I would like to do and still a lot of work to be done.

Greengrass is now an integral part of my life and I will stay with him as long as *Heartbeat* remains one of the most successful shows on television. There will be changes for sure: Nick Berry is leaving the show and new characters are already being developed, one a doctor, the other a new bobby. This will fundamentally alter the mix of the show and that is exciting, for new characters offer new opportunities for scripts and story lines.

Claude himself may develop. We have long talked about a 'spin-off' series and I have this idea of Claude coming into some small amount of money which he will use to set himself up as a racehorse trainer — a very dodgy racehorse trainer, of course. He would move only a few miles or so from Aidensfield and that would give him the opportunity to pop back into *Heartbeat* from time to time. All this, of course, is a matter for Yorkshire Television to consider.

I do have one serious professional ambition outside television. Television has been good to me and made me financially independent, which, back in the dark days of the 1960s, seemed a highly unlikely prospect. Now, I feel, is the time to put something back into the profession that has been so kind.

I doubt that I will ever retire, for putting my feet up in front of the fire is not an idea that appeals to me. I would like to go back into the theatre, that world which I adopted at such terrible cost to me and my family. But not as an actor.

Now is the time, I feel, to give some other actors the chance to get on to the ladder which, after many faltering steps, finally took me to the top. To do this, I have long been considering going into theatre production, backing plays with both my money and my judgment. Not, I hasten to add, as a dilettante 'angel' trying to buy prestige with cash, but as a hands-on producer with control. This time, let the other so-and-sos argue with me. It will be interesting to see the other side of the coin.

Personally, my life has been better than I ever had the right to expect. I have had two wonderful wives, the second of whom allows me to cherish the memories of the first. I have two loving, supportive and entertaining children and my grandchildren. For them, I have been able to provide everything my own parents would so much have loved to provide for me.

I have my semi in Sapcote and other homes I can visit at any time I wish: my daughter's converted farmhouse in my home county, the French *maison de maitre* I helped my son to buy, and my wife's Hollywood style bungalow in, well, Hollywood.

All in all, not a bad sum total for an urchin from Rat Alley.

Most of all, though, I have my self respect. I was a damn fool once, and deserved the punishment that I received. But I have paid my debts and, along the way, I have made a few people laugh, which is as great a gift as a man can give.

Even in the bad days, I never sacrificed my principal of giving good value for the people who paid to watch me perform. When it was necessary to fight, I fought and, as often as not, I succeeded.

So I stood up. I was counted. But I have not been counted out ...YET!

Index